W9-DBC-520

DATE DUE			
JAN 23 '84			

THOMAS A. BRYSON

Seeds of Mideast Crisis
The United States Diplomatic Role in the Middle East During World War II

McFarland & Company, Inc.
Jefferson, North Carolina
1981

By the same author

Coedited with Robert W. Sellen, *American Diplomatic History: Issues and Methods* (1974)

American Diplomatic Relations with the Middle East, 1784-1975: A Survey (1977)

Walter George Smith (1977)

United States/Middle East Diplomatic Relations, 1784-1978: An Annotated Bibliography (1979)

An American Consular Officer in the Middle East in the Jacksonian Era: A Biography of William Brown Hodgson, 1801-1871 (1979)

Tars, Turks, and Tankers: The Role of the U.S. Navy in the Middle East, 1800-1980 (1980)

Library of Congress Cataloging in Publication Data

Bryson, Thomas A   1931-1980
Seeds of Mideast crisis.

Bibliography: p.   Includes index.
1. World War, 1939-1945 — United States.
2. United States — Foreign relations — Near East.
3. Near East — Foreign relations — United States.
4. World War, 1939-1945 — Diplomatic history.
I. Title.
D769.1.B79   327.73056   80-15896
ISBN 0-89950-019-6

McFarland & Company, Inc., Publishers
Box 611, Jefferson, North Carolina 28640

to

Anne, Olivia, & Tommy

Table of Contents

Preface

At the present time the United States is deeply involved in the Middle East. The growing dependence upon oil from the Arab world, the commitment to Israeli sovereignty, the longstanding effort to dampen intraregional strife hinging on the Arab-Israeli conflict, the diplomatic support of Middle Eastern lands against abridgement of freedoms by an outside power, continued access to communication and transportation routes in the region, and the deployment of the Sixth Fleet in Middle Eastern waters, all constitute the foundation of America's Middle Eastern policy.

While the American heritage in the Middle East has its origins in the early days of the republic, it has only been in the period during and since World War II that United States interests in the Middle East came to be of vital importance. Prior to the war the United States had a multiplicity of interests in the Middle East. The activities of merchants, missionaries, educators, mariners, and oil companies were uppermost in the minds of foreign policy-makers. Policy was directed toward the protection of these interests and was shaped by a number of basic guiding principles.

World War II has been described as a watershed in this nation's Middle Eastern policy. During the war American policymakers began to view the region as vital to national security. Winning the war constituted a primary goal. Supplying Lend-Lease aid to the Soviet Union through Iran, denying the Germans access to the rich petroleum resources in the Persian Gulf, and preserving the integrity of the various countries in the region were considered policies in the national interest. This term is defined as those policies that protect the national security of the United States and promote the economic well-being of the American people. Never before in the country's history had this region been vital to the American national interest.

War's end found American policy-makers striving to create a comprehensive regional policy, one that encompassed all of the nations of the Middle East. As used herein, this region includes the belt of Muslim states across North Africa—Morocco, Algeria, Tunisia, Libya, and Egypt—the nations of the Arab core—Saudi Arabia, Palestine, Jordan, Syria, and

Iraq—and the states of the northern tier—Turkey and Iran. Some historians believe that the United States possessed no regional policy beyond that dictated by the broad guidelines such as the "open door," protection of American rights in the mandates, freedom of the seas, and those contained in the Altantic Charter and the United Nations Declaration.

But historians have differed widely in their interpretation of this nation's Middle Eastern policy in World War II. There are those who argue that the United States had no comprehensive policy that extended beyond specific policies toward the several countries in the region and those dictated by the basic guiding principles. They hold that, having no comprehensive policy, the State Department was quite willing to follow the British initiative in an area that consititued the hub of the British Empire. Other writers suggest that the United States not only began to formulate specific policies in the Middle East during the war, but that it made a definite break from British tutelage. This policy extended to an aggressive oil policy in Saudi Arabia and Iran, and independent poitical aims in Palestine, Iran, Turkey, Syria, and Lebanon. Indeed, they argue that the United States not only opposed British imperialism but began to formulate a basic, region-wide policy in the closing days of the war. The revisionist school of historians takes an altogether different tack, asserting that American policy-makers adopted a strategy well calculated to reduce the British position in the region in order that American economic interests might prosper. This policy was allegedly designed to protect and increase American oil holdings in the region and to open up markets hitherto closed by the imperial limitations of the European nations.

The purpose of this study is to examine the unfolding of American Middle Eastern policy during World War II. This presupposes that there was in fact no region-wide policy at the outset of the war, but that during the conflict the policy-makers in the Department of State began to envision not only an American policy *vis-à-vis* each of the countries in the region, but to develop a policy that encompassed the region as a whole. Inasmuch as the policy-making process is not an abstract exercise performed by computers but rather the result of a meeting of the minds of men, an attempt will be made to identify those persons who contributed to the formulation of policy.

As American policy began to develop on a country by country basis and on a regional scale, it is possible to relate policy formulation during World War II to policies that now govern United States relations with the Middle East. To a large degree the two are interrelated, with wartime policy providing a foundation for that which followed during the postwar era.

Preface

No author is without a debt of gratitude to others for assistance in completing his book. I am no exception. I wish to acknowledge the assistance of Susan Smith, inter-library loan librarian at my college, for providing many needed sources. Anne Chowns helped me in using U.S. government documents related to my subject. Jackie Davis and Jane Sapp also provided numerous yeoman chores in the library that were beneficial. The manuscript was greatly improved by the critical readings of Robert W. Sellen, professor of history at Georgia State University. A grant from the West Georgia Faculty Research Council was most helpful in completing this work. Albert S. Hanser, my department chairman, graciously provided released time from the classroom to enable me to work on this book. Mary Ivey provided useful assistance by typing portions of the manuscript. My wife Anne not only gave the manuscript a good reading, but took on many family chores while the work was in progress. My children Tommy and Olivia continued to evince an interest in the "newest book."

Thomas A. Bryson

West Georgia College
Carrollton, Ga.

Chapter 1

Introduction

The genesis of America's Middle Eastern diplomatic ties is to be found in the early days of the republic. Relations between this nation and the Middle East can be divided into three eras. The initial period, 1784 to 1941, is characterized by a lack of political involvement in the region. Policy-makers were guided by dictates of the Monroe Doctrine and protection of missionary and educational interests constituted the main themes of the diplomatic record. To be sure, trade expansion was an important consideration, for during the early nineteenth century, diplomatic overtures and naval power aimed to eradicate the Barbary menace that threatened commerce in the Mediterranean. Support for quests for economic concessions in Turkey before and after World War I and for American oil companies in the 1920s also marked the emphasis on commercial expansion. In a sense policy-making in the 1920s marked a transition, for it was during this time that the nation's diplomatists began to give higher priority to commercial expansion than to furthering the aims and aspirations of the missionaries and philanthropists and their lobby. During the years of America's involvement in World War II, 1941 to 1945, this country's foreign policy-makers were concerned with winning the war and in perpetuating continued American access to the sources of petroleum in the Middle East. This period marked a watershed in the nation's Middle Eastern diplomatic intercourse, for protection of private noneconomic interests gave way to considerations of the national interests. During the years since World War II, national security interests, as related to the Middle East, have continued to remain uppermost in the minds of policy-makers. Containment of the Soviet thrust into the Middle East, preservation of transportation and communication routes, the need to stabilize a region torn by strife over the creation of Israel, and a growing dependence on Middle Eastern petroleum resources to heighten the economic recovery of our European allies constitued main themes in U.S. Middle Eastern diplomacy.

In taking a closer look at the America's Middle Eastern experiences, we find that as early as the colonial period Americans had established ties

1

in the Middle East. The New England colonies had a considerable commerce with the Barbary states which amounted to one-sixth of their total export in wheat, one-fourth of their export of dried and pickled fish, and which ran from eight to one hundred ships per year.[1] In the aftermath of the Revolution, American trade with the British West Indies — a most important segment of the colonists' trade — was disrupted, and New England merchants sought to replace that commerce with trade in the Baltic, the Orient, and the Mediterranean. Soon American ships sailed the cold dark waters of the Baltic and cruised the warm blue reaches of the Pacific, but American commerce with the Mediterranean lands was obstructed by the Barbary corsairs. The United States initiated a Middle Eastern diplomacy in May 1784, when Congress appointed a special commission, consisting of Benjamin Franklin, John Adams, and Thomas Jefferson, to negotiate treaties with the Barbary states. Between then and 1789 American diplomacy was largely unsuccessful, for the treasury lacked the funds to pay the tribute to complete the treaties with Barbary that were so necessary to commercial intercourse. After the adoption of the Constitution of 1787, and the implementation of Alexander Hamilton's economic plan, Congress had the money to support a diplomatic policy *vis-à-vis* Barbary, and the wherewithal to build a Navy to project naval power into the Mediterranean to implement that policy. Between the years 1795 and 1816 the United Sates alternated between using diplomatic overtures and the application of naval power in treating with the Barbary states. This era gave rise to the famous naval displomats — Edward Preble, Stephen Decatur, William Bainbridge — who treated with Barbary at the mouth of a cannon and wrote large in the annals of American diplomacy as they achieved the freedom of the seas for American merchant ships in the Mediterranean.

But American diplomacy with the Middle East was not entirely commercial, for during the nineteenth century and the early years of the twentieth, a long train of missionaries, educators, mariners, naval officers, military advisers, technical experts, archaelogists, diplomats, and oil men journeyed to the Middle East, there to fulfill this country's manifest destiny in a region that would have great import for the nation in the middle years of the twentieth century.

American missionaries originally arrived in the Levant in 1820. In the years following the negotiation of the Turco-American Treaty of 1830, the American Board of Commissioners for Foreign Missions dispatched more than sixty missionaries to the Middle East. They were scattered across the region from Greece to Persia and from Constantinople to Syria and Palestine. They found the Muslim population opposed to the reception of the Christian Gospel, and so they turned their attention to education and medicine. Soon the missionaries and their helpers were operating schools and clinics in Anatolia, Perisa, Syria, Lebanon, and Egypt. Although unsuccessful in evangelizing the Muslims, the missionaries directed their energies to the native Christian peoples of the Middle East, namely the Armenians, the Greeks, the Nestorians,   the Copts, and the various Christian peoples of Lebanon. The missionary educators emphasized cultural traditions and native languages, and in so doing they stimulated the rise of modern Arab nationalism, as well as the embryonic emergence of nationalism among the Armenian peoples.[2]

While the schools were important in imparting to the peoples of the Middle East the rudiments of education, it was the founding of Robert College in 1863, Syrian Protestant College in 1866, and Constantinople Women's College in 1871 that gave the missionaries a vital role in training a cadre of leaders that would speed the peoples of the Middle East toward progress and modernity. In so doing, they provided the region with a vanguard of trained people who formed the foundation supporting the pillars of the modern Middle Eastern nation state.

It was only natural that the missionaries taught their college students the concepts of western political thought. The subject peoples of the Ottoman Empire—the Arabs, Armenians, Bulgarians, Greeks, Cretans—having received ideas that stimulated their own cultural nationalism and imbibed the theories of Locke, Jefferson, Hume, and Paine, began to evince a yearning for the right to a national destiny. The United States would serve as the model for the classrooms and for the subject peoples. As the subject minorities initiated their national movements to achieve self-determination, their leaders tendered requests to Washington, beseeching the United States government to use its good offices on their behalf. While the missionaries championed their cause, the official policy in Washington was one based on the Monroe Doctrine and the teachings of the Founding Fathers. American officials sympathized with the cause of the subject peoples, but could only remain aloof in keeping with the long-standing policy of nonintervention. It was during the Greek Revolution that Secretary of State John Quincy Adams enunciated the official American policy regarding the subject peoples, later incorporated in the Monroe Doctrine. In a ringing peroration, Adams declared:

> Wherever the standard of freedom and independence has been or shall be unfurled, there will her [U.S.] heart, her benedictions, and her prayers be. But she goes not abroad in search of monsters to destroy. She is the well-wisher to the freedom and independence of all. But she is the champion and vindicator only of her own. She well knows that by once enlisting under other banners than her own, were they even the banners of foreign independence, she would involve herself beyond the power of extrication, in all the wars of interest and intrigue, of individual avarice, envy, and ambition, which assume the colors and usurp the standard of freedom.[3]

Subsequently, President James Monroe declared official policy in the Monroe Doctrine. While private American groups, including the missionaries, both championed the cause of the republican Greeks and provided them with substantial quantities of relief supplies, official Washington remained aloof. This precedent of public nonintervention and private relief during the days of the Greek quest for independence was repeated during the time of the revolts of the peoples of Crete in the 1860s, the Bulgarians in the 1870s, during the Armenian disturbances in the 1890s and in the period 1915-1927, and at the time of Zionist efforts to achieve the creation of a Jewish national home pursuant to the Balfour Declaration in the era following World War I.

With the passage of time, the missionary lobby became formidable, and its representatives had entrée in offices at the Department of State, in the White House, and in the halls of Congress. So powerful had the lobby become by 1900 that diplomat Lloyd Griscom declared that "the missionaries had been among the first to learn how to exert pressure in politics — even the head of our State Department used to quake when the head of a Bible Society walked in."[4] Of course the peak of the missionary lobby's power came during the administration of President Woodrow Wilson, the son of a Presbyterian minister who had matured in the midst of clergy and missionaries. Lobbyists had personal contact with Wilson, with influential members of Congress, and with officials in the Department of State. Their all-consuming goal was to realize American acceptance of a mandate for Armenia. Although failing to achieve their goal, the missionary lobby continued to press the government to act on behalf of the Armenians.[5]

While the missionaries certainly constituted a major force in shaping American Middle Eastern policy prior to World War II, there were others as well. American citizens gave technical assistance to nations in the Middle East as early as the 1830s. That decade found shipbuilder Henry Eckford building warships for the Turkish Sultan to replace those sunk at the 1828 battle of Navarino Bay. Following the American Civil War, both Union and Confederate officers made their way to Egypt, there to advise the Khedive on ways to modernize his army. In the aftermath of World War I Near East Relief personnel began to teach vocational education to the orphans in their many centers in Turkey. While this technical assistance was given by private American citizens, nevertheless it constituted the forerunner of technical assistance tendered by the United States government both during and after World War II.[6]

To be sure, private American interests gave officials in Washington good cause for providing diplomatic and naval support. Early accounts of American diplomatic agents in the Middle East indicate that one of the State Department's major concerns was the protection of missionary interests and those of other American citizens. Although it is true that the missionaries were compelled to rely upon British diplomats for protection from time to time, nevertheless the American diplomatic network later proved effective in providing adequate protection. On occasion these diplomats called on ships of the United States Navy to extend protection in the form of naval power.[7]

In the early days of the nineteenth century ships of the Mediterranean Squadron were directed to the Middle East to deal with the Barbary menace. Thereafter, these ships sailing in small groups or operating singly, used the base facility at Port Mahon in the Balearic Islands. At times, American diplomatic agents called upon the ships to proceed to certain ports to protect American citizens and property. Most notable of these occasions was the British bombardment and occupation of Egypt in 1882, when ships of the Mediterranean Squadron not only evacuated countless American citizens, but Blue Jackets landed and helped to restore order to the city of Alexandria following the cessation of hostilities.[8] After the turn of the century, American warships were present in Middle Eastern waters in larger numbers. In 1904 no less than a dozen warships were present at Tangier, Morocco, to facilitate the settlement of the episode involving Jon Perdicaris, a man claiming protection by right of naturalization. Later that year, American vessels called at Smyrna to support American diplomatic efforts to protect missionary schools in the Ottoman Empire. Perhaps the most impressive visit of American warships to the Middle East was the passage of the Great White Fleet through Mediterranean waters in 1909, when the sixteen battleships called at numerous Middle Eastern ports. During World War I American warships provided relief to Jews, Arabs, and Armenians, and after the cessation of hostilities, the American Naval Detachment in Turkish Waters, operating singly or in groups of two or more, provided numerous services to American citizens in the Middle East.[9] In addition to protecting American interests, American naval officers became their country's diplomatic representatives afloat. The furtherance of American commerce was one of the major goals of these officers, and to Admiral Mark L. Bristol, the U.S. High Commissioner in Turkey from 1919 to 1927, go highest laurels for his efforts to further trade in the Middle East.[10]

Admiral Bristol's activities on behalf of commerce were in line with the precedents set during the Taft years. While it is true that American oil interests were not active in the Middle East in the prewar era, nevertheless other commercial interests were busily pursuing economic goals that attracted official support. The administration of President William H. Taft supported the group led by Rear Admiral Colby M. Chester, a retired U.S. naval officer, who attempted to obtain an extensive economic concession in the Ottoman Empire. The effort to obtain a concession calling for the development of mineral resources, including oil, and a railroad, received the President's imprimatur, for Chester's policy was harmonious with the large policy of "Dollar Diplomacy" which constituted United States policy in both Latin American and East Asia. The effort to obtain the Chester concession proved abortive, but it heralded government support for commercial interests that became the hallmark of United States policy in the 1920s when the Department of State employed the Open Door policy for the advantage of American oil interests in the Middle East.[11]

While State Department representation of the interests of the Chester group indicates that American policy was formulated in response to the needs of interests groups, there were occasions when policy was the direct result of an official government initiative. This was the case at the Algeciras Conference, an international forum convened to consider the Moroccan problem. President Theodore Roosevelt ordered American representatives to attend, for he desired to use American good offices to preserve world peace, then threatened by German opposition to the French presence in Morocco, a reality created by the Anglo-French *Entente Cordiale* of 1904. Too, Roosevelt hoped thereby to indicate American support for the Anglo-French accord.

Support of the Chester Concession and participation in the Algeciras Conference marked a greater American role in the Middle East, one that heralded increased interests in that region during World War I. In the war years American missionary interests once again assumed a dominating role in the shaping of American Middle Eastern policy. The outbreak of hostilities in 1914 caused the missionaries no end of troubles, but they were fortunate in having Henry Morgenthau as the American Ambassador in Turkey. He ably represented their interests in Washington, where President Woodrow Wilson gave a sympathetic ear to the missionary cause. The missionary lobby was responsible for the establishment of Near East Relief, a philanthropic organization that raised funds to assist the destitute Armenians who had been subjected to deportation, starvation, and massacre by the Turks who viewed them as a disruptive, pro-Russian influence in the Ottoman Empire. The organization raised over $100 million in relief funds. President Wilson had close ties with Near East Relief, and government agencies gave it fullest cooperation during and after the war. It was during Wilson's tenure in the White House that the missionary lobby reached perhaps the high-water mark of its influence in official government circles in Washington.[12] Following American entry into the war, the missionary lobby influenced the President's decision not to intervene in the war in the Middle East, for such a declaration of war against Turkey would have resulted in Turkish reprisals against the missionaries who operated schools and hospitals.

In addition to being receptive to the needs of the Armenians, the President also lent a receptive ear to the wishes of American Zionists whose influence was also apparent during the Wilson years. Palestinian Jews were cut off from channels of commerce, supply, and funding after the outbreak of war. American Zionists spearheaded an effort to obtain government sanction of the employment of ships of the U.S. Navy to supply these Jews with materials necessary to their survival. The effort marked the genesis of Zionist influences on American foreign policy. As the war progressed, and it appeared that the Zionists' goal of creation of a Jewish national home in Palestine was a distinct possibility, Zionist pressure on the President increased. Zionist influence persuaded the President to abort Ambassador Morgenthau's 1917 mission to seek a separate peace between Turkey and the Allies. Jews reasoned that a British military offensive against the Turks in Palestine was much more in line with ultimate Zionist goals. American Zionists also influenced Wilson's approval of the Balfour Declaration, a British-sponsored statement calling for the creation of a Jewish national home in Palestine.

Armenians and Zionists received much of the President's attention, but his plans for the postwar Middle East were more comprehensively set forth in his Fourteen Points. Point XII provided that the "Turkish Portions of the Ottoman Empire should be assured a secure sovereignty," but that the national minorities, the non-Turkish people under Ottoman hegemony, should be assured the right of self-determination. Wilson journeyed to Paris, determined to obtain justice for subject nationalities, but he had not reckoned on the secret treaties made by the Allies to slice up the Turkish empire. Faced with the problem of reconciling a Middle Eastern solution with the aims of the Allies and the goals of Wilson, the Paris Peace Conference adopted the mandate solution presented by Prime Minister Jan Smuts of South Africa. To determine the wishes of the peoples about their poitical future, Wilson caused a fact-finding commission to tour the Levant. Known as the King-Crane Commission, it presented a report on the disposition of the subject peoples that varied greatly with the aims of the Allies. But the report was suppressed at the bidding of the French.[13]

But Wilson erred from the principle of self-determination in permitting the Greeks to invade and occupy the western portion of Anatolia around the port city of Smyrna. The Greek incursion set off a chain of events that led to the rise of Turkish nationalism under the aegis of Mustapha Kemal and the ultimate downfall of the Allied settlement for Turkey. The Turks not only opposed Allied occupation of Anatolia but also the creation of an Armenian state under the American mandate.

Ultimately, Wilson was compelled to withdraw altogether from the Middle East, for not only had a reluctant Senate failed to approve the Versailles Treaty, containing the League of Nations Covenant, but it also rejected outright the President's bid to accept an Armenian mandate. His health broken, his peace plan in shambles, Wilson could only issue faint pronunciamentos concerning the disposition of the Middle East. The European powers worked their will, dividing up the Ottoman Empire into mandates, thus neglecting the bid of Armenians, Jews, and Arabs for the right of self-determination of peoples.

Although the United States government withdrew from the negotiation of a final Middle Eastern settlement, it nevertheless remained interested in political developments in the region during the interwar years. The missionary-relief lobby continued to plead the Armenian cause and for government protection of its operation of schools, hospitals, orphanages, and technical-vocational programs. High on the list of priorities of the State Department in this period was an on-going effort to secure the rights of missionaries to carry on their work in the Middle East. To be sure, American diplomats encouraged the missionaries to accommodate themselves to the emergence of the vital force of nationalism which manifested itself during the interwar years in the Middle East. That the missionary-relief lobby was still a viable force in shaping an American Middle Eastern policy is evidenced by the lobby's successful effort to bring about Senate opposition to the Turco-American Treaty of Lausanne. The failure of this treaty caused the State Department to obtain a *modus vivendi* with the Turks that provided for continued American trade with Turkey.

However, during the decades of the 1920s and 1930s, commercial expansion was uppermost on the list of political priorities in the State Department, and American Foreign Service Officers did not permit the interests and aims of missionaries to interfere with the attainment of economic and commercial goals. Indeed, Admiral Mark Bristol, U.S. High Commissioner to Turkey, considered that American economic involvement in the former Ottoman Empire was of the greatest necessity to the continued prosperity of the American people.[14] But perhaps the most significant example of government assistance to American economic interests came with the State Department's support of American oil interests during the interwar period.

The American quest for Middle Eastern oil was prompted by the belief that wartime depletion of American domestic oil reserves would result in a postwar shortage. In 1919 and again in 1920 members of the U.S. Senate demanded that the State Department initiate steps to remove all restrictions placed by the foreign governments on American oil exploration. The Wilson administration, followed by those of Harding and Coolidge, utilized the Open Door as a tool for driving a wedge into the Middle East that would enable American oil interests to obtain access to valuable oil reserves in Iraq. This was part of an aggressive postwar

American quest for oil in the Dutch East Indies, Mexico, Venezuela, Colombia, Peru, and of course the Middle East. For over a decade the State Department, working in tandem with executives of several large American oil companies, utilized the Open Door to obtain a position for American oil interests in the Iraq Petroleum Company. Although American entry into this international oil consortium was eventually realized in 1929, the five American companies were regulated by the famous "Red Line Agreement," a self-denying clause that prohibited all members from independently exploring for oil beyond an area marked on the map by a red line.[15]

The American quest for oil also ran into obstructionist tactics in Persia (Iran), and it was not until after World War II that American interests would gain access to the rich Iranian oil fields.

But success was not to be denied the American oil concerns, and the Gulf Oil Company, in partnership with the Anglo-Persian Oil Company, obtained a rich concession in the Sheikhdom of Kuwait, one that later proved to be one of the richest oil finds in the Middle East. But the most lucrative concession went to the Standard Oil Company of California. Known to all as SOCAL, it obtained an exclusive concession to explore for oil in Saudi Arbia. By the end of the 1930s, SOCAL's geologists had located oil in commerical quantities, and it was producing oil in sufficient quantities to obtain access to overseas oil markets. To ensure access to these markets, SOCAL brought the Texas Company into its organization, ultimately renamed the Arabian-American Oil Company (ARAMCO) in 1944. Also SOCAL was fortunate in obtaining a concession in the oil-rich sheikhdom of Bahrain, an island in the Persian Gulf adjacent to Saudi Arbia.

By the outbreak of World War II in 1939 the American interest in Middle Eastern oil was considerable. In that year approximately 15 percent of the oil produced in Middle Eastern oil fields was for the accounts of American petroleum companies. And so it was only natural that with the onset of World War II that American oil concerns would require continued State Department efforts to protect their reserves in the Middle East, reserves which would later prove vital to the Allied war effort.

Assistance to American petroleum companies was but one instance of State Department support of commerical interest in the Middle East. When Admiral Cobly M. Chester and his associates resumed their effort to obtain a concession in Turkey, the Department once again lent its backing to this venture. At length, the concession was awarded for the construction of railroads and the exploitation of mineral resources along the right of way. But failure to raise the necessary capital resulted in the cancelation of the concession in December 1923.[16]

American commercial interests were also busy elsewhere in the Middle East. In Iran, several American concerns participated in the building of the Trans-Iranian Railroad from the Caspian Sea to the Persian Gulf. While one of the American companies did not realize full compensation for its efforts, nevertheless the project was to prove important during World War II when countless thousands of tons of American Lend-Lease material would travel over this vital transportation link to the Soviet Union.[17] In Turkey, several American companies established branch factories, and in the interwar period the products of the Ford Motor Company, the Curtis Wright Corporaton, and the Standard Oil Company were being distributed throughout the Anatolian peninsula.

But commerce was not the only American interest in the Middle East in the years between the wars, for American Zionists continued to lobby in Washington, urging the U.S. government to use its good offices to persuade Great Britian to implement the Balfour Declaration to the end that a Jewish national home might be created in Palestine. Britain had occupied Palestine during the war, and in 1922 she received a League of Nations mandate for that land. As a sop to disappointed Arabs, she created the state of Transjordan in 1928, with the Emir Abdullah, a member of the Hashemite dynasty, as ruling monarch. But the State Department refused to heed the pleas of American Zionists, continuing to regard Palestine as a British problem. Impervious to Congressional pressure and the importunities of the Zionist lobby, the Department acted merely to protect American rights in the Palestinian mandate.

With the advent of the 1930s, the rise of Adolf Hiter, and Germany's calculated program to destroy the Jewish community in that country, American Jews stepped up their petitions to Washington. In 1939, the British Foreign Office issued a White Paper, repudiating the British pledge to implement the Balfour Declaration, and setting forth a policy that would limit Jewish immigration to Palestine. American Jews inundated the White House with messages, asking that the President use his influence to realize Zionist goals. In spite of their lobbying and flooding the country with propaganda on behalf of the Zionist program, the United States government adhered to the policy that Palestine was a British problem and the United States would continue to pursue a policy of nonintervention.[18]

Thus, during the interwar years American diplomatists continued to acknowledge the supremacy of British and French influence in the region. For this reason their reaction to the pleas of Armenians, Jews, and Arabs was one of aloofness. While American policy-makers sympathized with peoples' aspirations to self-determination engendered by many years as wards of the Ottoman Empire, and then subject to the mandates of Western powers, the U.S. government would not move to help them realize their goals. Nevertheless, the State Department was ever vigilant to see that private American interests, both economic and philanthropic, were protected in all parts of the Middle East.

Although the peoples of the Middle East evinced a strong nationalist spirit during these years, the State Department continually cautioned American interests in the Middle East to accommodate their aims to the nationalistic aspirations of the Turks, Persians, Egyptians, and others. Not only was there a willingness to accommodate to the nationalism of the Middle Eastern peoples, but there was also a continued unwillingness to accept as permanent the British and French imperial positions in the Levant. At the outbreak of war in 1939, there was a strong anti-imperial feeling in the Department of State, where many of the Foreign Service Officers were convinced that conditions would develop in such a fashion as to offer the United States a golden opportunity to take advantage of the large funds of good will toward Americans in the Arab states, Turkey, and Iran in order that American business might capture new markets and realize large profits at the expense of the British and the French.[19]

As the outbreak of World War II approached, policy-makers in Washington had not as yet developed a comprehensive, region-wide policy. To be sure, the traditional guiding principles continued to point the direction that policy-makers would take. But as yet no steps had been taken to develop policy statements on American interests in a region that would see great change with the oneset of hostilities in 1939. Of course, there had developed during the prewar years a tendency to formulate policy on a country by country basis. Perhaps the lack of a comprehensive policy can be explained by a tendency to recognize that Great Britain had major interests in the region, the United States had few, and foreign policy needs simply did not call for a regional policy.

While the age-old tradition of nonintervention had guided policy-makers in Washington from the inception of republic, the American involvement in World War II in the Middle East would change that tradition. The onset of hostilities would create a new power configuration in the Middle East and create new economic needs. First, the leadership of the world-wide Zionist movement would pass to the United States during the war. The disclosure of Hitler's barbarous treatment of European Jewry would harden the purpose of American Zionists, who in the postwar era would demand United States diplomatic support for the implementation of the Balfour Declaration. Endorsement of and backing for the realization of Zionist goals would irreversibly involve the United States in the growing political complexities in the Middle East in the postwar years. Second, during the war years American policy-makers would perceive a growing shortage of oil in the United States and demand an aggressive oil policy that would ensure access to Middle Eastern oil sources in the postwar era. John A. DeNovo observed that "by 1939, oil and Zionism were the two most potent factors operating to out mode traditional American noninvolvement in the Arab Middle East during the course of the war."[20]

While the factors of oil and Zionism would thrust the United States irrevocably into the Middle East, it was considerations of wartime strategy that first placed the Mddle East high on the list of American foreign policy objectives. Following the fall of France in 1940, the United States maintained diplomatic relations with the obnoxious Vichy regime. Vichy controlled French North Africa, the French fleet, and other French colonies, a number of which were in the western hemisphere. Diplomatic ties plus the extension of economic aid enabled this country to lay the foundation for the Allied invasion of North Africa and for the subsequent reentry of French forces into the war against the Axis.

Following the Japanese bombing of Pearl Harbor, the United States declared war on Germany, Japan, and Italy. Immediately after Pearl Harbor, Prime Minister Winston S. Churchill crossed the Atlantic to discuss wartime military objectives with President Franklin D. Roosevelt. In the historic Washington Conference, known by the code name of ARCADIA, Churchill and Roosevelt established the prototype for the summit conference that would serve the two leaders so well in subsequent conferences. The strategy talks centered around ways and means of launching an attack against the Germans in 1942 to relieve the Russians who were so badly pressed by Hitler's legions on the Eastern Front. The decision to launch an Anglo-American invasion of French North Africa, tentatively agreed upon by Churchill and Roosevelt, ultimately was to involve the United States in the war in the Middle East.

Chapter 2

Anglo-American
Strategic Considerations

Immediately after the Japanese attack on Pearl Harbor, Prime Minister Winston S. Churchill, accompanied by an entourage of military advisers, traveled to Washington to discuss Anglo-American strategic considerations that ultimately led to a joint Anglo-American amphibious landing in French North Africa in November 1942, known as Operation TORCH. Most often referred to as the ARCADIA Conference, this "summit" meeting was to be the first of many between the two Allied leaders. The conference permitted the American and British leaders to exchange their views, and it initiated the six-month period of debate that culminated in Operation TORCH.

While traveling on *H.M.S. Duke of York* to Hampton Roads, Virginia, Winston Churchill produced three position papers on the future course of the war. One dealt with the Atlantic Front, another with the Pacific Front, and the third treated military possibilities for the year 1943. For the Atlantic, the Prime Minister anticipated an Anglo-American invasion of French North Africa, a stroke that would deny the Germans Dakar and other principal French West African ports. This strategy called for cooperation with the forces of the French military command in North Africa. His plan envisioned the employment of fifty-five thousand British troops, consisting of two divisions and an armored contingent, and required that the United States dispatch an equivalent of three infantry divisions and one armored division to Northern Ireland to complete their training for future participation in the Anglo-American landing in North Africa.[1]

Churchill and company landed at Hampton Roads on December 22 and promptly flew to Washington. That evening the Prime Minister met with President Franklin D. Roosevelt, and immediately the men and their staffs launched into a discussion of Churchill's scheme for an Anglo-American invasion of North Africa. Of course Roosevelt had not yet had a chance to study Churchill's papers for the future conduct of the war.

13

Churchill records that this meeting, which included Cordell Hull, Secretary of State, Sumner Welles, Under Secretary of State, Harry Hopkins, President Roosevelt's personal adviser, Lord Beaverbrook, British Minister of Air, and Lord Halifax, British Ambassador to Washington, "cut deeply into business."[2] Churchill noted that there was support for his plan, for it was agreed that it "was vital to forestall the Germans in Northwest Africa...." Fearing an incursion into that region that would give the Germans the port of Dakar from which to launch forays against the Western Hemisphere, President Roosevelt asserted that he favored committing American land forces to battle as soon as possible and the plan for an invasion of North Africa met with his approval.[3]

At the first plenary meeting of the two political leaders and their military staffs on 23 December, Churchill again brought up his plan for an invasion of North Africa. Reiterating his talk of the evening before, the Prime Minister declared that Britain had the requisite troops ready for an invasion. He asked for American cooperation in this venture by moving troops to Northern Ireland. The President responded, saying that he "considered it very important to morale to give this country a feeling that they are in the war, to give the Germans the reverse effect, and to have American troops somewhere in active fighting across the Atlantic."[4] A subsequent meeting of the President and Prime Minister and their military advisers on January 4, 1942, indicated that there was some measure of agreement about moving ahead with an Anglo-American invasion of North Africa later in 1942.[5] The President again broached the matter at a meeting on January 12, saying that reports from North Africa suggested that French Army officers were interested in plans for an invasion. He advised that overtures be made to them and that a "fairly well settled time table" should be established for the forthcoming operation.[6]

Of this 12 January meeting, Churchill recorded that "there was complete agreement upon the broad principles and targets of the war." He wrote that "a tentative time-table had been worked out for putting ninety thousand U.S. and ninety thousand British troops ... into North Africa. It was settled to send two American divisions to Northern Ireland." But James MacGregor Burns wrote that Roosevelt's enthusiasm for the North Africa operation had cooled following ARCADIA, indicating that General George C. Marshall and Secretary of War Henry L. Stimson had influenced his thinking on strategic questions.[7]

Although plans for an Anglo-American invasion of North Africa had been discussed, there was much tough negotiating ahead before plans were confirmed, for General Marshall, Chief of Staff, was opposed to launching an invasion of North Africa which would utilize the forces so urgently needed for an invasion of Northern France — an operation he envisioned as necessary to Germany's final defeat. Marshall firmly believed that the Allies should strike across the English Channel and then aim at the heart of Germany. This strategy, he believed, would bring the war to an early end. But there should be no side shows as anticipated by the British plan for an invasion of North Africa.

While American and British military chiefs would continue the debate on future strategy, ARCADIA ended on a positive note. The Americans and British had reaffirmed their war plans in the Declaration of the United Nations, dated January 1, 1942. The Anglo-American planners were fully committed to a strategy of defeating Germany first, and were at least temporarily in agreement about a joint invasion of North Africa. They believed that the creation of a Combined Chiefs of Staff, to operate in Washington, would further enhance the war effort.[8]

But the aura of good feeling that accompanied the ARCADIA Conference soon dissipated, for General Dwight D. Eisenhower, working under General Marshall, had developed an elaborate strategy which called for using the British Isles as a base for the launching of an invasion of Northern Europe. Eisenhower expressed the War Department's thinking in January 1942: "We've got to go to Europe and fight — and we've got to quit wasting resources all over the world — and still worse — wasting time. If we're to keep Russia in, save the Middle East, India, and Burma, we've got to begin slugging with air at Western Europe, to be followed by a land attack as soon as possible."[9]

This plan had the support of General Marshall and Secretary Stimson, and on April 1 General Marshall presented the plan worked out by General Eisenhower and his staff to the President. Assisted by Stimson and Hopkins, Marshall succeeded in winning the President's endorsement of the plan for an Anglo-American invasion of Northern Europe in 1943. Roosevelt ordered Hopkins and Marshall to travel to London to discuss the plan with British military leaders and win their agreement.[10]

The Hopkins-Marshall mission departed Baltimore on April 4. Given the code name "Modicum," it included numerous military and civilian advisers. The party traveled via Pan American Clipper to Bermuda and Scotland, arriving at London on the morning of April 18. Marshall and Hopkins promptly went into conference with the Prime Minister. The basis of the conversation was the memorandum prepared by Eisenhower and his staff for the invasion of Northern Europe in 1943. The two Americans found the Prime Minister in agreement with the Eisenhower plan. Hopkins impressed upon Churchill the reality that the plan had the President's firm approval, that it was necessary to launch an invasion of Europe as soon as possible in order to relieve the pressure on the Russians and strike at the heart of Germany. General Marshall argued vehemently for two attacks on the continent: The first, known as SLEDGEHAMMER, would be launched in the autumn of 1942. It was to be considered an emergency measure, taken only if German victories on the battlefield threatened to cause the collapse of the Soviet Union. The second invasion, called ROUNDUP, would be a much larger operation and would be scheduled for the spring of 1943. This landing would constitute the main thrust at the heartland of Germany. Any operation in North Africa the General considered as peripheral and met with his opposition.[11]

On April 14, the Anglo-American leaders met in extended session. After a lengthy discussion of world-wide strategic considerations, the Prime Minister agreed that the two nations' plans for a 1942 operation would need to be governed by developments on the Russian Front.[12]

In reality the British Prime Minister's agreement was hedged. He could not help recalling the bloodbath that had accompanied British fighting in Flanders fields and on the bloody Gallipoli Peninsula in World War I. While agreeing in principle to an Anglo-American invasion of France, he opposed premature action in 1942 that might lead to a stalemate. Recalling the experience of the Canadians at Dieppe, he firmly believed that a cross-Channel attack must carry a preponderance of British and American military might to ensure a firm beachhead that might quickly he expanded. Too, he continued to dread a possible German-Japanese link up in the Middle East, an action that would remove the vital oil reserves of that region from the Allied list of economic assets. Although Hopkins and Marshall assumed that they had won Churchill's unqualified approval, they were mistaken, for much hard negotiating remained ahead for the Anglo-American military planners before finally determining a strategy for 1942.[13]

In May 1942, Russian Foreign Commissar V. M. Molotov paid a hasty visit to London, inquiring of the Prime Minister if the Anglo-American allies planned to launch an invasion of France in 1942 that would divert some forty-odd German divisions from the Russian Front. Churchill expressed the difficulties of such an operaton.[14] For his part, he began to develop even stronger reservations about an Anglo-American invasion of the continent in 1942. Meeting with his military staff and with his cabinet, the Prime Minister concluded that there was no possibility of mounting an invasion of France in 1942, but that 1943 offered much more auspicious circumstances for such an operation. He concluded that during 1942 only French North Africa provided the Anglo-Americans sufficient prospects for an operation against the Germans.[15]

With these reservations in mind, the Prime Minister journeyed to Washington in June 1942 to persuade the American President of the impracticality of an invasion of France for 1942 and of the need to reconsider the invasion of French North Africa. Accompanied by Field Marshal Sir John Dill, by Sir Alan Brooke, chief of the Imperial General Staff, and by Major General Sir Hastings Ismay, Churchill departed on his trans-

Atlantic flight on June 17. Following their arrival in the United States, the British and their American hosts carried on their meeting at two levels. The Combined Chiefs of Staff held their meetings in Washington, while the President and Prime Minister conferred at the President's home at Hyde Park, New York, and later at the White House. There were also informal conferences between lower echelon American and British military men. Differences of opinion over strategic goals caused the Americans and British to spar over the merits of the 1942 and 1943 landings in Northern France and the alternative combined operation for French North Africa in 1942. The British officers were unalterably opposed to any landing in France in 1942, while the Americans considered an operation in North Africa to be merely peripheral.[16]

On June 20, the President's private train bore him, the Prime Minister, and advisers to Washington, there to continue the high-level talks. The following morning found the Anglo-American leaders in conference. During the meeting, news arrived of the fall of the British forces at Tobruk in North Africa. This news was shocking and it proved to be a catalyst. The Prime Minister asked the President for as many Sherman tanks as he could spare. General Marshall proposed to send three hundreds tanks and one hundred 105-mm. guns by fast convoy to the Middle East.[17] Irritated by the fall of Tobruk, the Prime Minister turned his attention again toward persuading the President to revive the plan for the North African invasion for 1942. Plans for this operation had been set aside after the ARCADIA Conference, but the President seems to have retained his belief that the Middle East offered possibilities for the employment of American troops against the Germans in 1942. After a lengthy meeting on the 23rd, Roosevelt suggested to Marshall the possibility of sending an American military force to the Middle East to take over the area between Tehran and Alexandria.[18]

On the following day General Marshall invited the Prime Minister and his military advisers to attend American Army maneuvers at Fort Jackson, South Carolina. The maneuvers impressed the British negatively, for they concluded that the untried American troops were not yet ready for combat against the experienced German divisions. Churchill and party returned to Washington and then set out on the long flight to London.

Aware of the greenness of American troops in the field and that British troops in Egypt were falling back to El Alamein only sixty short miles from Alexandria, the British Prime Minister was convinced that North Africa rather than France held out the brightest prospects for Anglo-American arms for 1942. And so when General Marshal dispatched General Eisenhower to London on June 23 as Commanding General of United States Forces, European Theater, with orders to prepare to launch a second front against the Germans in Northern France, Churchill wasted little time in asserting his opposition to the American plan. The Prime Minister announced to Eisenhower that SLEDGEHAMMER was not in the offing for 1942 and that only a landing in North Africa offered real prospects for victory. Churchill advised Roosevelt on July 8 that British military leaders were absolutely opposed to SLEDGEHAMMER for 1942 and that only Operation GYMNAST, the planned operation for a landing in North Africa, held out hope for an effective means of drawing off German troops from the Eastern Front. Learning of British intransigence, General Marshall turned to a desperate expedient. He considered turning America's full military might toward the Pacific to prosecute the war against the Japanese if the British continued to prove obstinate. But the President was determined to pursue a Europe First policy, and he so informed the General on July 14.[19]

Aware that American and British military chiefs were still at loggerheads on matters of strategy, Roosevelt decided to send Hopkins, Marshall, and Chief of Naval Operations Admiral Ernest J. King to London to iron out Anglo-American differences, with a view to launching a joint attack against the Germans in 1942. The President was now thinking seriously of the North African operation. This was General Marshall's understanding and it was also Churchill's conclusion. The Prime Minister wrote that "I had made a careful study of the President's mind and its reactions for some time past, and I was sure that he was powerfully attracted by the North African plan."[20] Indeed, President Roosevelt's memorandum for the guidance of Hopkins, Marshall, and King cautioned that all "available U.S. and British forces should be brought into action as quickly as they can be profitably used." He urged that "it is of the highest importance that U.S. ground troops be brought into action against the enemy in 1942." If Operation SLEDGEHAMMER is out of the picture, then the Anglo-American planners should consider taking steps to cut off German occupation of French North Africa.[21]

With the President's words carefully considered, Marshall, Hopkins, and King departed for London on July 16 to meet with the British and determine the course of strategy that would guide Anglo-American forces for the next two years. The outcome of the London talks would be the decision to launch a joint invasion of French North Africa in the fall of 1942, thus ultimately delaying the larger invasion of Northern France until 1944. The likely outcome was presaged in the July 20 talks with the British. Prime Minister Churchill presented a powerful argument against launching SLEDGEHAMMER in 1942. If this operation were scrapped, then he suggested that thought be given to an occupation of French North Africa to head off a possible German intrusion into the vital region. Marshall and King reiterated their argument for a cross-Channel attack in 1942 to succour the hard-pressed Russians. At the opening of the second meeting on July 22, General Marshall announced that the Anglo-American military chiefs had reached a deadlock in their talks and that he had cabled the President for further informaton.[22]

The President duly replied, relating that he was not surprised over the stalemate on SLEDGEHAMMER, and urged his delegation to arrive at some decision with the British that would result in the employment of American forces against the Germans in 1942. He suggested that they consider an operation in North Africa. On the following day, Roosevelt cabled a longer and more detailed instruction, asserting that he now supported the launching of the North African combined operation for the autumn of 1942. When the President learned from Hopkins that there was some hesitancy about pushing ahead with Operaton GYMNAST, Roosevelt replied that the Anglo-American planners should proceed at once to make plans for the GYMNAST landings which should occur not later than October 30.[23]

On July 25 the British Chiefs of Staff accepted the American proposal to establish a planning organization for the invasion of French North Africa and for the cross-Channel attack. Operation GYMNAST was now rechristened Operation TORCH. Before departing for the United States, Marshall advised Eisenhower that he favored placing him in charge of Operation TORCH and the subsequent planning for the cross-Channel invasion. Formal confirmation of Eisenhower as supreme commander was not settled until August 14, when the President notified the General of his appointment.[24]

The President had thought that the July 25 decision on TORCH was final, but there was still considerable opposition to the plan. Marshall and Stimson and their military advisers continued through early August to oppose TORCH. They not only mistrusted the President's judgment, but they also believed that he had been misled by the Prime Minister into favoring an operation that was merely peripheral to the larger task of striking a mortal blow at Germany across the English Channel. The Chief of Staff was of the opinion that the amphibious convoy directed to deliver the troops and equipment on North African beaches would be compelled to cross the U-boat infested waters of the Atlantic and land troops on beaches made treacherous by bad weather. To meet the needs of Operation TORCH he was compelled to equip a force by robbing from other American units and a convoy that was due to sail for Russia in October. Too, TORCH constituted a drain on American manpower resources badly needed in the Pacific theater. There was also a considerable difference between Churchill and Roosevelt about the scope of the North African operation. The President anticipated that the major landing force would be American and that it would come ashore at Casablanca. The Prime Minister argued that British forces should also land simultaneously in Algeria. However, by August Marshall and Stimson swung into line and threw their weight behind TORCH, and the President and Prime Minister worked out their differences. Ultimately, the date for TORCH was pushed back by General Eisenhower to November 8, a date determined by military and not political considerations.[25]

The President's cables to Hopkins in London indicated a keen interest in the forthcoming North Africa operation. This interest was long-standing, and diplomat Robert Murphy recorded that the President was "delighted that the African enterprise finally was underway." While Murphy credited Churchill with influencing the President, he said, "Roosevelt had been more responsible for the ... venture than anyone else, and despite his innumerable preoccupations elsewhere he had found time to read our reports..."; and "the North African expedition appealed to his sense of adventure, especially as it involved a major naval operation."[26] Indeed, the President's interest was real, and historian Arthur Funk observed that Winston Churchill was aware of this concern. The Prime Minister "knew perfectly well that possessions in Africa had held for President Roosevelt a special charm. Churchill could sense, with that incredible intuition of his, that the correct line with the President should be North Africa, and again North Africa, and again and again North Africa."[27]

In order to understand Roosevelt's predilection for North Africa, we need to examine the memoirs of diplomat Robert Murphy, who traces very well the President's growing infatuation with the French colonies in North Africa. The President's pro-Vichy policy was based on strategic considerations. He hoped to keep the French fleet intact and it and the colonies out of German hands. He concluded that North Africa was the most likely point from which French troops might be once again employed against the Germans. The President's flirtation with Vichy has aroused a storm of controversy among historians.[28]

In the autumn of 1940 the President had ordered Robert Murphy, counsellor of the U.S. Embassy at Paris, to return to the White House for consultation. Roosevelt directed him to make a tour of French North Africa and to report back directly to him about political conditions in that region. Murphy records that American policy vis-à-vis French Africa became in fact "the President's personal policy. He initiated it, he kept it going, and he resisted pressures against it, until in the autumn of 1942 French North Africa became the first major battleground where Americans fought Germans."[29] It seems that the President believed that French North Africa could become a center of anti-German activity. If the French in Africa could be split off from the Vichy government in France, supplied with up-to-date American weapons, and induced to launch an attack against the German forces fighting the British in Africa, then the cause of freedom would be served. A movement led by the renowned General Maxime Weygand, the French delegate in Africa, might well become full blown by enticing the French fleet to play a decisive role in the war.[30] So important did the President regard French North Africa that he directed Murphy to by-pass the State Department and report to him alone.

Murphy arrived at Algiers on December 18, 1941, and spent slightly over two weeks visiting French officials at Dakar, Algiers, Tunis, Casablanca, and Tangier. He interviewed General Weygand and negotiated the famous Murphy-Weygand Accord, an agreement which would permit the employment of French assets frozen in U.S. banks to buy such items as cotton cloth, sugar, tea, and petroleum. The French argument for these goods was predicated on the assumption that the Germans would occupy French Africa. The French could then use these vital goods to placate the Arab populace and induce them to support the French resistance to the Nazis. Murphy concluded that the French Army in Africa could prove valuable to the United States. Thus it was in the American national interest to render economic aid to the French. He cabled to the President his report on January 17, 1941. He recorded that the President read his findings closely and used them as the basis for his North African policy.[31]

The Murphy-Weygand Accord received much opposition from the British, who approved the agreement to allow ships to pass through the British blockade with goods bound for the French African territories provided that the United States appointed a team of American diplomatic agents to ascertain that the goods did not fall into German hands. The State Department promptly recruited twelve vice consuls to serve as observers or controllers. These men were immediately dispatched to North Africa, placed under Robert Murphy, and put to work; six served in Morocco, four in Algeria, and two in Tunisia.[32] These men were given the rank of vice consul, and Murphy styled them as "rank amateurs." They served a three-fold function: they controlled the distribution of American goods in their respective areas: they collected vital military and political intelligence that was later used to aid the planners for Operation TORCH; and they created a "Fifth Column" to support the Anglo-American landings in North Africa in November 1942.[33]

In addition to the above, Murphy considered it absolutely necessary to maintain good relations with Vichy, for a successful policy would at all events depend upon the endoresement of the regime of Marshall Henri Philippe Pétain, the Vichy head of state. On hearing from President Roosevelt personally that a North African operation was being discussed, Murphy knew clearly what to do. In addition to obtaining Vichy's permission for an Anglo-American landing, he must also alert his group of pro-American, anti-German French military and government officials. But his task was not without difficulty, for the American press was critical of the pro-Vichy policy of the President, and when he conferred in London with General Eisenhower, the Allied commander for TORCH in

September 1942, he learned that the General had some reservations about the wisdom of making the landings in North Africa.[34] Eisenhower also had reservations about entrusting to the French allied plans and the November 8 date for the invasion. However, a presidential directive to Murphy spelled out the American intention to place a landing force in French North Africa to prevent the Germans and Italians from taking over the area and placing weapons and bases in the region from which to strike at the Western Hemisphere. It guaranteed that the French would continue to govern the area. But it asserted that the invasion force would be purely American in make-up.[35]

More will be said of Murphy's negotiations with the French authorities, but it is now necessary to discuss other goals that Murphy and his vice consuls were directed to achieve. Not only did this diplomatic team check out the distribution and use of American goods, but they also gathered military intelligence. Kenneth Pendar, one of the vice consuls, recorded that "we kept an eye on American goods; we gathered all the information we could."[36] The vice consuls also collected military maps, data on the depth of French African ports, the best beaches for landings, the position of French coastal batteries, the movement of tides and currents, the positions of French warships, the disposition of French troops, the condition of roads, bridges, airfields, and the attitude of French political and military figures.[37] During his time in Africa, Murphy also put together a network of French officials, both civil and military, that made up his "Fifth Column." In spite of Washington's hot and cold support of the African policy, Murphy recorded that "our French friends plotted with us for almost a year." This cloak-and-dagger activity essayed to win the support of the French military arm in North Africa that constituted 125,000 regulars and some 200,000 reservists for the Anglo-American landings.[38] In the process of putting together this subversive group, Murphy formed his "Group of Five." Through this mélange of right-wingers, republicans, and varied socieconomic backgrounds, he made contact with resistance forces in Morocco, Algeria, and Tunisia. The "Five" could work together because of their common desire to establish a government in North Africa free of Vichy control.[39]

But much of the military was adamantly loyal to Pétain, and Murphy's effort to win over the top echelon of admirals and generals did not bear fruit. Many military units were under the control of the French Navy; commanded by Admiral Michelier, the Navy remained largely loyal to Vichy. Murphy's efforts to gain the Navy's endorsement was a failure, and the French Navy hotly contested the Anglo-American landing in November 1942. Murphy was also unable to win over General Auguste Nogues, French resident general in Morocco, who also offered stiff opposition to American forces that came ashore in the landings. But it was Admiral Jean

François Darlan, the French five-star admiral who was Minister of Marine on whom Murphy concentrated his attention. The reason for the American Vichy policy was to win over such a high ranking military leader as Darlan who would support the Anglo-American war effort in Africa. Darlan could bring the French military force in North Africa and possibly the French fleet at Toulon into the war on the side of the Anglo-Americans. But an understanding with the French admiral was long delayed, for he was not yet trusted. In the meantime, Murphy turned his attention to gaining the support of General Henri Giraud. At length he was able to obtain the General's agreement to participate in the Allies' African strategy. Ultimately, General Eisenhower, with his strong sense of compromise as the key to harmony, hit on the idea of bringing Darlan and Giraud into the picture as joint rulers, and he worked out a plan that would elevate the admiral to a kind of French High Commissioner over French possessions in North Africa, and give to General Giraud command of all French military forces.[40] Giraud, then residing in France, appointed General Charles Emmanuel Mast to represent him in Algiers, and Murphy wasted no time in advising Mast that the time had come for talks between American and French military officials, with a view to bringing France back into the war.

Murphy arranged for an October meeting at a farmhouse near the town of Cherchell, about seventy-five miles west of Algiers. There, a group of French military leaders, headed by General Mast, met Eisenhower's deputy commander, Major General Mark Clark, and Brigadier General Lyman Lemnitzer. This meeting was one of the most chronicled cloak-and-dagger conferences of the war. The American officers landed by submarine and proceeded to the place of rendezvous with the Frenchmen. The meeting produced mixed results. The French were advised of the landing but were not given specific dates and times. They asserted that General Giraud desired to be placed in overall command of the Allied military force that was to come ashore on French colonial soil. They detested Darlan and presented an argument for Giraud's heading the operation. During the Cherchell talks, which were concluded on October 23, French police burst into the house looking for smugglers, and General Clark records that the conspirators had to take cover in an empty wine cellar![41]

With the invasion a scant two weeks away, Murphy had to work out some agreement between Darlan and Giraud and at the same time win over General Alphonse Juin, a high French officer reportedly pro-American. Admiral William Leahy, the President's Chief of Staff at the White House, advised Murphy on November 2: "The decision of the President is that the operation will be carried out as now planned and that you will do your utmost to secure the understanding and cooperation of

the French officials with whom you are now in contact."[42] In compliance
with his orders, Murphy advised General Giraud that it was imperative
that supreme command of the Allied forces be held by an American.[43] But
his task was difficult, for time and time again the French high command
had announced that it would resist any invasion.[44] In addition, as time for
D-Day drew near, General Giraud had not yet arrived in North Africa.
Ultimately, he reached Gibraltar, and it required two days of intense per-
suasion on the part of generals Eisenhower and Clark to gain Giraud's acceptance of working with the Allied command structure. With Giraud
brought into the picture, it only remained to gain a working relationship
with Admiral Darlan to reach the goal of French support for the landing.[45]

On the night of the invasion, the British Broadcasting Company
broadcast the spine-tingling words in French, "Allo, Robert Franklin
arrive." This was the prearranged code signal to alert Murphy and his network of resistance workers that the TORCH landings were in process. Murphy alerted his workers and they began to take over key points in Algiers.
He then contacted General Juin, the pro-American officer who had given
his word of honor to the Germans not to participate in the war against
them. Murphy advised him that the landings were then in progress. Juin
was cooperative and he assisted Murphy in making the approach to
Darlan. When apprised of the course of developments associated with
TORCH the French Admiral became apoplectic, asserting that he had given
his oath to Pétain and that he could not revoke it. Murphy urged him to
request permission from Pétain to support the American landing. The
French message to secure Pétain's endorsement was never answered, and
Murphy was ultimately taken prisoner by the French. But when Admiral
Darlan was advised that Americans were indeed landing all along the
Algerian and Moroccan coasts in superior numbers, Murphy was released
and Darlan agreed to make a contact with the American military forces.[46]

Murphy arranged for Major General Charles W. Ryder, commander of the Eastern Task Force that had landed on the beaches some ten
miles west of Algiers, to meet with Admiral Darlan and General Juin.
Following a brief but strained interchange, both parties signed a cease-fire
that stopped the fighting in the immediate area of Algiers.[47]

While this was fortuitous, the French had offered sharp resistance
to the Anglo-American landings. This was particularly true in Morocco
where the obdurate General Nogues commanded the French Army and
Navy. In the Western Task Group, Americans came ashore at three points,
marked on the map by Safi, Fedhala, and Mehedia. Naval resistance
was particularly effective, compelling the American naval armada to fight
the heated little battle of Casablanca in which American naval and air forces sank French ships and killed Frenchmen. The landings in Algeria were
mixed Anglo-American affairs, with the Royal Navy taking responsibility

for the operation. Resistance to this operation was brief. Although the Anglo-Americans made many mistakes, they accomplished the largest amphibious operation yet undertaken. It had been skillfully planned and well executed with a minimum of training. Its accomplishment in the face of French resistance and on beaches plagued with high waves was a tribute to the planners and to the men who executed the landings. While losses were sustained, they were minimized by the cease-fire arranged by Robert Murphy, thus vindicating the American Vichy policy to win French support for the landings.[48]

Although Murphy's assistance in arranging the ceasefire averted continued fighting around Algiers, two other explosive problems needed to be solved. It seems that General Mark Clark, Eisenhower's deputy, had made an agreement with General Giraud, giving the Frenchman the top command of French forces that would be subordinate to the supreme Allied Commander, General Eisenhower. Since Murphy had initiated talks with Admiral Darlan, with a view to placing him at the head of all French forces, the Americans were in a diplomatic dilemma. Fortunately, General Giraud had no political ambitions and no desire to become embroiled in the political complexities that obtained in French North Africa. He advised Clark and Murphy that political problems were more than he cared to handle and that he desired only to be free to exercise command over French combat forces. He hoped that the problem could be resolved so that Darlan would serve as a French high commissioner, while, he, Giraud, would command all French military forces in North Africa.[49]

Final agreement between the French military leaders in North Africa and the Anglo-Americans was greatly facilitated by the German occupation of Unoccupied France following the TORCH landings. This agreement was reached on November 11 after several stormy interchanges between the parties, and it called for a general ceasefire throughout French Africa and cooperation between the French military forces and the Anglo-Americans. While the so-called "Darlan deal," worked out by General Clark and Admiral Darlan, came under fire in the United States and Britain, it nevertheless received General Eisenhower's approval. This agreement provided for unimpaired French sovereignty over North Africa and for the United States to train and equip eight French divisions in North Africa, for the equipping and training of three additional divisions in France, for the training and equipping of nineteen French air squadrons, and for the extension of supplies to the French Navy.[50]

While the agreement with Darlan is open to criticism because it was made with a former collaborator with the Nazis, it was nevertheless important to the Allied war effort. Darlan effected a cease-fire, placed French forces under Allied command, and delivered all of French North Africa, plus the French West African port Dakar, to the Allies. He also attempted to induce the French fleet at Toulon to come over to the Allies, but in this he was unsuccessful. Although his assassination on December 24 relieved the Anglo-Americans of the onus of the embarrassing "Darlan deal," both Murphy and Clark "agreed that Darlan had contributed as much as any Frenchman to the success of a highly speculative military and diplomatic venture."[51]

The "Darlan deal" was much criticized in the American and British press and in official circles in both Washington and London, but General Eisenhower accepted it for it gained the cooperation of the French in North Africa and obviated having to use Anglo-American forces to occupy, police, and pacify the region. Eisenhower cabled to Washington and London his reasons for accepting the agreement. He advised that French officers in North Africa were loyal to Marshal Pétain, but when Admiral Darlan gave them the word to support the Anglo-Americans and effect a cease-fire, fighting stopped, and the French forces in North Africa threw their support to the Anglo-Americans. Winning the endorsement of the local populace depended upon Darlan's leadership of the French colonial government. Without his leadership, Eisenhower claimed it would have been impossible to have gained the backing of the people and the endorsement of the French military establishment.[52]

However, the General's troubles in Africa were far from over, for in spite of the Clark-Darlan accord which guaranteed to leave French sovereignty unimpaired in North Africa—a condition that caused the American military authorities to have to rely on the French colonial regime—President Roosevelt advised Eisenhower and Murphy that in his view "we have a military occupation" and our Commanding General "has complete control of all affairs both civil and military."[53] The President's cable of course implied that the American military leader was responsible for the government of French North Africa—a violation of the accord made with Admiral Darlan. The War Department sent out a group of seventeen American military officers who were to govern Morocco, Algeria, and Tunisia. Eisenhower did not agree with the imposition of American authority upon the French, and he had the men reassigned, thus leaving the Darlan-Clark accord uncompromised and French authority intact.[54]

An interesting corollary to this Darlan accord occurred in Morocco, where Lieutenant General George S. Patton, commander of the Western Task Force, arranged for a cease-fire with General Auguste Nogues, commander of French troops in Morocco. In compliance with his orders, Patton was required to have the French commander sign "Treaty C," an instrument that would have ended the French protectorate in Morocco and caused no end of troubles to the Americans. Instead, Patton acted on his own authority, tore up the treaty, and established a good relationship with Nogues, permitting the Frenchman to continue in effect the French protectorate. Nogues proved valuable to the Americans, for he maintained order in Morocco, supplied the labor needed to unload American supplies, provided the troops necessary to safeguard transportation of goods, and assumed control of political matters, thus relieving Patton of the onerous burden of political control and leaving him free to prosecute the war.[55]

While Nogues was somewhat of an embarrassment to the Americans in North Africa, the death of Darlan and the subsequent selection of Giraud as his successor was anything but perplexing. The removal of Darlan by death relieved the American command of considerable complications. But the selection of Giraud was questionable, for he was a poor political leader. This man was more concerned with leading French troops on the battlefied. Ultimately, he agreed to share leadership with General Charles de Gaulle, whose political aptitude far overshadowed that of Giraud. Subsequently, de Gaulle relieved Giraud of his command and placed him on the back shelf of history.

But Giraud's assuming command did not remove the disappointment that General Eisenhower felt at the death of Darlan, for in addition to political problems he also had his difficulties on the field of battle. The American unwillingness to land troops in Tunisia and the inability of the French to move rapidly enough to offset a German invasion of that country made Eisenhower's task of linking up with the British Eighth Army, moving from the east, all the more difficult. The winter rains of North Africa and increased Axis reinforcements in Tunisia stalled his winter offensive during the Christmas season of 1942. To Eisenhower, with his orientation toward mounting a cross-Channel invasion of France to wind up the war, fighting in the winter mud of North Africa must have been frustrating. Little did he realize that as the year came to an end, the British were considering additional operations in the Mediterranean theatre.

The British preoccupation with a Mediterranean strategy needs to be understood in terms of the British World War I experience in the trenches of France, of the military configuration unfolding at the end of 1942, and in terms of British imperial aspirations. As 1942 ended, the new year held promise of an Anglo-American victory in North Africa. With a rapid growth of military strength in the region, it was only natural that the British desired to use the seasoned Allied force to prosecute the war in the Mediterranean. What is more, the Mediterranean was a major link in the British Empire. Gibraltar and Suez were important points along the way to British oil in Iran, to India, and to Australia and New Zealand. But the American outlook was entirely different. American military leaders were eager to move the focus of military operations against the Germans from the Mediterranean to Britian, where the English countryside would serve as an immense base to store the needed material and troops with which to launch a massive attack on the continent of Europe. The British were aware that generals Marshall and Eisenhower were both anxious to wind up the campaign in North Africa and set up bases in England, anticipating the day when a cross-Channel attack would be set in motion.[56]

As early as November Roosevelt told Churchill, "I believe that as soon as we have knocked the Germans out of Tunisia, we should proceed with a military strategical conference between Great Britain, Russia and the United States." Stalin was unable to attend, and in a letter to the Prime Minister of his (Churchill's) suggested inclusion of political questions on the agenda of the proposed meeting, Roosevelt wrote: "In view of Stalin's absence, I think you and I need no foreign affairs people with us, for our work will be essentially military." The Prime Minister agreed, and so the agenda at the Casablanca Conference in January 1943 was largely devoted to military-strategic considerations.[57]

The President and some of his party departed Washington on January 9, 1943, by special train for Miami, while others traveled by plane. The party then boarded two Boeing Clippers and made a 10-hour flight to Trinidad, where they refueled for the 9½-hour flight to Casablanca. The President's party included General Marshall, Admiral King, Lieutenant General H.H. Arnold, commander of the Army Air Corps, Harry Hopkins, Averell Harriman, and the President's son Lieutenant Colonel Elliott Roosevelt.[58]

The summit conference at Casablanca was significant because the two Allied political leaders worked out military policy that would have considerable bearing on the future conduct of the war. Robert Murphy recorded that the conference was conducted on two levels. At the Anfa Hotel Anglo-American military chiefs debated the war strategy while at Roosevelt's villa, he and Churchill discussed the intricacies of French politics with emphasis on North Africa.[59] Out of these two-level military and political talks emerged the determination to continue a Mediterranean strategy for two additional years. Churchill, with his remarkable intuition, recorded that although he knew that General Marshall was "keen" to end operations in the Mediterranean and resume plans and preparations for the cross-Channel attack, he was aware that the President was strongly in favor of giving the Mediterranean prime place. "He also seems increasingly inclined to Operation 'Husky' [the plan to invade Sicily]...."[60]

The Prime Minister's perception of Roosevelt's and Marshall's thinking on strategy was right. At a pre-conference meeting at the White House on January 7, General Marshall opposed continued operations in the Mediterranean, because German submarines would take a high toll of Allied shipping. He also disclosed that the British intended to pursue a

Mediterranean strategy, with a view to knocking Italy out of the war and bringing Turkey into the conflict. This strategy would likely involve an invasion of Sicily. The President was aware that the United States had some 800,000 to 900,000 men in North Africa, a number of whom would be needed for garrison duty once the Germans were defeated. He queried Marshall about what disposition should be made of the remainder—a clear indication that he was thinking along the lines of the Prime Minister and his military chiefs.[61]

When the conferees gathered at Casablanca, the Combined Chiefs of Staff went immediately into conference in a banquet room in the Anfa Hotel on January 14. For five days these meetings were punctuated with heated exchanges between General Marshall and General Sir Alan Brooke, chief of the Imperial General Staff. Marshall argued vehemently that the American chiefs looked with disfavor upon continued military operations in the Mediterranean and strongly urged mounting an operation from the United Kingdom that would strike at Germany over the beaches of Northern France.[62] Marshall's opposite number was well prepared and it was apparent to all assembled that the British had brought a well-conceived military formula for the continuation of the war in 1943. On January 14 Brooke launched into a lengthy discussion of goals that the British anticipated achieving in the coming months. These included continued aid to the Russians, a stepped-up aerial bombardment of Germany, and continued operations in the Mediterrnean, with a view to removing Italy from the conflict and involving Turkey. The Mediterranean, he suggested, offered many opportunities for landings on Sardinia, Sicily, Crete, or the Dodecanese. Brooke was obviously opposed to the premature launching to a cross-Channel attack in Northern France.[63]

Because the American chiefs were divided on strategic goals—General H.H. Arnold of the Army Air Corps favored an intensified bombing of Germany, while Admiral King favored an expanded naval war in the Pacific, and General Marshall wanted to concentrate on the cross-Channel attack—and their British colleagues were united in purpose, the British ultimately were successful in getting their plan accepted. The tide ran against the stubborn Marshall because the President was quite willing to compromise. He quite readily accepted the British argument that it was necessary to exploit opportunities in the Mediterranean by utilizing Anglo-American forces already on the scene. Yet, at the same time he asserted that it was necessary for the Allies to continue preparations for the cross-Channel attack.[64] At length, the Combined Chiefs prepared a draft memorandum which contained a list of strategic priorities for the coming year. It urged the defeat of the German U-boat threat, preparation for an invasion of Sicily in order to intensify pressure on Italy and possibly induce Turkey to enter the war, continued aid to Russia, an intensified aerial bombardment of Germany, and continuation of the offensive in the Pacific.[65] Late in the afternoon of the 18th, the Combined Chiefs presented their program to Churchill and Roosevelt at a meeting in the former's villa. Since the memorandum constituted the essence of the prearranged British plan, General Marshall permitted General Brooke to summarize the plan for those assembled. The President and Prime Minister discussed the plan *in toto*.[66] Ultimately, after much discussion and some revision of their original plan, it was resubmitted on January 23, the final day of the conference, to a meeting of the President and Prime Minister. It submitted a list of priorities and, in order of their importance, called for an intensified campaign against German U-boats in the Atlantic, continued supply of vital materials and weapons to the Soviet Union, the invasion of the island of Sicily during the summer of 1943, a continued build-up of troops and material in the United Kingdom for the forthcoming cross-Channel attack, and the continuation of operations against the Japanese in the Pacific.[67]

In addition to planning strategy for the Mediterranean for the coming year, the President and Prime Minister decided to complete the campaign in North Africa as expeditiously as possible. Although Eisenhower's army was bogged down in the mud of Tunisia where heavy December rains had delayed his campaign against the Germans, they decided that Eisenhower would retain the top command in the North African theatre, with General Sir Harold Alexander, the British commander in Africa, serving as his deputy as commander of combat forces, and Air Marshall Sir Arthur W. Tedder and Admiral Sir Andrew Cunningham given respective executive command over air and naval forces in the theatre.[68] Of this move, William H. McNeill concluded that the decision to retain Eisenhower was based on a British desire to maintain American interest in the Mediterranean and to avoid antagonizing French military leaders who would refuse to serve under British commanders. In terms of the overall wartime strategy for 1943, the decisions reached at Casablanca could not help but disappoint General Marshall and Harry Hopkins, both of whom were intent on building up for the cross-Channel operation which would be launched in late 1943. The Casablanca decisions now ruled out the possibility of a cross-Channel attack until 1944 and resulted in the continuation of Mediterranean operations for two more years. Of course their strategy would ultimately result in knocking Itay out of the war. Surprisingly, General Eisenhower approved the plan. This staunch advocate of cross-Channel strategy wrote that the attack in France could not have succeeded in 1943 and should not be made until the summer of 1944.[69]

While military subjects took up most of the time of the Anglo-American political and military chiefs at Casablanca, nevertheless they had to deal with political questions as well. The President's decision to announce that the Anglo-American allies would prosecute the war on the basis that the Axis Powers would be eliminated on terms of "unconditional surrender" was designed to reassure the Russians. This announcement was no surprise, for the President had discussed it with his advisers prior to coming to Casablanca.[70] This subject has been well discussed elsewhere, and since it does not bear on the American role in the Middle East, little more will be said about it, for some comment must be made about the Anglo-Amerian decision on the question of the French in North Africa. With the conference approaching an end, Roosevelt and Churchill were anxious to settle the French question, for neither man desired to return home with the charge of supporting Darlan hanging over his head. The President was not happy about the charges that he was pro-Vichy and a supporter of collaborationists. These charges blighted his liberal image.[71] While the President had many reservations about bringing General Charles de Gaulle into the picture, the British had none. The British had sponsored him, and Churchill pressured the General to come to Casablanca to the conference. There Murphy and Harold Macmillan, the British minister resident in Algiers, worked out a formula whereby de Gaulle and Giraud would exercise joint political and military leadership in French North Africa. The stage was set for the Prime Minister and President to witness a "shotgun marriage" between the two French leaders that would include the shaking of hands before photographers, a gesture symbolic of the merger of the two men. Ultimately, de Gaulle emerged as the leader and Giraud was removed from his command and all authority.[72] While the internal infighting between the forces of Giraud and de Gaulle is beyond the scope of this study, what is important is that the French forces participated in the Allied efforts to rid North Africa of the Axis menace and to continue the fight until victory was achieved.

Following the conference, the Allies sent cables to both Joseph Stalin and Chiang Kai-shek, reporting the results of the Casablanca Conference. Both cables emphasized the necessity for considering a Mediterranean strategy during the coming year, with Stalin being assured of the delivery of supplies through the Persian Gulf and Chiang assured of more material aid given to the Allied forces in India, Burma, and China.[73]

The conference concluded on a positive note, for the Americans and British were now planning to carry the war to the Axis Powers. During May of 1943 the Anglo-American forces finally brought the Afrika Korps to bay. Approximately one-quarter million Axis prisoners were taken in the final days of the North African campaign. During the concluding days of the conflict, Frenchmen and Arabs fought alongside Americans, Britons, and their Australian and New Zealand comrades. That the French forces and the North African Arabs participated in this joint effort is vindication of the American policy in regard to Vichy and of the task perfomed by Robert Murphy and his twelve vice consuls. While no American policy during World War II has been more closely scrutinized by scholars than the American "Vichy gamble," it does seem safe to conclude that it was a success. Very few American Foreign Service officers have ever had such impact on the determination of American policy as Robert Murphy.

One of the major purposes of initiating the North African campaign was to prevent the meeting of German and Japanese forces at some point along the rimland of Asia, a possibility that would give the Axis control of the rich oil resources in Iran, Iraq, and in the Saudi Arabian fields along the Persian Gulf. As Secretary of State Cordell Hull wrote, "The planning and the carrying out of the campaign in North Africa, where the Arab population predominated, and the establishment of important American supply lines to Russia through the Near East, showed the necessity for stability in the Near East, toward which end stability in Saudi Arabia was essential."[74]

Chapter 3
Saudi Arabia and the Oil Factor

American interests in the Middle East during the war included furthering the political aspirations of the various Arab states, but the United States also sought to preserve the American oil concession in Saudi Arabia, in addition to other American oil interests in Iraq, Kuwait, and Bahrein. To defend these objectives, it became necessary to extend financial assistance and technical aid to cement the ties between the United States and Saudi Arabia. In Saudi Arabia the oil factor played a much greater role in U.S. diplomacy than it did in other countries, for it was in this land that geologists of the California-Arabian Standard Oil Company (casoc) had located the largest proven oil reserves in the world. It was most necessary that these reserves be shielded from foreign intrusion.[1]

Before discussing the course of diplomacy during the war, a brief word should be offered to explain the American involvement in Saudi Arabia. In 1931 Charles Crane, the American philanthropist who had participated in the King-Crane Commission's investigation, visited Saudi Arabia. Crane greatly respected the Arabs, and he offered to King Ibn Saud the services of Karl Twitchell, an American mining engineer, to make a survey of the mineral resources of Saudi Arabia. Twitchell completed the survey, ostensibly to locate additional water resources in the arid land, and reported that the country was potentially rich in oil. The King ordered Twitchell to secure American financial resources for developing the oil. In 1932 he was able to interest officials of Standard Oil of California (socal) in making application for a concession. The King awarded the concession to the California-Arabian Standard Oil Company, a socal subsidiary in 1933. Work was begun and in 1938 casoc brought in the first well. Oil was soon being produced in commercial quantities, but the onset of World War II hindered production, thus reducing the King's royalties which had been diminished by the smaller number of pilgrims coming to the holy cities of Mecca and Medina.[2]

During the first year that the United States was involved in the war, the State Department took steps to protect this oil concession by establishing an American Legation at Jidda, by dispatching an agricultural mission to aid the Saudis, by placing antiaircraft weapons in Saudi Arabia to protect the American oil properties, and by extending financial aid to the hardpressed government of Ibn Saud.[3] The United States initiated this aggressive policy toward the Saudis because their land, with its valuable oil resources, was important to the war effort of the United Nations. Too, the King exercised enormous influences over the other Arab states where American troops were located, and he was regarded as the moral leader of all Arabs.

The establishment of an American Legation in Saudi Arabia was an important step along the way to protect the American oil concession in that remote land. American oil men reckoned that the British posed a real threat to their concession, and in the early 1930s they began to petition for a legation. Britain opened a legation as early as 1930, and other European and Middle Eastern nations also maintained diplomatic establishements in Saudi Arabia as well. It was only in 1939 that the State Department appointed Bert Fish, American minister at Cairo, to represent American interests in Saudi Arabia.[4] The oil officials then pleaded for a resident minister at Jidda. But this end was not to be realized right away, for Fish was eventually succeeded by Alexander Kirk, a career diplomat, who served as minister to both Egypt and Saudi Arabia. Finally, in response to the pleas of the oil interests, the President decided to appoint a chargé d'affaires, supported by a small staff, at Jidda. James S. Moose, Jr., then serving at Tehran, was assigned as consul and chargé at Jidda. Moose reported from Jidda that the Legation was opened on May 1, but required numerous supplies to perform the various consular functions.[5] His presence in Jidda greatly enhanced the prestige of the United States and enabled the country to maintain a representative to ensure constant vigilance over the nation's vital interests. Subsequently, the Secretary of State recommended to the President who immediately approved the appointment of Moose as minister resident in Jidda, the reason being that the American oil concession in that country constituted one of the largest oil reserves in the world and required the protection that only a ranking diplomat could offer. Given the influence of the King upon the Arab nations in the Middle East, it was "considered advisable to enhance the prestige of the American diplomatic representative at Jidda."[6] Eventually, Moose was replaced by Colonel William A. Eddy, the noted American Arabist who had served in the U.S. Marines in World War I, later taught at the American University of Cairo and at Dartmouth, and served as president of Hobart College.[7] His knowledge of the Middle East made him a most fortunate choice.

In early 1942 another occasion arose which enabled the United States to create more good will in Saudi Arabia. Ibn Saud requested the dispatch of a mission of technical experts to assist in the agricultural development of his country. The Department of Interior and the Department of Agriculture made available a team of experts to fulfill the King's wishes. Karl S. Twitchell was appointed as chief of mission, and his assistants were Albert L. Wathen, an irrigation expert with the Department of the Interior, and James G. Hamilton, an agronomist with the Department of Agriculture. The purpose of this mission was to examine the agricultural and related resources of Saudi Arabia, to provide advice to the Saudi government, and to report on the irrigation possibilities for putting more land into production.[8] The selection of Twitchell was wise, for he was both known to the King and had arranged for casoc to find oil in Saudi Arabia, and also had extensive on-the-ground technical experience in the Saudi desert during his earlier geological survey of the country's resources in the early 1930s. All three Americans had had experience with agriculture in the southwestern reaches of the United States, where semiarid climate and soil conditions were similar to those found in Saudi Arabia. The mission arrived in Saudi Arabia on May 10 and was welcomed by Ibn Saud who cordially extended it every courtesy.[9] After their audience with the King, the three men began their investigation. They visited many parts of the Arabian peninsula, and observed numerous possibilities for better use of the land, for irrigation development, and for improvement of the crops. The mission presented its report to the King on May 11. Considering that the mission had traveled some ten or eleven thousand miles, its report can be considered complete and as another accomplishment that would strengthen diplomatic ties between the United States and Saudi Arabia.[10] In an effort to continue the work recommended by the Twitchell mission, the U.S. government subsequently sent out a team of agriculturalists in the autumn of 1944. Headed by David Rogers of the Department of Agriculture, this team established a 3000-acre experimental farm. Using modern American agricultural practices, it demonstrated what could be done for farming in nearly barren Saudi Arabia.[11]

While the agricultural advisory work aimed at building good will, the Department of State took steps in another area to protect American oil concession rights and oil company personnel. The Department entered into negotiations with the Saudi government to permit American military advisers to enter the country to train Saudi troops in the use of antiaircraft guns supplied by the United States Army for the protection of the oil installations.[12] In addition, the Department moved to lighten the financial burden of King Ibn Saud in order to provide further protection for the American oil concession.

With the onset of hostilities in World War II, Ibn Saud's revenues were drastically curtailed by the sharp decrease in the number of pilgrims coming to the holy cities of Mecca and Medina where they paid taxes to the government. The war also reduced trade, because wartime shipping restrictions redirected commerce and supplies in the Middle East to meet Allied war needs. The King turned to officials of CASOC for immediate financial aid. In 1939 CASOC advanced him $1.7 million, but when the British increased their subsidy to the King, this caused CASOC officials to believe that the British posed a threat to their concession. James A. Moffett, associated with Standard Oil of California and chairman of the board of both the Bahrein Petroleum Company and its subsidiary California Texas Company and a friend of President Roosevelt, wrote him on April 16, 1941, to explain the plight of the American oil interests in Saudi Arabia. He related that the King required $6 million per year to help meet his budget of $10 million. He advised him that CASOC had invested $25.5 million in its oil exploration ventures, advanced $6.8 million in future royalties, and could no longer afford to offer additional funds to meet the King's needs. He asserted that his company feared Britian's growing influence in Saudi Arabia, a reality that could have adverse consequences for American petroleum interests in that country. Moffett postulated that he wanted to explore the possibility that the Import-Export Bank or the administrators of the new Lend-Lease Aid program would supply King Ibn Saud with funds. The President lent a sympathetic ear to Moffett, but replied that the law did not make provision for such a request. However, he pointed out that CASOC might deliver to the U.S. government from the King's account $6 million in oil products for the next five years. Further discussion with Secretary of the Navy Frank Knox disclosed that the U.S. Navy had no need for such an amount of oil from the Saudis. But the President was determined to do something for the American oil men, and he suggested that Federal Loan Administrator Jesse Jones, then arranging for a $425 million loan to Great Britain, advise the British to set aside a requisite amount of the loan proceeds to take care of the King's needs. Jones advised Moffett on August 11 that due consideration was being given to the needs of Ibn Saud. Jones directed Lord Halifax, British ambassador, to make arrangements to make provision for the King's financial needs out of the proceeds of the U.S. loan. CASOC officials were somewhat chagrined to learn from Jones that the government could not advance funds to the King under the Lend-Lease Act, and that there was no law that would allow the government to make a loan to him. They learned that the British were requested to make provisions for the King out of American funds. Thus CASOC officials advised the King that a large amount of money received from the British came only after the President had made special arrangements with the British to supply the King's financial needs out of funds lent to the British.[13]

Although CASOC officials were successful in obtaining financial aid for King Ibn Saud, they were not able to offset the growth in Saudi Arabia of British influence which constituted a threat to the American oil concession. The American oil men were convinced that the British were able to increase their influence in Saudi Arabia at the expense of the United States government. They firmly believed that in order to protect American interests in that country the United States government must extend Lend-Lease aid to the Saudis.

In early 1943 Harry D. Collier, president of CASOC, and W.S. Rodgers, chairman of the Texas Company, a partner in the CASOC Saudi venture, approached Secretary of the Interior Harold L. Ickes who was the newly appointed petroleum administrator. They informed him that Saudi Arabia had one of the largest reserves of oil in the world, and that Great Britain was trying to obtain a piece of the concession. Further, they related that they had been unable to obtain direct assistance from the U.S. government to protect American interests. Subsequently on February 8, 1943, Rodgers forwarded to Ickes a letter recommending that the United States extend to Saudi Arabia Lend-Lease aid. To give weight to his suggestions, Rodgers also saw the secretaries of Army, Navy, and State, urging upon them the need to extend Lend-Lease to the Saudis.[14]

Prior to the oil officials' approach to Ickes and the secretaries, the Near East Division of the State Department had already recommended that Saudi Arabia be authorized Lend-Lease aid. On January 9, Dean Acheson, Assistant Secretary of State, impressed upon Edward R. Stettinius, Jr., Lend-Lease administrator, the need to make Saudi Arabia eligible for Lend-Lease supplies. Lend-Lease, he said, would recognize the King's "loyal and courageous attitude and would facilitate the prosecution of the war." While Acheson emphasized the military benefits that might accrue to the United States, implicit in his request was the advantageous diplomatic position that would result from such public aid.[15] Stettinius promptly replied that he had written the President on January 11, recommending that Roosevelt determine that the "Defense of Saudi Arabia is vital to the defense of the United States so as to render" that country "eligible for assistance under the Lend-Lease Act."[16] President Roosevelt quickly replied to Stettinius that he "hereby" declared "the defense of Saudi Arabia is vital to the defense of the United States." A revealing essay by Irvine H. Anderson suggests that it was the State Department recommendation by Paul H. Alling, chief of the Near East Division, that prompted the President's action rather than the pleas of the oil company executives.[17]

The President's action pleased the officials of the Texas Company and Standard Oil of California, the co-owners of the concession, for it relieved them of further burdensome payments to the King, protected the American oil concession, offset the possibility of British encroachment on the concession, and shifted the burden to the American taxpayer. They were pleased to know the bureaucracy in this case moved rapidly.

On hearing from the Secretary of State that Saudi Arabia was eligible for Lend-Lease, Alexander Kirk, the American diplomat who served as minister to both Egypt and Saudi Arabia, reported from Cairo that the King desired Lend-Lease aid in the form of sixty trucks to transport foodstuffs and the gift of irrigation equipment. He suggested that the trucks and machinery could be furnished by the Middle East Supply Center, the joint Anglo-American economic control agency in Cairo. When authorization was issued for prompt delivery of the desired equipment and machinery, the King promptly relayed his appreciation for the material that was being forwarded under the auspices of MESC.[18] During World War II the United States government supplied the Saudi government a total of $33 million in Lend-Lease materials. The program went forward with little difficulty, but since the materials were being forwarded by the Middle East Supply Center of Cairo, some of the equipment arrived inscribed with British markings. Although the British were not trying to take credit for American Lend-Lease, some officials in the American Foreign Service exhibited sensitivity about receiving proper credit for the aid thus extended.[19]

Shortly after Saudi Arabia was made eligible for Lend-Lease, President Roosevelt extended King Ibn Saud an invitation to visit the United States early in October 1943 to discuss Lend-Lease needs. The King declined but dispatched his son, the Amir Faisal, future king of the Saudis. Following an official White House dinner on September 30, Faisal discussed with State Department officials the Lend-Lease requirements of Saudi Arabia. His visit concluded, the State Department decided to dispatch an American military mission to Riyadh, there to determine Saudi Arabia's defense needs in terms of Lend-Lease materials.[20]

In early October 1943 Ibn Saud extended an invitation for U.S. Army Headquarters Middle East to dispatch a team of experts to Saudi Arabia to survey that country's military requirements that might be fulfilled through the Lend-Lease Administration. The State Department was anxious that the mission expedite its work, for it had learned that the British planned to provide the King with fifty armored cars, five hundred machine-guns, ten thousand rifles and ammunition. Accordingly, Major General Ralph Royce, commander of American forces in the Middle East, took those steps to organize a mission to work with the Saudis.[21] March of 1944 found General Royce visiting the King at his camp north of Riyadh. The General delivered to the King samples of American arms that were to be turned over to the Saudis, presented to him a description of arms that could be delivered in the future, and discussed his probable military needs. Subsequently, Colonel Garrett B. Shomber took charge of the American Military Mission. He was presented to the King in May and his team was soon instructing the Saudis in the use of American weapons. Some hundred and fifty Saudi officers received training and the mission was so successful that it continued to the end of 1944. Eventually, the mission effected a medical survey of Saudi Arabia, thus adding to its accomplishments.[22]

While the shipment of military weapons was an important facet of American Lend-Lease aid to Saudi Arabia during the war, the largest item of Lend-Lease aid to that country was silver bullion or silver riyal coins. There was a shortage of coins in the country, and officials in the Division of Near Eastern Affairs at the State Department recommended the delivery of silver to the Saudi government because "the great political and strategic importance of the oil resources in Saudi Arabia" made it necessary to maintain "a sound economic system inside Saudi Arabia in order that these oil resources may continue to be available." The Saudis needed this money to pay government salaries and to maintain a sound fiscal system. The State Department arranged for John W. Gunter, a Treasury Department official, to go to Saudi Arabia in September and October of 1943 to examine Saudi financial problems. He determined that the gift or loan of silver would enable the Saudis to find relief for the shortage of coins, and he also drafted a long-range program to assist the Saudi government to establish a reliable financial system. An agreement was signed on October 3, whereby the United States Treasury would lend 4.167 million ounces of silver bullion. This was the first of several shipments, for all told the Treasury shipped 22,354,500 ounces of silver to the Saudis, out of which 21,323,250 ounces, valued at $15,139,507 was to be returned to the United States Treasury within five years after the cessation of the wartime emergency. Most of the silver riyals were minted in the United States. To ascertain that the United States government received credit for alleviating the coin shortages in Saudi Arabia, the U.S. Army delivered the initial shipments of newly minted coins in grand style, complete with a military procession and no little pomp and circumstance.[23]

Lend-Lease aid to the Saudis during World War II not only helped to prevent the bankruptcy of the King's government, but it also supplied him with the weapons and training that enabled him to put together the nucleus of a modern army. Too, American vital interests dictated that Lend-Lease aid was important. These interests determined that even after the cessation of hostilities and the termination of Lend-Lease aid to other countries, Lend-Lease supplies continued to flow to Saudi Arabia. American largesse was based on the assumption that the vast oil reserves in Saudi Arabia must at all costs be protected.

Saudi oil was becoming increasingly valuable, for some months after Saudi Arabia was made eligible for Lend-Lease, American industrialists, oil company officials, and government leaders, began to foresee an oil shortage for the United States. On June 10, 1943, Harold Ickes, petroleum administrator for war, advised President Roosevelt of an impending shortage of crude oil that would curtail activities of the American armed forces. He urged the President to take immediate action, with a view to acquiring ownership and management of foreign oil reserves. He suggested that the President direct the Secretary of Commerce, who headed the Reconstruction Finance Corporation, to organize a Petroleum Reserves Corporation which would be directed to acquire and manage foreign oil reserves. More specifically, he asserted that the United States government should obtain ownership of the large crude oil concession then held in Saudi Arabia, then estimated to have reserves of some twenty billion barrels — or one of the largest known oil reserves in the world.[24] Harold Ickes' warning was supported by a report made by Dr. Herbert Feis, State Department petroleum expert and adviser on economic affairs, who urged that American domestic oil reserves were being rapidly diminished by the war and that the United States government must consider new alternatives to supply future oil needs.[25] Ickes and Feis were not alone in suggesting government entry into the oil business; the Joint Chiefs of Staff and State, War, and Navy representatives felt likewise.

Accordingly, the Petroleum Reserves Corporation (PRC) was created by the Reconstruction Finance Corporation on June 30, 1943, and on July 6, 1943, Secretary of State Cordell Hull advised the President of a plan whereby the PRC could secure for the U.S. government "complete stock ownership of the California-Arabian Standard Oil Company." The representatives of PRC would be authorized to begin talks immediately with CASOC officials. Funds for the transaction would be supplied by the PRC.[27]

The President wasted little time, for on July 14, 1943, he convened a Cabinet-level conference to draft a plan for U.S. oil strategy of global dimensions. Feis was present and he discussed possible future oil policies with those assembled. The President announced that the secretaries of State, War, Navy, and Interior would serve as members of the Board of Directors of PRC and that Harold Ickes was to serve as president.[28]

Holding the powers of president of PRC, Ickes immediately began negotiations with Harry D. Collier and W. S. Rodgers, the chief executive officers of Standard Oil California and the Texas Oil Company, co-owners of the lucrative CASOC concession, for the purchase of one hundred per cent of the stock in CASOC. Collier and Rodgers expressed deep concern at this outright invasion of private enterprise by an official of the U.S. government. Ickes then reduced to seventy per cent the amount of stock desired by the government. Meeting continued opposition he reduced his figure to fifty-one per cent and finally to thirty-three and one-third per cent. He continued his talks all through the months of August, September and October 1943. At length, finding Collier and Rodgers adamant about retaining their respective company's holdings in CASOC, Ickes broke off the talks, with nothing to show for his efforts.[29] While the two oil companies had seemingly been willing to sell as long as the German desert army under General Rommel proved a distinct threat to their properties, with the Allied defeat of that army, the companies proved reluctant to part with their rich assets.

But Ickes continued to maintain an avid interest in the oil potential of Saudi Arabia, and in November 1943 he dispatched to that country a geological survey team headed by E.L. DeGolyer, a well-known petroleum geologist, to make a survey. The DeGolyer team reported in January 1944 that in their opinion the center of world oil production would shift rapidly to the Middle East. At about this time, Admiral Andrew Carter, petroleum administrator for the Navy, following a visit to Saudi Arabia and conferences with company representatives, recommended that the United States government build a pipeline from the Saudi oil fields to a port on the Mediterranean. Simultaneously, an official with CASOC advised Wallace Murray, chief of the Near East Division at the State Department, that the company planned to build a pipeline from the Gulf to the Mediterranean and that it desired State Department support for the project. There was considerable desire within government circles about the ownership of such a pipeline. Ultimately, it was agreed that the U.S. government would own the pipeline only for the duration of the war. With this dispute settled, Ickes moved ahead with talks, and on February 6, 1944, he announced that PRC had entered into an agreement with the Arabian-American Oil Company and the Gulf Exploration Company for the United States government to construct, own, and maintain a pipeline from the Persian Gulf to the Mediterranean. This pipeline would transport crude oil from American oil fields in Saudi Arabia and Kuwait. The two companies agreed to hold a reserve of one million barrels as a reserve available to the American military forces.[31] Inasmuch as the agreement required approval of the rulers of Kuwait and Saudi Arabia, the Department exercised its influence on the U.S. Congress to shelve the two pro-Zionist resolutions then in committee in order that King Ibn Saud would grant his approval to the agreement. More will be said about the Zionist facet of U.S.-Saudi relations later.[32]

The construction of the pipeline by the United States government was not yet a certainty, for Ickes' announcement of the proposed undertaking created a storm of protest in the press, in Congress, and in oil industry circles. Opponents asserted that the pipeline would not be completed until after the cessation of hostilities, that there was no shortage of domestic oil reserves, that it would involved the United States in the politically unstable Middle East, that it would depress oil prices on the domestic market, and finally that it heralded the entry of government into the private enterprise sector. Several important senators, James A. Moffett, and the Petroleum Industry War Council, an advisory board consisting of representatives of fifty-five American oil companies, attacked the plan. Even Herbert Feis opposed this move. Ralph T. Zook, President of the Independent Oil-Producing Association, also struck out at the pipeline as an invasion of the private sector. Opposition also came from an international source, for the British were unalterably against the government's building a pipeline. The press leveled criticism at the plan and a Senate committee held hearings on the project, showing that reservations about the project existed in Congress. Given the widespread opposition to the projected government-built pipeline, Harold Ickes wrote in December 1944 that the plan had received so much criticism that it seemed unlikely that the government would undertake the project.[33] Indeed, Secretary of State Hull advised Ambassador William Eddy in Saudi Arabia to confer with the King and to tell him that there was little possibility that the United States government would build the pipeline.[34]

While the U.S. government was compelled to bow out of the pipeline project, the oil companies thought well enough of the idea to move ahead on it. On March 14 W.S. Rodgers and Henry T. Klein, respectively the chairman and president of the Texas Oil Company, announced that the pipeline would be built by private enterprise. The owners of the rich oil concession in Saudi Arabia organized Trans-Arabian Pipe Line Company (TAPLINE) in July 1945 for the purpose of constructing a pipeline from the Persian Gulf to the Mediterranean. The builders of this 1040-mile artery faced three immediate problems: buying the necessary steel to complete the line at a time when steel was in short supply due to the demands of the war effort; obtaining the permission of those nations across which the pipeline would pass; and finding the capital to accomplish this multimillion dollar project.[35] The completion of TAPLINE is beyond the scope of this study, but a few words about it are necessary since it does bear on the subject of this work. W.J. Lenahan, a TAPLINE representative, obtained from Sir Alan G. Cunningham, British high commissioner for Palestine, an agreement to build the pipeline across the territory of the British mandate. He then entered into talks with Jordan and secured the right to build a portion of the line across that country for an annual fee of $250,000. Conversations with Lebanese and Syrian representatives were not immediately fruitful, but ultimately Lebanon agreed to permit passage of the pipeline for an annual payment of $180,000. Syria demanded more. A diplomatic crisis ensued, causing the principals to meet at Beirut, where James Wadsworth, American ambassador to Iraq, Lowell Pinkerton, minister to Lebanon, and Lenahan worked out a convention on September 1, 1946. But the situation was fraught with the strife that accompanied the Israeli war of liberation. Work on the pipeline was halted. Following the armistice between Israel and Egypt in January 1949, Lebanon and Syria acted to make construction through their territories possible. The agreement with Syria gave the company the right to construct and operate a pipeline for a period of seventy years, at the end of which time all property would revert to Syria. The company also agreed to pay a royalty on each ton of oil that moved over Syria.[36] The company also found it necessary to obtain the assistance of the U.S. government to build the thousand-mile pipeline, because the thirty to thirty-one inch steel pipe was in short supply. The Department of Commerce issued the requisite export license for TAPLINE to procure the twenty thousand tons of steel, in exchange for the company's agreement to supply oil at cost to the American military forces for a ten-year period after the completion of the pipeline.[37] To obtain the necessary capital to complete the project, ARAMCO entered into conversations with Standard Oil of New Jersey and with the Socony Vacuum Oil Company, whereby the two major companies received a percentage of ARAMCO stock in exchange for the $102 million necessary to build the pipeline. Ultimately, Jersey Standard and SOCONY obtained the necessary permission of their partners in the Iraq Petroleum Company to participate with ARAMCO in the Saudi venture and thus escape the restrictions imposed by the famous "Red Line Agreement."[38]

By permitting Jersey Standard and SOCONY to buy into ARAMCO and TAPLINE, the American oil group in Saudi Arabia moved ahead to complete the pipeline. Construction was completed in the autumn of 1950. The first oil reached the Lebanese port of Sidon, the western terminus, on November 10, and the first tanker was loaded on December 2. Costing some $200 million to construct, the pipeline can move about 310,000 barrels per day over the distance of 1040 miles from the Saudi Arabian oil fields on the Persian Gulf.[39]

While one goal of United States policy in Saudi Arabia during the war years was to ensure continued access to that country's abundant oil reserves, another was to see that Great Britain did not gain access to them. Cordell Hull recorded that rivalry with Britain in Saudi Arabia disturbed Anglo-American unity of purpose in the Middle East during 1944. He had received reports of British activities in Saudi Arabia which were prejudicial to American interests there. As early as November 1943 a State Department adviser on political relations addressed a memorandum to Secretary Hull, apprising him of the Anglo-American political rivalry in Saudi Arabia and suggesting that it could be remedied by an agreement "covering a range of petroleum problems of mutual interest in the Middle East...."[40] Hull was keenly aware that S.R. Jordan, the British minister at Jidda, was pursuing several courses at variance with American interests, and on April 3, 1944, he told the President that Jordan had "persuaded King Ibn Saud to remove certain key Saudi officials known to be friendly to the United States and to agree to appoint a British economic adviser and possibly a British petroleum adviser as well."[41] Later in the month

Alexander Kirk, American minister at Cairo, communicated to the Secretary that Saudi Arabia was rapidly becoming an arena in which Anglo-American adversaries were bidding for hegemony. For example, a British military mission was competing with the work of an American mission of a similar nature. Hull recorded that he urged the President to extend additional financial subsidies to the Saudi Government during 1944 to offset British intrusion. Hull eventually approached Lord Halifax, British Ambassador in Washington, and informed him that Jordan was "unacceptable" to American interests in Saudi Arabia. Jordan was ultimately transferred.[42] In point of fact, Hull had suggested to Halifax and to the President in December the need for an Anglo-American oil agreement that would include a settlement of differences stemming from the overzealous pursuit of new sources of petroleum.[43]

Hull's suggestion to the President was echoed by Harold Ickes, and also by members of the Petroleum Industry War Council (PIWC) who recalled the intense Anglo-American rivalry over oil in the Middle East in the aftermath of World War I. The President realized that government policy working through PRC to ensure continued access of the American government to Saudi Arabian oil had been a failure. He cancelled PRC and chose to work through diplomatic channels to protect American oil interests. Late in 1943 the Department of State invited the British government to send delegates to Washington to discuss mutual problems associated with the rivalry for oil. At first, the British were hesitant to send Cabinet-rank delegates to a conference in Washington, because the forthcoming Anglo-American invasion of Normandy consumed much attention in London. Following a lengthy exchange between President Roosevelt and Prime Minister Churchill, in which each assured the other of the intention to respect British oil holdings in Iraq and Iran and American holdings in Saudi Arabia, they agreed that the conference should be held. On March 7, 1944, the President issued an announcement of the forthcoming conference on petroleum. The President appointed Cordell Hull and Harold Ickes chairman and vice-chairman respectively of the forthcoming Anglo-American conference. The State Department appointed ten oil executives to act as advisers.[44] Preliminary conversations at the technical level were begun in April, anticipating the time when higher level talks would be held, with a view to drafting an Anglo-American oil agreement. Ultimately, a British committee of cabinet rank, headed by Lord Beaverbrook, arrived in Washington in July to conclude the negotiations. Cordell Hull presided over the initial cabinet-level meeting on July 25, but shortly thereafter turned the chair over to Ickes. A draft treaty was worked out in July, discussed by the President's advisers and announced on August 8, 1944. The Anglo-American Oil Agreement contained five principles setting forth the manner in which the United States and Britain would cooperate in the sphere of the international petroleum trade:

> (1) Petroleum supplies would be made available to all nations at fair prices.
> (2) Oil resources should be developed to encourage progress in the various host countries.
> (3) Equal opportunity should be afforded for exploration in areas not already under concession.
> (4) Signatories would respect concession contracts lawfully negotiated and in force.
> (5) International petroleum business would be conducted in an orderly manner to ensure that ample oil stocks are available to all nations.

This agreement also provided for an International Petroleum Commission, the function of which was to prepare estimates of petroleum supply and demand. It was intended to be voluntary in nature with no enforcement authority given to an executive body.[45]

The President received the agreement on August 22 and he transmitted it to the Senate two days later. Word of this accord aroused a storm of protest in the American petroleum industry. Oil executives felt that they had not been consulted. Some believed that the accord represented a step toward wholesale nationalization of the oil industry. Domestic producers feared that large-scale imports of cheap crude oil would depress their markets. The Senate returned the treaty to the President for revision, and Ickes traveled to England to renegotiate. It was resubmitted to the Senate, and the Petroleum Industry War Council and the American Petroleum Institute approved it. But opposition in the oil industry remained. The Senate did not commence hearings until June 1947. Although reported out of committee favorably by the Senate Foreign Relations Committee, the Senate did not act on it. It had received too much opposition from the domestic petroleum industry.[46]

During World War II the United States government firmly allied itself to American petroleum interests in their bid to protect and expand their Middle East oil holdings. But it ran into considerable opposition when it attempted to obtain outright ownership of the concession and when it attempted to enter into an international agreement that was construed by the oil industry as impinging on the private sector. American oil concesssion rights in Saudi Arabia were also complicated by another factor, and it is now necessary to look briefly at the impact of American Zionism upon United States relations with Saudi Arabia.

Although the Zionist movement and its impact on American-Saudi relations will be discussed in greater detail in a later chapter, a word does need to be said about it at this point. King Ibn Saud was considerably disturbed to learn of Zionist activity in the United States that aimed to create a Jewish national home in Palestine, a land inhabited in the main by Arabs. He so informed the President in April and May 1943. An American fact-finding mission to the Middle East disclosed that Zionist activities would surely create tension, disturb the stability in the Middle East, and thus harm the war effort. The President replied that he would take no action on the Palestine question without prior consultation with Arab and Jewish leaders. In January 1944, when House and Senate committees were considering two resolutions calling on the U.S. government to use its good offices to create a Jewish commonwealth, Secretary of State Hull, supported by Secretary of War Stimson and Chief of Staff General George C. Marshall, put pressure on the Congress to keep the resolutions in committee. His reason was that these measures could disturb negotiations with the King concerning the construction of a pipeline across Saudi Arabia. While the Zionist question was in abeyance during the remainder of the year the President made an effort to reconcile King Ibn Saud to the creation of a Jewish national state in Palestine at a meeting between the two heads of state when the President was returning home from the Yalta Conference in early 1945. The King's reaction was wholly negative, and the President was unsuccessful.[47]

In concluding this chapter of America's wartime diplomacy with Saudi Arabia, we can say that it was marked by approaches that were both traditional and innovative. As in the past, the Department of State supported American oil interests by cultivating close ties with the King. The extension of financial assistance and the delivery of Lend-Lease aid were motivated by the need to head off a British intrusion into Saudi Arabia that could threaten the valuable American oil concession. That the government considered purchasing the American oil concession in Saudi Arabia was a new departure, brought about by the need to ensure continued access to the abundant oil reserves in Saudi Arabia to satisfy the needs of American military forces. Because oil interests resented intensely this invasion of private enterprise, the President drew back and tried a different approach. The Anglo-American Oil agreement was the more tried and true approach taken by American diplomats in the past. But given the nature of the agreement, and given the mindset of American businessmen, this too was unacceptable. The government then fell back on reliance on the Open Door policy and on the efforts of private enterprise. Its support for the bulding of TAPLINE indicated the government's concern that the United States have continued access to the vast oil reserves of Saudi Arabia.

The close ties established between the United States and Saudis during World War II provided a large fund of good will in the Arab land. This reservoir of good will, in spite of Saudi reservations about the Zionist movement in the United States, was to lay the foundation of mutually acceptable relations in the Cold War era, a period that witnessed the aggressive outward thrust of communism frighten the conservative Saudis and cause them to draw even closer to the United States.

While the unfolding of American diplomatic relations with Saudi Arabia moved along a single line, uncomplicated save by the Zionist factor, the diplomatic intercourse with Iran was more involved. Indeed, Iran occupied the State Department and the executive branch of the government to a greater degree than any other country in the Middle East.

Chapter 4

Iran: The Political Cockpit of the Middle East

American relations with Iran prior to World War II can be characterized by diplomatic efforts to assist the activities of missionaries and oil men to achieve their disparate goals. The conversion of Shiite Muslims and securing an oil concession in Iran's northern provinces were two widely separated goals that interested officials at the State Department during the 19th and 20th centuries. For their part, Iranians viewed the United States as a possible diplomatic make-weight to strengthen Iran against separate British and Russian efforts to achieve hegemony, respectively in the southern and northern portions of the land of the Shahs. This effort to solicit American good offices proved futile, for policy-makers in Washington were persuaded by the Monroe Doctrine that involvement in Iran's international problems would only enmesh the United States in the diplomatic tangles of the Eastern Hemisphere. But in the 20th century, two missions undertaken by private American citizens, one headed by W. Morgan Shuster in 1911-1912 and the other headed by Arthur C. Millspaugh from 1922 to 1927, succeeded in making financial and political reforms in the Iranian government.[1]

With United States entry into World War II, there began to unfold a long, complicated diplomatic intercourse between Washington and Tehran. As the memoirs of Cordell Hull indicate, Iran received greater attention than any other country in the Middle East.[2] With Britain and Russia in occupation of that country, Iran became a veritable political cockpit. As the diplomatic record indicates, the United States had no comprehensive policy at the outset of hostilities, other than the traditional guiding principles—freedom of commerce and navigation, abstention from permanent alliances, self-determination of peoples, the principles of noncolonization and nonintervention as set forth in the Monroe Doctrine, the right of expatriation and naturalization, and the arbitration of disputes—that normally directed the nation's foreign policy makers.

48

During the war years, the American State Department concentrated on implementing those policies supportive of the war effort. Maintaining the vital "Persian Corridor" through which traveled the Lend-Lease aid to the embattled Soviets was a primary diplomatic goal. But the State Department also undertook steps to strengthen Iran that she might maintain her sovereignty, unimpaired by British or Russian diplomatic intervention. The extension of Lend-Lease aid to Iran, the dispatch of political, financial, and military missions to bolster the Shah's government, and the maturation of American diplomatic policy, all aimed at creating a stronger Iranian state. While President Roosevelt sought to improve the level of living in impoverished Iran, the State Department also aided American oil interests in their quest to secure concessionary rights in Iran. Policy was both pragmatic and idealistic. But the idealistic goal of bringing progress to Iran and maintaining that state's territorial integrity and political sovereignty was in the American national interest. United States policy in wartime Iran can be placed in three separate categories: first, priority was given to winning the war, the accomplishment of which aim involved shipping Lend-Lease supplies to Russia; second, the U.S. government extended political and economic support to the Iranian government to sustain that government's bid to maintain sovereignty in the face of British and Russian efforts to curtail that sovereignty; and third, the State Department supported the quest of American oil companies in Iran for new concessions.

Inasmuch as the main purpose of the Anglo-Soviet occupation of Iran was to neutralize German elements in that country and to establish a supply route over which aid could be extended to the Soviets, we need to take a look at the operation of the "Persian Cordidor." The British and Russians concluded the Tripartite Treaty of Alliance with Iran in January 1942. One clause of this treaty granted to Russia and Britain "the unrestricted right to use, maintain, guard and in case of military necessity, control in any way that they may require all means of communications throughout Iran, including railways, roads, rivers, and aerodromes."[3] The "Persian Corridor" proved to be a vital channel of supplies to the Soviet Union. It was one of five routes over which traveled some 19.3 million long tons of Lend-Lease aid from the United States to the Soviet Union during the years 1941-45. The Persian route was extremely important, for it could be utilized during all four seasons of the year. Three of the other routes to Russia were closed down during the winter months of the year. A total of 7.9 million tons of equipment was discharged at Persian Gulf ports between 1941 and 1945. Logistical experts have estimated that American deliveries through the "Persian Corridor" to the Soviet Union were sufficient to maintain sixty Soviet combat divisions in the battle line on the Eastern Front.[4]

The first American serivce troops reached the Persian Gulf region of Iraq and Iran late in 1941. Originally known as the Iraq-Iran Service Command of United States Army Forces in the Middle East (USAFIME), this command was redesignated Persian Gulf Service Command in August 1942. The PGSC was in charge of troops working in Iraq, Iran, and Saudi Arabia. It was responsible for service troops that moved supplies to the Russian Army through the "Persian Corridor." Major General Donald H. Connolly assumed command of the PGSC on October 20, 1942, and it was this officer and his staff who made PGSC an effective logistical weapon of war. Within eight months the number of officers and men in his command reached the impressive figure of 30,000. These men were responsible for maintaining the southern section of the Iranian State Railway, a motor transport truck service, an aircraft assembly plant, for unloading ships at Persian Gulf ports, and for a multiplicity of other tasks associated with a large regional service command.[5]

Inasmuch as President Roosevelt declared Russia eligible for Lend-Lease aid in 1941, British Middle East advisers suggested in 1942 that the United States should assume responsibility for maintaining a portion of the "Persian Corridor" to increase deliveries of arms and equipment to the Soviet Union. During the summer of 1942 President Roosevelt and Prime Minister Churchill engaged in an exchange of notes leading to American assumption of control over the southern section of the Iranian State Railway (ISR). Writing on August 22, 1942, Churchill asserted that he would welcome American responsibility for assisting with deliveries of aid to Russia.[6] On 15 September the President replied, "We are prepared to take over the Persian Railway and all plans now being developed."[7] The Iranian government consented to the American operation of the southern sector of the ISR in December.[8]

One of the major reasons for the United States' taking over the southern section of the ISR was to cut the losses of merchant ships carrying Lend-Lease aid to the Russian ports of Murmansk. On the Murmansk route no less than twenty-two out of thirty-three ships in a recent convoy had been sunk by German aircraft and submarines. American military leaders rightly believed that the ISR would be a more efficient means for delivering supplies to Russia. The ISR had been completed in 1939 and was a remarkable engineering feat. It extended some 865 miles from the southern terminus at Bandar Shapur north to Bandar Shah on the southeastern shore of the Caspian Sea.

The American Military Railway Service took over the southern sector of the ISR from the British in the spring of 1943 and handed it back to the Iranians in June 1945. From April 1943 to June 1945 the Military Railway Service (MRS) maintained a daily average of 3,397 long tons of freight destined to supply Russian forces. The ISR became a vital link in the

Lend-Lease aid program. By 1943 the MRS employed a staff of over one hundred to supervise five battalions of some 4,000 service troops and some 15,000 ISR native workers. It was responsible for maintaining the right of way, for servicing the rolling stock, for loading and unloading cargoes, for guarding against pilferage, and for operating the trains on schedule. When MSR terminated its operation in June 1945, it turned over to ISR approximately 8,000 cars. Its task completed, the Military Railway Service could rest on its laurels, knowing that it had transported to the armies of the Soviet Union three out of every five tons of equipment delivered via the "Persian Corridor." In so doing it maintained one of the most vital links between the Soviet Union and its western allies.[9]

Complementary to the operation of the Iranian State Railway was the increased number of wharfing facilities built by the U.S. Army to handle the growing railroad tonnage of Russian aid material. The War Department directed the work of Folspen, a private construction company that was responsible for building additional wharf berths at the port of Khorramshar, a number of road bridges, and other improvements that would facilitate the increased delivery of war material to the Russians. The discharge capacity of ports increased from 189,000 long tons in August 1942 to 399,500 long tons by June 1943. The increased capacity stepped up the tons of material shipped by the ISR to the Soviets.[10]

While the ISR provided the main artery for channeling Lend-Lease aid to the Soviet Union, the Motor Transport Service (MTS) operated another vitally important avenue. It began operations in March 1943 at which time some 400 trucks moved out of Andimeshk, driving toward the Soviet Union with cargoes of Lend-Lease equipment. The number of trucks involved in this logistical operation rose by fall to about 2,500 vehicles and reached around 6,000 in September 1944. Many of the drivers were natives, and it was inevitable that some pilferage would result. When the MTS terminated its operation in the summer of 1945, it could claim a good record. It had carried cargoes amounting to 618,946 long tons, of which 408,460 long tons were carried to the Russians. To accomplish this task, T.H. Motter estimates that it would have required a line of Army 6 X 6 trucks lined up from Baltimore to Chicago.[11]

Much of the equipment delivered to the Soviet Union was assembled at plants in Iran, including many American trucks. Approximately 400,000 trucks were delivered to the Soviets during the years 1941 to 1945. Of this number, close to 45 percent traveled via the "Persian Corridor." Approximately 88 percent of these were assembled at American plants at Andimeshk and Khorramshahr from March 1942 through April 1945.[12]

In addition to operating truck assembly plants, the United States government also maintained through a private contractor an airplane assembly plant. The government supplied to the Soviets 14,834

American aircraft. Of this number, approximately one third, or 4,874, were delivered via the "Persian Corridor," with 995 being flown in and 3,879 being shipped by train. Plants were operated at Basra, Shuaiba and Abadan. Eventually, a plant was put into operation at Tehran. In April 1943 the U.S. Army Air Corps assumed responsibility for operating the plant at Abadan.[13]

In addition to prosecuting the war effort by maintaining the "Persian Corridor," the United States government also implemented a number of policies to support the political integrity of Iran. American foreign policy objectives were well stated by Secretary of State Cordell Hull in a memorandum to the President in August 1943. Hull recommended that the United States continue assistance to Iran to maintain political and economic stability for the purpose of preventing either Russia or Great Britain from taking action that "will seriously abridge, if not destroy, effective Iranian independence." Hull suggested that the "best hope of avoiding such action lies in strengthening Iran to a point at which she will be able to stand on her own feet, without foreign control or 'protection,' and in calling upon our associates, when necessary, to respect their general commitments under the Atlantic Charter and their specific commitments to Iran under the treaty of Alliance of 1942...." The United States, Hull concluded, "must adopt a policy of positive action in Iran, with a view to facilitating not only the war operations of the United Nations in that country but also a sound post-war development."[14]

As early as 1942 the United States had begun to extend aid to Iran in the form of shipments of grain. In February Allah Yar Saleh, chief of the Iranian Trade and Economic Commission, wrote Wallace Murray, chief of the Division of Near Eastern Affairs, asserting that there was a shortage of wheat in Iran. Murray assured him that he would investigate possibilities of furnishing wheat for Iran.[15] In the following month, Sumner Welles, acting secretary of state, advised Louis G. Dreyfus, U.S. minister in Iran, that arrangements were being made to send to Iran 20,000 tons of wheat at the rate of 2,000 tons monthly.[16] Wallace Murray looked into the shortage of grain in Iran and discovered that the British had promised to deliver 8,000 tons monthly, but were making good on 6,000 tons, leaving a 2,000-ton shortfall. He learned that the shortage of shipping was responsible for the inability of the British to meet their commitment. On May 1 he met with Saleh and advised him that steps were being taken to ascertain that the British lived up to their agreement to deliver the prescribed amount of grain.[17] Subsequently, the State Department used its good offices to procure an Anglo-American declaration, ensuring that the governments of the United States and Britain would guarantee to supply the necessary quantity of grain to make up for any shortage.[18]

American aid to Iran came in another area that would assist in the distribution of grain. A large country that depended on transportation by motor truck, Iran relied upon American trucks and tires to carry her food-stuffs to distant regions. With the onset of hostilities, this supply was dried up by wartime necessities and the shortage of shipping. To alleviate the shortage and to assist with the distribution of grain, the United States government acted quickly, and on July 1 an *aide-mémoire* was sent to the Iranian Legation in Washington, advising that steps were being taken to ensure the shipment of trucks and tires to Iran to meet minimum needs. During the current year Iran could expect to receive a total of 68,000 tires. The U.S. government would also be prepared to receive Iranian requests for trucks and for spare parts to repair trucks not then in operation.[19]

The means whereby the United States government channeled aid to Iran was the Lend-Lease Administration. On March 10, 1942, President Roosevelt advised E.R. Stettinius, Lend-Lease administrator, that he declared the defense of the government of Iran to be vital to the defense of the United States.[20] Although Lend-Lease aid made it possible for the Iranians to receive grain and the tires and trucks to assist in the distribution of that grain to outlying districts, there nevertheless developed an alarming crisis in Iran. As early as December 1942 Minister Louis G. Dreyfus reported from Tehran that riots had developed in response to the shortage of food. By mid-1943 that crisis had deepened. In September 1943 James M. Landis was appointed American director of economic operations in the Middle East. He diagnosed Iran's problems in November in a report to Harry Hopkins, special presidential adviser, pointing to the lack of food and the means for the distribution of this food to be central to Iran's instability. Landis immediately ordered General Connolly to designate a group of officers and enlisted men under his command to assist in the transport of cereal and other food stuffs for civilian needs and to assign fuel and oil stocks for the Iranian motor trans-portation system.[21] The President further authorized the U.S. Army to broaden General Connolly's authority to furnish equipment and forces to aid the Iranians in such projects as road repair and construction, the digging of irrigation ditches, and the offering of technical advice. While the President authorized Lend-Lease aid to Iran, the American Embassy in Tehran approved the extension of Lend-Lease goods to the Iranian Army and Gendarmerie because two American military missions operating in Iran were able to direct the use of this material and ensure that it was em-ployed in a satisfactory manner.[22]

While the Iranians wanted Lend-Lease aid to alleviate the distress among the people whose demand for food led to riots and instability, they wanted a trade agreement with the United States because of the prestige that would accrue to the Iranian government.[23] In January 1942 Allar Yar Saleh, Iranian trade commissioner in Washington, approached the State

Department with a view to obtaining a trade agreement that would show that Iran is an independent country and a "going concern."[24] A lengthy exchange between the State Department and the Iranian government ensued, leading ultimately to the negotiation of an agreement on April 8, 1943. The agreement accorded both signatories reciprocal concessions. Based on the Open Door policy, this agreement, the second made by the United States in the Middle East after that with Turkey, marked a new direction in Iran's international relations. Iran was fast turning away from the German connection and obtaining a greater degree of freedom from the British and the Russians. Iranians regarded American aid through Lend-Lease channels and military and economic missions, plus the trade agreement, as buttressing an independent Iranian State, free of the restrictions imposed by foreign powers.[25]

Inasmuch as mention has been made of the operation of American military and economic missions in Iran, it is now necessary to discuss these, for they did indeed play an important role in strengthening the ties between the United States and Iran and in establishing a greater degree of Iranian independence.

As the Iranians hoped to use Lend-Lease aid to reduce British and Russian influence in their country, so they also requested the United States to send economic and military advisers to strengthen the internal administration of the Shah's regime.[26] The State Department approved the dispatch of these missions to Iran, for the presence of missions there would enable the United States to counteract pro-Axis feeling in Iran that might result in closing down the "Persian Corridor," and they would also provide a means of obtaining a regular channel of intelligence on Iranian affairs.[27] Conversation between Minister Dreyfus and the Iranian Foreign Office and exchanges between the Iranian Minister in Washington and the Secretary of State disclosed the need for advisers to reorganize the Iranian police force, both rural and urban, modernize Iranian finances, and to restructure the system of supply in the Iranian army. In addition, the Iranians made known their desire for the services of a military aviation officer, a military engineering officer, and several agricultural experts.[28]

The U.S. government was happy to assist the Iranians, and in May of 1942 the Department of State informed the Iranian minister in Washington of its efforts to obtain the service of Colonel Norman Schwarzkopf, a graduate of West Point in 1917 who had subsequently served as director of rural police for the state of New Jersey. He had made his name in the Lindbergh kidnapping case and was recognized as a leading American authority in the area of rural police work. At the time, this officer was working in Iran and was familiar with some of the problems inherent in the work of his mission.[29] Concerning Schwarzkopf's fitness for and interest in the mission, Wallace Murray advised Minister Dreyfus on August 24 that the former policeman was interested in the position and was keenly aware of the situation in Iran. A few months later the Department worked out the details of Schwarzkopf's mission and ascertained that he would serve as an adviser in reorganizing the Imperial Iranian Gendarmerie (the rural police force), with the rank of assistant to the Interior Minister, for a one year period with the option of renewal.[30]

On October 21, 1943, the Majlis — the Parliament of Iran — passed a law authorizing the Iranian government to employ eight American army officers to assist the Ministry of the Interior to reorganize the rural police force. The mission was to continue its work for at least two years. The agreement between the United States and Iran was signed on November 27, 1943 and was extended through the exchange of notes on September 6, 1944, and again on September 29, 1945, and subsequently.[31] Schwarzkopf was most effective. Of all the American advisers in wartime Iran he accomplished the greatest number of reforms, remaining in the country until 1948. His achievements came in spite of numerous handicaps that included illiteracy, lack of funds, opium addiction, conflict between the Iranian Army and the Gendarmerie, bureaucratic opposition to reform, and the fact that Schwarzkopf's rank was far less than his powers as assistant to the Minister.[32] In addition to Schwarzkopf, there was a complementary mission dispatched to Iran to work with urban police, and the mission was headed by L. Stephen Timmerman. While Schwarzkopf and Timmerman were American officials and cooperated with the American Legation, they were not connected with the Legation or with the U.S. government. As a postscript to Schwarzkopf's wartime mission, it should be pointed out that in the postwar era Iran, supported by the good offices of the State Department, pressured the Soviets to evacuate the northern province of Iran. Following the Soviet withdrawal, Colonel Schwarzkopf, at the head of the Iranian Gendarmerie, entered the disputed area and began the process of restoring Iranian rule to the area.[33]

In addition to securing American advisers to reorganize rural and urban police forces, the Iranians also initiated action to obtain an American officer to reorganize the finance and supply functions of the Iranian Army. This officer would serve as a kind of quartermaster general. In May 1942 the War Department designated Major General John N. Greely as intendant general to undertake the work of advising the Iranian Army. The following month, Minister Dreyfus notified the State Department that Greely was acceptable to the Iranian government.[34] The Iranians then pressed ahead with securing the services of an American military mission for the purpose of reorganizing the training of the Iranian Army. The War Department was unable to undertake the dispatch of an

American military mission to Iran. It did recommend the appointment of Major General Clarence S. Ridley, an engineering officer who had served as governor of the Panama Canal Zone and as chief of the Puerto Rican Hurricane Relief Commission, to succeed General Greely, whose tenure in Iran was short.[35] Ridley's mission also achieved success, for his considerable experience in dealing with people enabled him to win the support of both the Shah and Premier Ahmad Qavam. The Iranian Minister of War, Field Marshall Amir Ahmadi, attributed Ridley's success to the general's simplicity, dignity, hard work, good leadership, and ability to win the support and confidence of Iranian leaders.[36] While its function was to work with the Iranian Quartermaster Corps, it seems that the most notable accomplishment of the Ridley mission was the motorizing of the Iranian Army, an accomplishment which Iranian officers recognized as being of great value.[37]

The outstanding problem faced by the Ridley mission was the dispute between the War and State Departments over the continuation of the mission beyond the termination date of March 1, 1945. The Iranians desired the continuation of the mission in order that it might further the work of reorganizing and building up the Iranian Army. E.R. Stettinius, acting Secretary of State, recommended to Colonel Henry L. Stimson, Secretary of War, that the mission to Iran be continued beyond the expiration date, because the "protection and advancement of our interests in Iran will require the strengthening of the Iranian security forces so that order may be maintained in this area, where world security might be threatened, after the withdrawal of Allied troops."[38] By way of epilog, it should be pointed out that in the aftermath of the Russian withdrawal from Azerbaijan, Major General Robert W. Grow, who headed the American Military Mission after the retirement of General Ridley, advised the Shah's military forces when they effected the reoccupation of Azerbaijan in 1947, a fact that shows the wisdom of retaining the mission in Iran beyond the date of its expiration.[39]

While the Schwarzkopf mission and the American Military Mission were noteworthy, that of Arthur C. Millspaugh proved the most important and also the most controversial of the American missions sent to Iran. As early as June 9, 1942 Prime Minister Ahmad Qavam queried Minister Louis Dreyfus about the possibility of having an American financial mission, headed by a man of the caliber of Dr. Arthur C. Millspaugh, come to Iran to effect a number of financial reforms in the government.[40] Within a matter of sixty days, the Department of State determined that Dr. Millspaugh, who had headed the financial mission to Iran in 1922-1927, was the logical choice for the post. Secretary of State Hull advised Dreyfus that Millspaugh had also indicated a willingness to accept the post if he is acceptable to the Iranian government.[41] Following an exchange of dispatches, on October 5 Ali Sohaili, Iranian Foreign Minister, advised Dreyfus that Millspaugh was acceptable, and on November 30 the Department of State announced that Millspaugh had been appointed to head a mission to Iran that would include experts in the fields of taxation, accounting, budgetary control, customs and tariffs, general economic mattes, and general financial matters. Ultimately, the Iranian Majlis passed a law on October 24, 1943, that authorized the formation of a mission of sixty Americans to be sent to Iran for a period of four years to undertake financial reforms there.[42]

While Millspaugh was hired by the Iranian government and was in no way a representative of the U.S. government, the Department of State took great interest in his mission. Inasmuch as the Nazi army was then approaching the Caucasus, thus posing a possible military threat to Iran, the Department expected Millspaugh to put "stiffening" into the Iranian government in order that it might make a greater contribution to the overall war effort.[43]

Millspaugh's mission was multifaceted. It had the task of ensuring that adequate food supplies were available for the people, and to this end it worked to improve internal transport facilities both by road and by rail. It also had charge of the prices of grain, cotton, tea, sugar, and tobacco and over the wages of government workers in factories and mines. It controlled all rents. Finally, it was responsible for reforms in financial administration in the upper level of government.[44] But Millspaugh recorded that his mission accomplished its work under difficult circumstances, for it met with numerous obstacles posed by officials of the Iranian government and by the Soviets who were in occupation in the northern provinces of Iran.[45]

One facet of opposition to the Millspaugh mission was Soviet-inspired. The Soviets, jealous of the British sphere of influence in southern Iran, desired to dominate the northern provinces. During the war the Red Army occupied the northern sector and commandeered Iranian arms factories in that area. In addition to dominating food production in the northern sector, the Soviets also tried to control the economy there by using the Red Army as an instrument of policy. The Soviets were opposed to the Millspaugh mission, and they attacked it through the pens of Soviet-inspired newspaper editors, through pro-Soviet members of the Majlis, and by administrative interference in the northern sector.[46]

But there were other factors militating against the success of the Millspaugh mission. The Majlis was the main opponent of the reform-minded mission staff. In the Majlis were representatives of the Tudeh party, the pro-Soviet political instrument, who resented the thrust of the mission. There were also large landowners who opposed the government's grain collection program. In addition, wealthy merchants and cabinet members hoped to guard prerogatives that might be annulled by reforms. But one of the main factors contributing to Millspaugh's eventual downfall and resignation was the gap between Millspaugh's own perception of his task and the perception of Iranian government officials. It seems that the American expert desired to effect genuine economic reform, while the Iranian leadership hoped that the mission would result in deeper American involvement in Iran, the better to offset British and Russian influence. Given widespread opposition to his mission, Millspaugh resigned on June 23, 1944, the Majlis passed the law cancelling his powers on February 28, 1945, and he departed the country on that date.[47]

While Millspaugh did make progress in the area of fiscal control, food supply, and internal transport, he claims that he could have effected greater change had he not been opposed by so many diverse elements and had he received greater support from the State Department.[48] But Department of State officials viewed Millspaugh as an employee of the Iranian government, and believed that they could not interfere in an internal affair of a sovereign nation, in the final analysis a problem between Millspaugh and his employer[49]

Although the presence of the Millspaugh mission in Iran was an internal problem, the presence of U.S. Army troops in that country was definitely a matter that concerned both the Iranian and U.S. governments. When 5,000 American service troops landed at the Iranian port of Khorramshahr without giving prior notification to the government in Tehran, the Iranian Minister for Foreign Affairs immediately suggested to Minister Louis G. Dreyfus that the United States should adhere to the proposed Anglo-Soviet-Iranian Treaty of Alliance.[50] A draft of the pact was forwarded to the State Department, and Cordell Hull advised Dreyfus that the Department desired to study the proposed agreement before taking action on it. Since no immediate action was forthcoming, Mohammad Reza Shah Pahlavi wrote the President that he hoped the United States would adhere to the Tripartite Pact which was based on the principles set forth in the Atlantic Charter. Further, he desired that the American troops would serve in Iran on "a footing of equality" with Great Britain and the Soviet Union.[51] Thus began a long exchange of notes between the two governments in which the Iranian Foreign Office tried to obtain United States adherence to two agreements. The first was the Tripartite Pact of Alliance. The second covered the status of U.S. forces in Iran, exempting American forces from the criminal jurisdiction of Iranian courts. No agreement was ever made. General Connolly had a smooth working relationship with the Iranian government, and he remarked to

Minister Dreyfus that Iranian-American relations were perfectly satisfactory, as they were.⁵² For a time the United States government considered making an executive agreement to cover the military presence in Iran. This suggestion was never acted upon. Perhaps one reason that militated against United States adherence to the Tripartite Pact was the Iranian insistence that the U.S. would be bound to defend Iran against foreign invaders. This stipulation arose from a possible German threat to Iran. But the State Department was unwilling to go to this length. In March 1942 Sumner Welles, acting Secretary of State, asserted to the Iranian minister in Washington that the United States had adhered to the provisions of the Atlantic Charter and that it did not seem appropriate "to make any public declarations concerning the independence and integrity of Iran."⁵³ Perhaps another reason for failure to sign the Tripartite Pact was centered on the fact that the United States had not definitely formulated a policy on Iran. Several historians are in agreement on this point.⁵⁴

A long-range American policy toward Iran developed gradually during the war years. As early as January 1943, a position paper prepared by John D. Jernegan of the Division of Near Eastern Affairs suggested that the United States needed to take cognizance of the presence of Russia and Britain in Iran. Given the presence of these two powers which might well circumscribe the freedom of Iran in the postwar period, Jernegan argued that the United States "alone, is in a position to build up Iran to the point at which it will stand in need of neither British nor Russian assistance to maintain order in its own house. If we go at this task wholeheartedly," he asserted, "we can hope to remove any excuse for a post-war occupation, partition, or tutelage of Iran." In concluding his paper, Jernegan suggested, "We can work to make Iran self-reliant and prosperous, open to the trade of all nations and a threat to none."⁵⁵ Jernegan's proposals became the basis of Department policy toward Iran, as evidenced by Cordell Hull's note to the President on August 16, 1943. Hull forwarded a policy statement that incorporated Jernegan's suggestions; the statement pointed out that Britain and Russia had "historic ambitions" in Iran that have made "that country a diplomatic battleground for more than a century." If the British and Russians were offered a free hand, it is likely that either one or both will take action that "will seriously abridge, if not destroy, effective Iranian independence. That such action would be contrary to the principles of the Atlantic Charter is obvious." To avoid British or Russian hegemony, the Secretary suggested that the "United States should adopt a policy of positive action in Iran, with a view to facilitating not only the war operations of the United Nations in that country but also a sound post-war development."⁵⁶ That the United States would adopt a forward policy in Iran in the aftermath of the war is evident in the Secretary's policy statement.

The two policy papers can be considered as the foundation of long-range American policy *vis-à-vis* Iran. When the three Allied leaders gathered at Tehran on November 28, 1943, Prime Minister Ali Sohaili advised that the Iranian government wanted a three-power declaration respecting Iranian sovereignty. The President welcomed such a suggestion, for a declaration would solve the long-standing problem concerning the legal status of American troops in Iran. Accordingly, on December 1 he affixed his signature to the Declaration of Tehran, a statement that ensured U.S. support for Iran's territorial integrity and political sovereignty. This statement bound Britain, Russia, and the United States to "respect the independence, sovereignty, and territorial integrity of Iran." In addition it called for the extension of economic assistance to Iran.[57] This declaration accomplished several purposes. First, it assured the Iranians that the United States would support Iranian sovereignty. One historian characterized it as one of the greatest achievements of American diplomacy in Iran, for the Iranian government was assured that the United States seriously supported the continued existence of a state long threatened by the British and the Russians.[58] Second, the declaration, issued at the suggestion of the Americans, assured the Iranians of economic support.[59]

Having obtained a three-power declaration on the territorial integrity of Iran, the United States further demonstrated its view of the growing importance of that country. In addition to raising its legation to an embassy, the President determined to make of Iran a test case to show what the United States could accomplish in an underdeveloped state by pursuing an unselfish policy in the postwar era. Prior to departing Iran, the President wrote to General Patrick Hurley, ordering him to make a fact-finding tour in Iran, with a view to determining means to strengthen Iran which might serve as a pattern for use in "our relations with all less favored associated nations."[60] Hurley had been originally ordered by the Secretary of State to bring about a greater degree of coordination among the various American agencies in Iran. The President, on the advice of his advisers in NEA and that of his Secretary of State, had now decided to broaden policy in Iran. Hurley had submitted to the President a report on Iran in May 1943, and it was this report that had whetted the President's interest in Iran.[61] But Hurley's second report, dated December 21, 1943, had greater impact on the President. Hurley argued that since it was the intention of the United States "to sustain Iran as a free, independent nation" based on the democratic, capitalistic system, the United States should continue to furnish expert advisers to Iran. He pointed out that the British were issuing American Lend-Lease supplies in Iran in a manner that was disadvantageous to the United States. He recommended that the U.S. distribute Lend-Lease supplies so as to obtain due credit. Inasmuch as Iran possessed rich oil reserves, Hurley suggested that the State Department be prepared to "advise the Iranian government concerning the character and other qualifications of every applicant for a concession."[62]

On January 12, 1944 President Roosevelt forwarded General Hurley's report on Iran to the Department with the comment: "I was rather thrilled with the idea of using Iran as an example of what we could do by an unselfish American policy. We could not take on a more difficult nation than Iran. I would like, however, to have a try at it."[63] That action was taken on Hurley's Iranian recommendations in the area of Lend-Lease was evidenced in a letter by Secretary of State Edward Stettinius.[64] It seems reasonable to believe that General Hurley's reports influenced the President immensely, for in 1944 the United States government began to implement policies designed to bolster Iran. By the extension of additional aid to that country, the U.S. could raise the level of living of Iranians and secure that country for the private enterprise system. A stronger Iran could then withstand the pressures placed on her by the Soviet Union and and Great Britain, as well as those internal dissident political forces. Hull reported that American assistance to Iran was greatly increased in 1944. In July 1944 Acting Secretary Stettinius prepared for the American chargé d'affaires in Iran a summation of American policy toward that country. He stated that the President and the Department had considered Iran "as something of a testing ground for the Atlantic Charter and for the good faith of the United Nations." A strong Iran would enable the United States to share "more fully in Iran's commerce and in the development of its resources." To that end the Department maintained an "interest in the present negotiations for a petroleum concession in Iran."[65]

While the United States had not yet formed a firm policy on Iran, it is clear that the rudiments of a policy were emerging in 1943 and 1944. To be sure, much of U.S. Iranian policy — the President's desire to use Iran as a case study for the implementation of programs that might serve as a pattern in other underdeveloped nations — would appear to be wholly idealistic, yet there is much more to this policy that is pragmatic. Iran was one of the most important oil-producing nations in the world, and, as Cordell Hull recorded: "one facet of our diplomacy consisted in supporting the efforts of American companies to obtain petroleum concessions there. The War and Navy Departments, alarmed by statistics tending to prove the depletion of the United States oil fields, and feeling that the oil of the Near East, because it lay closer to the Far East then the Western Hemisphere fields, might be vitally necessary in the war against Japan, strongly urged that the Near Eastern potentialities be developed."[66] It is now necessary to discuss the Department's support of American wartime efforts to obtain oil concessions in Iran.

The Iranian government hoped to involve the United States officially in Iran by commercial means, for in February 1943 the Iranian commercial attaché in Washington queried the Standard Vacuum Oil Company to determine if that company desired to obtain a concession in Iran. In November 1943, Standard-Vacuum communicated with the Department of State its intention to send a representative to Tehran, with a view to negotiate with the Iranian government for an oil concession. Cordell Hull advised the oil company that the Department looked "with favor upon the development of all possible sources of petroleum." He said the Department had no objection to the forthcoming negotiations.[67] Accordingly, the Standard-Vacuum Company sent a representative to Tehran in early 1944 with the knowledge that the State Department gave its approval. In the spring of 1944 he was joined by a representative of the Sinclair Oil Company. Matters related to oil negotiations were soon complicated by the British Royal Dutch Shell Company's effort to obtain an oil concession. But Iranian Premier Sohaili desired to give the concession to an American concern, for he did not want the British to control the entire southern coast of Iran. The Department of State was impartial and supported both American oil companies.[68] In the meantime the Iranian government had retained A.A. Curtice and Herbert Hoover, Jr., two American petroleum engineers, as oil consultants to study the two American proposals. But the two American companies were slow in making their presentations, and Richard Ford, the American chargé d'affaires in Tehran, was most critical of the oil companies for using lower echelon representatives to negotiate for the oil concession.[69]

The quest for oil in Iran was further complicated in February 1944, when the American chargé cabled the Department that the Soviet Union opposed the granting of a concession to an American oil company in Northern Iran. Actually the two American companies were negotiating for concessions in southern Iran, but in March or April the Standard-Vacuum Company representative expressed the desire to obtain a concession in one of the northern provinces. The Iranian government advised that discussion of a concession in the north would have to await the departure of Soviet troops after the end of hostilities.[70]

During the spring and summer of 1944 talks between the Iranian government and the two American oil company representatives progressed satisfactorily. By August they had reached the point at which Ford advised the Department that the companies should send to Iran their highest level executives to close the negotiations, because "competent authorities state prospects of proposed concession area have no equal in Middle East, but to gain this rich prize for American interests will require quick action...."[71]

Further negotiations between the American companies and the Iranians were to be obstructed by the arrival of Vice Commissar for

Foreign Affairs Sergei I. Kavtaradze in Tehran on September 15, 1944. The Russians had been excluded from the oil talks in which American and British representatives had been engaged with the Iranian government, even though the Iranian government had granted in 1916 an oil concession to Akakiy Khoshtaria, a citizen of Russian Georgia.[72] On October 1 Kavtaradze bypassed the cabinet and the Majlis and entered into talks directly with the Shah. The Russian proposed that the Iranians grant the Soviets an exclusive concession over a five-year period for oil exploration in a 200,000 square kilometer area of northern Iran stretching from Azerbaijan to Khorassan. The Shah replied that the proposal was beyond his competence and should be taken up with the Prime Minister and appropriate cabinet official.[73]

The Soviet diplomat now turned to Prime Minister Saed and pressured him to give a reply within three days. The Iranian was not to be intimidated, and he announced at a special session of the Majlis on October 8 that his cabinet has agreed to postpone all oil concession negotiations until after the war.[74]

On learning of the Iranian decision Secretary of State Hull urged Ambassador Leland B. Morris to advise the Iranian government that the United States government accepted its decision as one made in good faith, but expected that "if and when the Iranian Government is in a position to consider applications for such concessions, the applications of American nationals will receive no less favorable treatment than the applications of the nationals or government of any other country."[75]

On October 12 Prime Minister Saed told the representatives of the American and British companies and Kavtaradze of the Iranian decision to postpone the award of oil concessions until the cessation of hostilities. This statement set off a chain of events leading to a crisis. The Russian diplomat denounced the Iranian government, an attack that was repeated in the Soviet press. The pro-Soviet Tudeh party sponsored demonstrations in Tehran, and the Red Army troops stationed in the capital city paraded through its streets and avenues. The capital's leftist press also attacked Saed for opposing the grant of concessions.[76]

Washington was concerned lest the growing tension between Iran and the Soviet Union interrupt the war effort. That the Department supported the Iranian decision is evident in the letter sent by Stettinius, acting Secretary of State, to Ambassador Averell Harriman in Moscow, advising the Soviet Union that the United States was convinced the Iranians were acting in good faith. Further, the U.S. was concerned that this matter would not violate the Declaration of Tehran, signed in December 1943.[77] The Department could not take too strong a position in Iran, for to do so would weaken the Soviet-American alliance. Dissension of any kind would only act to obstruct the prosecution of the war effort. For this reason the State Department refused an Iranian plea that the United States take a strong stand against the Soviets.[78]

Although Washington took a low-key approach to the crisis, officials at the State Department and in Tehran were apparently not aware of the growing Soviet pressure on Saed. When advised by the Soviets that two Russian officers had been killed and that unless remedial measures were taken by the Iranians the Soviets would take appropriate action to suppress the anarchy perceived in Tehran, Prime Minister Saed resigned. Soviet pressure on Iran ceased and the crisis ended.

What can be said of the wartime quest for oil in Iran? It did produce an international crisis, but given the wartime imperative of the need to continue the coalition, the U.S. did not elect to make an open breach with the Soviets. It is difficult to say that the U.S. had any restraining action on the Soviets. R.K. Ramazani concludes that the Soviets were successful, for they brought to an end the possibility of Americans and British obtaining concessions in Iran and they compelled the resignation of Prime Minister Saed. Finally, the Soviets were successful in thwarting the Iranian bid to further involve the United States in Iran through the grant of a lucrative oil concesssion.[79]

However, the American wartime quest for oil rights in Iran has caused a storm of criticism. Edward M. Mark asserts that the Soviet quest for a sphere in northern Iran was in response to the American bid for an oil concession. The Russians wanted to obtain a sphere in the north in order to obtain an oil concession in the region following the removal of Soviet troops.[80] Equally critical are works by Gabriel and Joyce Kolko and George Kirk, who suggest that American wartime policy in Iran was primarily motivated by political considerations, rising out of the need to find new sources of petroleum to supplement American domestic oil reserves that were badly depleted by the war.[81] In an earlier book, Kolko asserted that oil assumed top priority in American foreign policy objectives in the Middle East during World War II. The American bid for a wartime oil concession in Iran caused Russia to respond in an aggressive manner in that country.[82] This criticism raises the question about American policy *vis-à-vis* Iran during World War II. What was the real nature of this policy? Although Cordell Hull maintained that U.S. policy aimed at defending Iran, he clearly stated that this policy called for steps that would maintain Iranian independence from possible British or Russian abridgment. To that end, Hull declared that the United States commenced Lend-Lease shipments to Iran. While prosecution of the war effort was a paramount goal, Hull asserted that "one facet of our diplomacy consisted in supporting the American companies to obtain petroleum concessions there."[83] Concerning the quest for oil, Arthur Millspaugh, head of the U.S. financial mission to wartime Iran and critic of American foreign policy, claimed that although "oil occupied a prominent place among the national objectives of the United States," the primary American effort in wartime Iran was to support the war effort. He recorded that the United States had a long tradition of disinterest in Iran, asserting that it was free of political motives in that country. Rather, he pointed out that President Roosevelt was motivated by a missionary zeal to raise the level of living under the Atlantic Charter. But Millspaugh was most critical of U.S. wartime policy in Iran, observing that it was outdated, marked by confusion and vacillation, poor organization, and a lack of coordination between State and War Departments.[84] Also critical of U.S. policy was the assessment presented by George Lenczowski, who claimed that the lack of a firm, well defined policy in Iran actually encouraged Russian expansion.[85]

What seems clear about policy formation is that the United States did follow the British lead in the early days of the war. While policymakers in Washington pursued a policy independent of Britain later on, they were reluctant to take a hard line against the Soviets, for President Roosevelt desired to build a bond of mutual trust between the United States and the Soviet Union in order that the latter would cooperate with the West in the postwar world. The extension of technical, military, and economic assistance, together with the Declaration of Tehran, indicated the willingness of American leaders to bolster the internal regime of Iran, to the end that it might remain free and independent, conditions necessary to the satisfaction of future U.S. economic goals. At all events, U.S. wartime policy in Iran developed a large reservoir of good will in that country, confirmed the Iranians in their view that the United States was a disinterested power serving to thwart the aggressive tendencies of Britain and Russia in the postwar era, and gave them hope for assistance that Iran might move toward modernity. This amicable relationship established during the war set the stage for the long period of good relations between the United States and Iran during the Cold War era.

The rapprochement between the United States and Iran that emerged in the closing days of World War II and the early days of the Cold War laid the foundation for the close ties between Washington and Tehran. But given the reality that the Shah exercised autocratic rule in Iran, this relationship was essentially between the United States government and one ruler. Perhaps a valuable lesson can be learned from equating a diplomatic relationship between a nation and a ruler, for during the closing days of the 1970s the Shah was ousted by a populace grown weary of a repressive tyrant who denied his people the freedoms taken for granted in the United States. Officials in Washington had so closely identified with the Shah that the formation of a viable relationship with a new government proved difficult.

Chapter 5

The Thorny Palestine Question

During the interwar period, American Zionists urged the United States government to apply pressure to Britain, in regard to the mandate for Palestine, to implement the Balfour Declaration to effect the creation of a Jewish national state. But the State Department remained aloof from the Palestine problem, maintaining that it was a British diplomatic puzzle and that its main concern was the protection of American interests in the mandate. After the cessation of hostilities in World War I, the British had occupied Palestine, and the Supreme Allied Council awarded to Britain a mandate for that country at the San Remo Conference in April 1920. In 1922 the League of Nations approved the mandate, with the provision that Britain should create a Jewish national state. This stipulation assumed that Britain would facilitate Jewish immigration to Palestine. As consolation for the disappointed Arabs, Britain created Transjordan in 1928, with the Emir Abdullah as reigning monarch. The United States acted to ensure that American rights in the Palestinian mandate were protected. Although a 1922 Congressional resolution called on the U.S. government to use its good offices to support the creation of a Jewish national state, the State Department turned a deaf ear to such pleas. In 1924 it concluded the Anglo-American Convention respecting Palestine which provided for the protection of American rights in the mandate.[1]

In spite of the Department's attitude that Palestine was a British problem, American Zionists maintained pressure on Washington. But weakness characterized their cause, for it was plagued by factionalism. After the 1929 Arab riots in Palestine, American Zionists became more vocal, but their pressure on Secretary of State Henry L. Stimson produced nothing more than a repetition of earlier announcements that the United States would not take up the Zionist cause. During the 1920s the Department adhered to the tradition of noninvolvement, to the assumption that Palestine was a British question, and to the Anglo-American agreement respecting American rights in the mandate. But in the decade of the 1930s, with the rise of Adolf Hitler and the pressure of the Nuremberg Laws

66

which placed German Jews outside the law, the Palestine question loomed larger in American-Middle Eastern relations. During the 1930s, with Jewish immigration on the rise, Arabs feared Jews would overrun Palestine. In 1936 Arabs rioted to voice their displeasure, whereupon the British appointed an official investigating body, known as the Peal Commission, to look into the causes of unrest. In 1937 it recommended the partition of Palestine into two states, one Jewish, the other Arab. Continued Arab disturbances in 1938 compelled the British Foreign Office to issue in 1939 the famous White Paper, a document that aimed at appeasing the Arabs by repudiating the Balfour Declaration and restricting Jewish immigration to Palestine to 75,000 during the during the next five years. It also placed limits on Jewish acquisition of farmland.[2] Although American Jews pressured Secretary of State Cordell Hull to fulfill Zionist goals, American Jewish political consciousness was not sufficient in 1938 and 1939 to obtain endorsement of their cause. The Department of State did not voice objections to the British 1939 White Paper. Thus in the months immediately prior to the onset of World War II, American Zionists were a weak force in the nation's policy-making process.[3] At the outbreak of war the United States continued to regard Palestine as a diplomatic conundrum to be solved by the British.

Following the opening of hostilities American Zionists and members of Congress compelled the State Department to reassess the official position on the Zionist question. Cordell Hull described the issue as "delicate," one that posed a real dilemma to the U.S. government.[4] On the other hand, there was the burning desire of American Zionists to create a homeland for the Jews who were being subjected to the barbarities of Hitler's Germany. On the other hand, Zionists could upset the Middle East by their continued lobbying, thereby hindering the Allied war effort. With Europe embroiled in war, the leadership of the world Zionist movement passed to the United States, where Zionist adherents hoped that the American government would throw its support behind the creation of a Jewish national state. This goal was at odds with the wishes of American oil men whose companies had promises of untold riches beneath the desert sands of the Middle East. Following the precedent of his predecessors, President Roosevelt did not regard Palestine as an American problem, and he maintained a detached posture in keeping with the guiding principle of nonintervention. But Zionists soon brought the Palestine issue before the American government and people.

In 1941 Emanuel Neumann, director of public relations for the American Emergency Council for Zionist Affairs, took the lead in the formation of the American Palestine Committee (APC), an organization that consisted of numerous members of Congress and was headed by Senator Robert F. Wagner of New York. In 1942 on the 25th anniversary of the enunciation of the Balfour Declaration, the APC, which now included sixty-eight senators and two hundred members of the House of Representatives, endorsed a statement that opposed the British White Paper restrictions on the Zionist program.[5]

While this was a first step in the use of political power to achieve its goals, perhaps the most important action taken by American Zionists was the passage of the Biltmore Program at New York City in May 1942. The Biltmore Conference was addressed by such leading Zionists as Chaim Weizmann, David Ben-Gurion, and Nahum Goldman. Ben-Gurion, one of the executives of the Jewish Agency, urged that Zionists drop the concept of a binational state, because Arabs would only dilute the effectiveness of a purely Jewish state. The Conference moved to achieve the goals of the Basel Program of 1897 which included the recognition of Jewish people to settle and colonize Palestine, and the creation of an organization to unite world Jewry in support of the Zionist movement. It also called for the rejection of the White Paper of May 1939.[6] With a definite program in mind, American Zionists now set about the task of winning the support of American Jews. The chore of calling American Jews to a meeting at Pittsburgh fell to Henry Monsky, the staunch Zionist president of B'nai B'rith. He invited thirty-four national Jewish organizations to send delegates to a conference at Pittsburgh in January 1943. Representatives of about one million American Jews assembled at the steel city on January 23-24, 1943, for the purpose of putting together support for a commonly accepted program for Palestine. They also set about the task of forming an American Jewish assembly to win Jewish support for the Zionist program. Out of this historic meeting came the American Jewish Conference which convened on August 29, 1943, and affirmed its endorsement of the Biltmore Program. It could claim to speak for the overwhelming majority of American Jews.[7] Having gained the support of American Jews for a comprehensive Zionist program, American Zionist leaders now turned their attention to winning the endorsement of the American public and the United States Congress.

During the remainder of 1943 the American Jewish Conference organized an effective canvass to raise funds and put together the machinery necessary to sway American public opinion through various propaganda organizations. Zionists could count on the Yiddish press, on twenty national periodicals, and on part of the American press to present material compatible with the Biltmore Program. The Zionists also employed pamphleteers and writers to prepare material favorable to their goals. They distributed some one million leaflets and pamphlets to American libraries in 1943 and 1944. The American Jewish Conference effectively used mass meetings and protest rallies to get its message across. It employed professional public opinion and propaganda methods to win public and congressional support for the Biltmore Program. Its leadership was almost the same as that of the American Zionist Emergency Council. To AZEC fell the chief task for educating the American public about the Jewish problem and Zionist solutions. Under the astute direction of Emanuel Neumann, the AZEC worked to achieve greater public support for Zionist aims. It too used organized pressure instruments aimed at eliciting the support of state legislatures, the endorsement of mass public rallies, and the affirmation of various professional groups such as university professors.[8]

In the late summer of 1943 the American Jewish Conference and the AZEC undertook to counteract the British White Paper which would bring to a halt all Jewish immigration to Palestine in April 1944. Zionists employed a wide range of propaganda techniques to mobilize American public opinion. Local emergency committees were encouraged to make contacts with their congressional delegations, stressing the importance of repudiating the British restrictions. Supported by more than two thousand Zionist leaders across the nation, the AZEC was able to secure a barrage of anti-White Paper resolutions from national Jewish organizations and also from civic groups such as the Rotary, Optimist, Elks and Lions clubs. Further, the Emergency Council enlisted nationally known members of the acting profession, such as Victor Jory, Gene Kelly, Joseph Cotton, Eddie Cantor, and Edward G. Robinson to deliver messages in radio programs in favor of the Zionist plan. In summary, this exercise in building public suport made it possible for Zionists to move further in the political field in 1944 by arousing the national consciousness of Jewish Americans and the sympathy of non-Jewish Americans.[9]

It is now necessary to discuss the growing Arab reaction to the rapid acceleration of Zionist activities in the United States in 1943. The passage of the Biltmore Program and the intense propaganda campaign mounted by American Zionists for the purpose of bringing American public opinion into support of Zionist goals aroused intense Arab reaction and made it necessary for the Department of State to take a position on the Palestine question. No longer could Washington afford to evade this issue which it had for so long regarded as primarily a British problem.[10]

To determine the Arab reaction to Zionist activities in the United States and the depth of anti-Jewish feeling in the Middle East the Joint Chiefs of Staff dispatched Lieutenant Colonel Harold B. Hoskins, a man conversant with the politics of the Middle East and a fluent speaker of Arabic, on a mission to the Middle East in late 1942. Hoskins warned of renewed fighting between Arabs and Jews in Palestine because Arabs feared that Jews would turn Palestine into an exclusively Jewish state. The Haganah, the Jewish Army in Palestine, was well armed with modern weapons obtained from the Vichy French. Further, the Arabs feared that the pro-Zionist sentiment in the United States would ultimately result in supporting the Zionist move to create a Jewish state. Only by the insertion of a large military force in Palestine could a Zionist state be imposed upon the Arabs. Hoskins argued that a joint Anglo-American statement should be issued that would assure the Arabs that no final decision on the Palestine question would be taken until the conclusion of the war and that any postwar decision would be taken only after full consultation with both Arab and Jewish leaders. The President and the Department of State endorsed this report which became the cornerstone of American policy on the Palestine question."

Brigadier General Patrick J. Hurley, personal representative of the President, submitted another report on Palestine on May 5, 1943. He warned that Arabs viewed Jewish migration to Palestine as a sort of imperialism, and that Arabs were of the opinion that the United States sponsored the founding of a Jewish state. Arabs, he concluded, "viewed the founding of a Jewish nation as a violation of the Atlantic Charter and of the fundamental principles of Americanism...."[12]

The Department also received reports late in 1942 and early 1943 that Arab leaders were disturbed about reports that the Zionist leaders were actively seeking official United States endorsement of the creation of a Jewish state in Palestine. Nuri as-Said, Prime Minister of Iraq, protested to the American Minister in Iraq about pro-Zionist statements originating in the United States.[13] Alexander Kirk, U.S. ambassador to Egypt, reported that the Egyptian government was considerably exercised at what it perceived to be the U.S. role in abetting the cause of Zionism in Palestine. He warned that force might well be required to quell disorders growing out of Arab and Jewish competition for Palestine. He asserted that Prince Mohammed Ali, heir to the Egyptian throne, had voiced numerous reservations about the pro-Zionist statements emanating from the United States.[14] But the warning that gave gravest concern came from King Ibn Saud of Saudi Arabia in May 1943. The King asserted that Jewish Zionists were trying to seize Palestine, a land to which they had no clear and perfect title by virtue of long-standing Arab settlement in that country from earliest times. He cautioned that Palestine "would forever remain a hotbed of troubles and disturbances" if Palestine became an exclusively Jewish state. He condemned Jewish propaganda and urged the President to call a halt to Jewish immigration to Palestine.[15] The President replied on May 26, setting forth American policy based on the advice of Colonel Hoskins' previous reports. He advised that no settlement would be made in Palestine before the end of the war and that no decision "altering the basic situation in Palestine should be reached without *full consultation* with both Arabs and Jews."[16] This communication to the King should be regarded as the genesis of the formulation of American policy on Palestine by the U.S. government which had previously based policy on the broad generalities of the Atlantic Charter. The "full consultation" formula was to be the hallmark of U.S. policy until the conclusion of the war.[17]

Inasmuch as the "full consultation" approach was acceptable to the British, the Department of State initiated steps during the summer of 1943 for the United States and Britain to issue a joint statement, advocating that no final decision regarding Palestine would be made until the conclusion of the war, and that any decision would be made only after "full consultation" with both Arabs and Jews. On June 9 Secretary Hull urged upon U.S. Ambassador John G. Winant in Great Britain the need to press the British to join the United States in issuing a joint statement on Palestine.[18] The President approved the text of a draft statement prepared by the Department, but the matter was ultimately dropped. It seems that news of the proposed statement leaked to Zionist leaders who "immediately bombarded high governmental officials with protests." Hull referred the matter to the War Department, but Secretary of War Stimson concluded that the military situation that obtained in the Middle East in 1943 did not "warrant the issuance of the statement and it was cancelled."[19]

Zionist leaders in the United States not only opposed the issuance of a joint Anglo-American statement on Palestine, but they also achieved one other important goal. Because the 1939 British White Paper immigration terms were due to expire in March 1944, whereupon Jewish immigration to Palestine would cease, Zionists pressed the State Department to obtain an extension. Hull advised Lord Halifax, the British ambassador in Washington, on December 13, 1943, that the U.S. government would be pleased to see the deadline extended. Hull pointed out that there were some five million Jews in the United States who were sympathetic with the plight of Jews in Europe. Moreover, the U.S. government "could not help but be thoroughly sympathetic with the Jewish request not to terminate the immigration provisions of the White Paper on March thirty-first...." Lord Halifax replied that the British government had indeed been planning to extend the deadline, because not all of the immigration certificates had been used.[20] In April 1944, Wallace Murray, chief of NEA, accompanied by Foy Kohler, Dr. Isaiah Bowman, and Robert Coe, attended a meeting in London at which Sir Maurice Peterson, under secretary of state for foreign affairs, advised that Whitehall intended to maintain immigration during the war years because the number of immigration certificates was more than ample to handle the current rate of immigrants.[21]

The immigration problem temporarily settled, the President turned his attention to another facet of the convoluted Palestine problem. Having received two communications from King Ibn Saud, both expressing opposition to the creation of a Jewish state in Palestine, the President discussed the Palestine situation with Dr. Chaim Weizmann, president of the World Zionist Organization. Roosevelt determined that the time had come when he should make an approach to King Ibn Saud to bring him together with Dr. Weizmann for the purpose of working out Arab-Jewish differences in order that the Palestine problem could be settled amicably. To this end, he ordered Colonel Hoskins to approach the King.[22] Accordingly, Hoskins visited King Ibn Saud in August 1943 and put to him the possibility of entering discussions with Dr. Weizmann or some other representative selected by the Jewish Agency for seeking a solution to the Palestine problem. The King refused to see Dr. Weizmann because he simply could not afford to support any Jewish claims to Palestine.[23] Subsequently, Hoskins returned to Washington and discussed the matter with the President, touching mainly on his conversation with the King. He pointed out that the King had a position of moral leadership in the Arab world and his prestige extended to the whole of Islam as well. During the conversation, the President suggested a trusteeship for Palestine, one that would make that land a "real Holy Land for all three religions, with a Jew, a Christian, and a Moslem as the three responsible trustees." He said that he was aware that such a plan might not meet the approval of American Jews.[24]

The President's suggestion of a trusteeship solution to the Palestine problem caused considerable discussion in the Department. Wallace Murray forwarded a memorandum of this idea to Assistant Secretary of State Adolph Berle and to E.R. Stettinius, acting Secretary of State during Cordell Hull's absence at the Moscow Conference. Murray noted that the handling of Palestine as a Class "A" Mandate was a failure due to two strongly competing nationalistic movements. The President's suggestion that Palestine be viewed "in a religious rather than a political light may also be sound and at any rate is thoroughly worth exploring." He sugested that the British remain as the mandatory power for Palestine, but that since the mandate concept for the independence of Palestine was a failure, Palestine should be "regarded primarily, for the time being, as a sacred respository of the interests of Christianity, Islam, and Judaism." He urged that a governing body of Christians, Jews, and Muslims be appointed to work under a British governor. Stettinius forwarded Murray's recommendations on to Hull on the latter's return from Moscow, with the comment that the was "considerably impressed by the President's philosophy on this problem."[26]

With regard to the trusteeship proposal which had been thoroughly studied by NEA, Hull recorded that "the impossibility of bringing the Jews and Arabs together on a common, friendly ground at that time, and the danger of stirring the sands of the Near East by a premature attempt to settle the question of Palestine made it wiser to postpone action until a more propitious time."[27]

While it was feasible to postpone action on the trusteeship proposal, there was another problem that confronted the Department and the President and demanded immediate attention. Zionist pressure on Washington was strong in late 1943, and on January 27, 1944, two identical resolutions concerning Palestine were introduced in the House of Representatives by James A. Wright, a Pennsylvania Democrat, and Ranulf Compton, a Connecticut Republican. These two measures put the United States Government on record as favoring the establishment of a national home in Palestine and that it would "use its good offices and make appropriate measures, to the end that the doors of Palestine shall be opened for free entry of Jews into that country...." A similar resolution was introduced in the Senate by Robert F. Wagner, a New York Democrat, and Robert A. Taft, the Ohio Republican. The former was referred to the House Committee on Foreign Affairs, while the latter was referred to the Senate Foreign Relations Committee.[28] The introduction of these two resolutions led to an immediate reaction in the Arab world and to immediate concern in the executive branch of government.

The Arabs responded vociferously. On February 9 the Egyptian ambassador in Washington registered concern that the resolutions would open up the question of Palestine, an issue that the President assured him would be postponed until war's end.[29] Ambassador Loy Henderson reported from Baghdad that Nuri as-Said, Iraqi Prime Minister, and Mahmood Subhi al-Daftari, Iraqi Foreign Minister, and numerous members of the government had expressed concern that the resolutions would cause unrest in the Arab world.[30] The American chargé in Damascus reported that members of the Syrian Parliament had voiced concern about the resolutions and that the Parliament had passed a resolution, asserting that passage of the American resolutions would "shake all confidence in international justice and those good hopes guaranteed by the Atlantic Charter."[31]

Both Secretary of War Stimson and Secretary of State Hull expressed their feelings on the resolutions to Senator Tom Connally, chairman of the Senate Foreign Relations Committee. Stimson asserted that the resolution is a "cause of deep military concern to the War Department," and that its passage would be "apt to provoke dangerous reprecussions in areas where we have many vital military intersts."[32] Following the lead of Stimson, Hull wrote two days later that, given the military considerations put forward by the Secretary of War, "it is believed that without reference to its merits no further action on this resolution would be advisable at this time."[33] King Ibn Saud, King Abdullah of Transjordan, and the King of Yemen voiced their opposition to the resolution in no uncertain terms.[34]

It appears that the strategy of the executive branch was to give the War Department full rein to kill the resolution in an executive session of the Senate Foreign Relations Committee. Under Secretary Stettinius so advised Hull, saying that General Marshall was conversant with matters in the Middle East and the impact the resolutions would have on American forces in that area.[35] Marshall was indeed apprised of the serious impact that passage of the resolutions could have on American forces in the Middle East, for on February 22, 1944, Assistant Secretary of War John J. McCloy sent a memorandum to him, asserting that the resolution could exacerbate an already tense situation in Palestine between Arabs and Jews. Outbreaks of violence could cause the Allies to "pin down troops for garrison duty" at a time when these troops are badly needed for duty in Italy. Disruption of the flow of vitally needed oil would surely follow in the wake of an Arab-Jewish conflict. Protection of refineries and pipelines would require "a substantial number of troops to protect them in the event of disorders."[36] Because of the impact that passage of the resolutions could have on the war effort, General Marshall testified before the Senate Foreign Relations Committee along the lines set forth in McCloy's memorandum.[37] As a result the resolution was withdrawn. Further action on the resolutions in the House was not forthcoming, for a letter from Secretary of War Stimson to the committee chairman advised that "further action on them at this time would be prejudicial to the successful prosecution of the war."[38]

While the matter of the Palestine resolutions was settled quietly in committee, there remained the problem of reassuring the Arab heads of state about U.S. policy toward Palestine. Under Secretary Stettinius suggested to the President and to Hull that the time had come for the United States to clarify its position on the issue by the issuance of a joint Anglo-American statement.[39] The suggestion fell on deaf ears, for the President did not wish "this matter raised at this time. He reiterated his position that he considers the problem as entirely a military one."[40] And so it fell to the Department of State to issue statements to the various Arab governments to the effect that the United States government would make no decision on Palestine until the conclusion of the war and then only with full consultation with both Arabs and Jews.[41]

The President was alarmed over the consequences that the resolutions could have on the American war effort in the Middle East, but he had to make some statement that would placate the Zionists because 1944 was an election year. On March 9, 1943, Rabbi Stephen S. Wise and Rabbi Abba Hillel Silver, co-chairmen of the American Zionist Emergency Council, who were becoming concerned about the position of the executive branch of the government toward the resolutions, interviewed the President. Roosevelt gave them a statement designed to pour oil on troubled waters:

> The President authorized us to say that the American Government has never given its approval to the White Paper of 1939.

The President is happy the doors of Palestine are today open to Jewish refugees, and that when future decisions are reached, full justice will be done to those who seek a Jewish National Home, for which our Government and the American people have always had the deepest sympathy and today more than ever, in view of the tragic plight of hundreds of thousands of homeless Jewish refugees.[42]

The President's statement aroused a storm of protest in the Arab world, to which Secretary of State Hull replied that the statement mentions a "Jewish national home rather than a Jewish commonwealth as referred to in the resolutions recently introduced into Congress." Hull cautioned that while it was true that the U.S. government had never given its endorsement to the White Paper of 1939, it is also true "that this Government has never taken a position with regard to the White Paper." In conclusion, he added that the U.S. government has no intention of altering its determination to make no decision on Palestine "without full consultation with both Arabs and Jews."[43]

While disappointed that the resolutions had been locked up in committees, Zionist leaders pushed ahead with their task. It was their hope to insert into the platform of both political parties in the 1944 presidential election campaign planks supportive of the Zionist position in Palestine. Dr. Silver achieved his purpose at the Republican convention on June 27 with a statement that called for opening Palestine to unrestricted Jewish immigration in order that the Balfour Declaration of 1917 might be implemented in full.[44] Dr. Wise worked among the Democrats who included a plank much shorter, but more to the point: "We favor the opening of Palestine to unrestricted Jewish immigration and colonization, and such a policy as to result in the establishment there of a free and democratic commonwealth."[45] The Department of State promptly received word from Damascus, Baghdad, Beirut, and Cairo that the Arabs were chagrined that Zionists were taking advantage of the American political process to achieve their goal in Palestine.[46] The Secretary of State had warned the President that he thought it advisable "for leaders of both parties to refrain from making statements on Palestine during the campaign that might tend to arouse the Arabs or upset the precarious balance of forces in Palestine itself."[47] Although Hull said the Palestine issue did not enter the campaign, nevertheless the President did make one statement that can only be construed as politically motivated. On October 15, 1944, he addressed to Senator Wagner a message that was to be conveyed to the Zionist Organization. The President referred to the Democratic plank of July and asserted that

efforts will be made to find appropriate ways and means of effectuating this policy as soon as practicable. I know how long and ardently the Jewish people have worked and prayed for the

> establishment of Palestine as a free and democratic Jewish common-
> wealth. I am convinced that the American people give their support
> to this aim and if reelected I shall help to bring about its realization.[48]

This statement might be considered as politically motivated or it might
set forth the President's views on this emotional issue.

Regardless of the true nature of Roosevelt's statement, it caused an
instant reaction in the Middle East, where an Arab Chamber of Commerce
in Jerusalem canceled an appointment with an American special economic
mission to the Middle East, Syrian press and public expressed much alarm
that the President intended to violate the principles of the Atlantic Charter, and a Cario newspaper proclaimed a boycott against American
goods.[49] Wallace Murray, highly exercised at the publication of the
President's letter and the reaction it caused among Arab political leaders,
addressed two memoranda to Under Secretary of State Stettinius on October 27, asserting that the "prestige of the United States in the Arab world
will undoubtedly seriously deteriorate by reason of official declarations in
this country by the President ... supporting the establishment of a Jewish
commonwealth in Palestine." The endorsement of a Jewish state, Murray
continued, "goes beyond any previous official American pronouncement
on Palestine, which have been limited to expessing sympathy with the idea
of a Jewish national home rather than a Jewish Commonwealth." This was
a patent violation of the "full consultation" formula, and unless counteracted "would seriously prejudice our ability to afford adequate protection to
American interests in the Near East." He called attention to the likelihood
that "the basic long-term American economic interest in Saudi Arabia will
be seriously threatened and possibly jeopardized." King Ibn Saud would
very likely question previous American statements to him about its future
policy *vis-à-vis* Palestine. Murray concluded with a warning that the
Soviet Union had been "showing growing interest in the Near East" and,
given Soviet opposition to Zionsim, it is likely that they will make
political capital out of Arab opposition to Zionist aspirations in
Palestine.[50] Murray's conclusions received support from Loy Henderson.
Writing from Iraq, the American minister warned that the President's
statement of intentions with respect to Zionist plans in Palestine could
only have an adverse effect on U.S. relations with Iraq. If the United
States government "would prefer the support of the Zionists to the friendship of the Arabs, the Iraqis would have the choice of complete subservience to Great Britain or the establishment of close relations with the
Soviet Union."[51]

If Department officials in NEA were upset about the reaction to the
President's October statement to Senator Wagner and the concomitant
reaction in Arab capitals, they were even more concerned to hear that
Secretary of War Stimson withdrew his objection to Congressional

passage of the two Palestine resolutions. On October 10, 1944 Stimson wrote in the foreword to a pamphlet on Palestine prepared by Representative Sol Bloom "that the military considerations which led to my previous action in opposing the passage of this resolution are not as strong a factor now as they were then. In my judgment, political considerations now outweigh the military, and the issue should be determined upon the political rather than the military basis."[52]

At the reemergence of the congressional resolutions, the State Department took the initiative in keeping them bottled up in committee, for the Department received word from Egypt that some five hundred members of various Arab groups from Egypt, Tunisia, and Morocco had met to send President Roosevelt a protest against American policy on Palestine.[53] Acting Secretary Stettinius advised Senator Wagner that he had discussed the resolutions with the President who thought that the delicate situation in the Middle East surrounding the murder of Lord Moyne in Cairo dictated against bringing the resolutions out of committee. Stettinius advised the President that in his opinion Senator Wagner would press for passage of the resolution but that "Senator Connally will be able to persuade the committee not to take action on it at this time."[54] Stettinius testified in secret session before the Senate Foreign Relations Committee on 6 December, explaining the delicate situation in the Arab world and urged that the committee make a statement to the effect that passage of the Palestine resolution at this time would be unwise.[55] The committee took no action on the resolution on the 6th and since no action was forthcoming during the week, the Department issued a press release on December 11 setting forth its views on the resolution with the simple statement that it did not consider that passage of the measure at the present time would be wise.[56] The Department's action was in harmony with the thinking of the President who had written Senator Wagner on December 3 that he was aware that the Jews wanted to go to Palestine where they would be met by "approximately seventy million Mohammedans who want to cut their throats the day they land. The one thing I want to avoid is a massacre or a situation which cannot be resolved by talking things over."[57]

The whole matter of the congressional resolutions on Palestine created a split in the Zionist leadership. Moderates were opposed to bringing them up at this time, for they considered the timing bad. However, Rabbi Silver, in favor of action, promptly resigned from his position of leadership in the Zionist Organization of America and the American Zionist Emergency Council when Zionists did not continue to press for action.[58] Nothing further was heard on the resolutions, and it must have come as a relief to the Department and to the President who was then preparing to leave for the Yalta Conference. On the eve of the conference, Stettinius wrote the President, advising that pro-Zionist statements in the United States had produced a "strong reaction in the Near East." The Secretary warned that "if this trend should continue, it would seriously prejudice our ability to afford protection to American interests, economic and commercial, cultural and philanthropic, throughout the area. It ... would have a very definite bearing upon the future of the immensely valuable American oil concesssion in Saudi Arabia, where the King's opposition to Zionism is well known." He pointed out that "the Russians are showing a growing interest in the Arab world and are quite plainly anxious to expand their influence in the area, particularly toward the Persian Gulf. Such expansion would of course be in the direction of the oil fields in Saudi Arabia and Bahrein as well as those in Iran, Iraq, and Kuwait. The Soviet Union has never endorsed Zionism."[59] The Department also prepared a paper on Palestine for the President's use at the conference. The paper suggested that the United States adhere to previously stated policy of not arriving at any decision on Palestine that "would endanger the war effort and jeopardize American interests in that area." Further, that the Powers at Yalta should not set out a Palestine policy without "full consultatation with both Arabs and Jews in accordance with commitments made both by us and the British."[60] However, the question of Palestine was not discussed at Yalta. Evan Wilson concludes that the President felt that Palestine was the type of issue that should be dealt with by the future international organizations, a position that he adhered to in his conversations with Colonel Hoskins.[61]

While the Presdient did not intend to discuss Palestine at Yalta, he did plan to visit King Ibn Saud on his return trip and take up the matter with him. Prior to departing for Yalta, the President requested James M. Landis, director of economic operations in the Middle East, to supply him with information that might enable him (the President) to "Bring about a rapprochement between Arabs and Jews on the Palestine problem." Landis replied promptly, warning that King Ibn Saud "feels very intensely about this subject." Further, that unless Roosevelt were prepared to make some "far-reaching proposals," he had best avoid discussing the Palestine question. He suggested that Palestine must "become an international responsibility. The British cannot be asked to carry it alone, nor can a steadfast policy be set and adhered to without whole-hearted Russian support."[62]

On his return trip from Yalta the President arranged to meet with King Ibn Saud in the Great Bitter Lake in the Suez Canal on board the U.S.S. *Quincy* (CA-71), the heavy cruiser which had taken him from the United States to Yalta and was to return him to the United States. As the destroyer U.S.S. *Murphy* (DD-603), carrying the King and his entourage, drew alongside the *Quincy*, the crew manned the rails of *Quincy* but no salutes were fired. The King crossed the gangplank to meet the President, and the two leaders conversed on deck for over an hour. The President refrained from smoking in the presence of the King, but he did smoke two fast cigarettes on the elevator down to the compartment where the formal meeting was to take place.[63] Colonel William A. Eddy, a fluent speaker of Arabic and the U.S. minister to Saudi Arabia, acted as personal interpreter for the President. His record of the conversation is interesting and he recorded that the President and the King "got along famously together." In their talks, the President asked the King for his advice regarding the Palestine problem and the matter of Jewish refugees. The King replied that they should be returned to their homes and displaced Jews should be provided homes in the Axis countries which had dispossesssed them. He expressed the opinion that Arabs and Jews could not get along together in Palestine. He asserted that Arabs hoped the United States and its Allies would base their Palestinian decisions on justice. The President replied that he "would do nothing to assist the Jews against the Arabs and would make no move hostile to the Arab people." He said that he could prevent neither speeches and resolutions in the Congress nor pro-Zionist editorials in the free American press. The President concluded with some comments on farming which he said greatly interested him, and expressed interest in irrigation, tree planting and water power which he hoped could be developed in many countries at the conclusion of the war.[64]

Following the President's return to the United States, he addressed a joint session of Congress on March 1, stating: "Of the problems of Arabia, I learned more about the whole problem, the Muslim problem, the Jewish problem, by talking with Ibn Saud for five minutes than I could have learned in the exchange of two or three dozen letters."[65] During the two remaining months of his life the President continued to give the Palestine problem and its tangential effect on Saudi Arabia his attention.

In that time President Roosevelt was subjected to enormous pressure by memoranda from the Department of State, from Congress, and from the AZEC. He obviously had reservations about the establishment of a Zionist state in Palestine, for he agreed with Colonel Hoskins' views "that a Zionist State in Palestine could be installed and maintained only by force."[66] But the President seems to have been speaking out on this issue in a way that would satisfy his particular hearer, for on March 16, 1945, Rabbi Wise, disturbed by his statement to the Congress, requested him to clarify his position on Palestine. The President replied that he had made his position on Zionsim clear in October, that he had not changed his position, and that he would "continue to seek to bring about [the] earliest realization"[67] of a Zionist state in Palestine. The President was obviously referring to the statement he had made in his letter to Senator Wagner in October of the previous year. The Rabbi then issued the President's statement to the press. Arab reaction was immediately forthcoming, for the President had seemingly departed from the "full consultation" formula. From Iraq the Department of State received word that Prime Minister Nuri as-Said expressed his keen disappointment in the President's statement.[68] In Damascus, Syrian university students rioted, demonstrating their opposition to what they perceived as the President's reversal of his position by opening the doors of Palestine to unlimited Jewish immigration.[69] Roosevelt's statement also vexed the staff at NEA and Wallace Murray dispatched a memorandum to Acting Secretary of State Joseph C. Grew, warning that "in the face of the situation, the continued endorsement by the President of Zionist objectives may well result in throwing the entire Arab world into the arms of Soviet Russia."[70]

So concerned was the Department that Acting Secretary Grew sent out a circular to American posts in the Middle East, advising that the "President's statement refers to possible action at some future time. Further that all Arab Governments were assured of the President's previous statement that "no decision altering the basic situation of Palestine should be reached without full consultation with both Arabs and Jews."[71]

During the month of March, six Arab leaders sent a collective letter to Roosevelt, setting forth arguments supporting the Arab position on Palestine. The State Department prepared replies, reassuring the addressees that the United States continued to adhere to the policy of "full consultation."[72] The President died at Warm Springs, Georgia, on April 12 while in the process of signing these notes to the Arab leaders. Those notes not signed by Roosevelt were returned to the White House for the signature of President Harry S Truman.[73]

Following the death of Roosevelt, Truman was the recipient of pressures from the Department of State, from Zionist leaders, and from the Congress — all of this in a growing climate of increased conflict in Palestine between Arabs and Jews. The Department undertook in the month of April to press its views on the new President. Acting Secretary Grew persuaded Truman to sign and send out to Arab leaders the letters prepared for President Roosevelt's signature.[74] Grew also sent to the President a memorandum explaining that although President Roosevelt "at times gave expression to views sympathetic to certain Zionist views, he also gave assurances to the Arabs ... that in the view of this Government there should be no decision altering the basic situation in Palestine without full consultation with both Arabs and Jews."[75]

But the Department was not alone in trying to get the ear of Truman, for on April 20, 1945, Rabbi Wise called on the White House and pleaded with him to support unlimited Jewish immigration to Palestine. A larger number of Jews in Palestine, Wise explained, was necessary if the Zioinst goal of a Jewish state were to be realized.[76] The President was well aware of Zionist aims, for Secretary of State Stettinius had briefed him on Zionist goals, explaining that leading Zionists were going to call on him to press for unlimited immigration to Palestine.[77] President Truman was sympathetic to Zionist plans, for he seems to have felt bound by President Woodrow Wilson's endorsement of the Balfour Declaration to assist in the founding of a Jewish national state.[78] Although the State Department continued to urge adherence to the "full consultation" formula, with the added suggestion that the United Nations Organization should handle the thorny Palestine question, Truman nevertheless endorsed the Zionist plan of unlimited immigration to Palestine.[79] In the summer of 1945 Truman prepared to leave for the Potsdam Conference with Prime Minister Churchill and Premier Joseph Stalin. To assist him at the conference the Department of State had prepared briefing papers. The one on Palestine suggested that the President should not press the Zionist viewpoint but should seek merely to determine what the British intention was.[80]

Influenced by David K. Niles, his adviser on minority affairs, and Eddie Jacobson, his former business partner, the President elected not to follow the advice of the State Department and other high-level members of the executive branch. At the Potsdam Conference, Truman wrote Prime Minister Churchill of the interest of the American people in the Jewish question, urging that Britain lift the 1939 White Paper restrictions to permit the immediate entry of 100,000 Jewish immigrants from the camps in Europe. In taking this tack Truman departed from his predecessor's policy of "full consultation."[81] Clement Attlee soon replaced Churchill, and he advised that he would give the matter his careful consideration. Attlee later urged Turman to dispatch U.S. military forces to Palestine to help carry out those measures necessary to maintain the peace. Truman refused.[82]

But as World War II drew dramatically to a close following the dropping of two atomic bombs on Japan, the President received a report from Earl G. Harrison, U.S. representative on the Inter-governmental Committee on Refugees, that profoundly influenced his thinking on the Palestine problem. Harrison reported in late August that most Jewish displaced persons wanted to migrate to Palestine. He urged that 100,000 certificates of immigration be issued for this purpose, as recommended by the Jewish Agency, the quasi-official Zionist governing body in Palestine. In compliance with Harrison's recommendation the President wrote Attlee on August 31, 1945, urging the British Prime Minister to permit entry of the Jewish refugees.[83] A reply from Attlee was not immediately forthcoming.

In the interim there was a debate in Truman's cabinet, where State, War, and Navy Department officials and the Joint Chiefs of Staff all concurred that U.S. support for the creation of a Jewish state was at variance with American national interests. Opponents of a pro-Zionist stance in the White House argued that American support for a Zionist plan in the Middle East would give the Soviets entry into that region where disappointed Arabs would turn away from the U.S. A pro-Zionist position in the U.S. government, they argued, would also jeopardize Arab good will at a time when the West would become increasingly dependent upon Arabian oil to sustain economic recovery and prosperity when Western oil reserves were badly depleted.[84] Particularly fearful of the consequences of a tilt toward the Zionists were Secretary of State James F. Byrnes, George F. Kennan, State Department adviser on Soviet affairs, and Secretary of the Navy James Forrestal.[85]

The course of events in the postwar era leading to the founding of the State of Israel is beyond the scope of this study. Suffice it to say in summary that President Franklin D. Roosevelt seems to have adhered to the principle of "full consultation" to the time of his death, although Secretary of State Cordell Hull asserts that Roosevelt was contradictory in that he "talked both ways to Zionists and Arabs." Whatever Roosevelt's shortcomings, Hull states that he did not permit the Palestine question to embroil Arabs and Jews in armed conflict, thus turning "the whole of the Near East" into an Armageddon between Arabs and Jews, and greatly obstructing the war effort.[86] However, Under Secretary of State Sumner Welles has suggested that the President never swerved from his plan to create a Jewish national state by using economic assistance to win Arab support for such a solution.[87] But one of the President's close advisers, David K. Niles, remarked that had President Roosevelt lived there were serious doubts in his (Niles') mind that an independent Jewish state would have come into being.[88] What seems clear in the midst of these conflicting interpretations is that the President, having failed to enlist King Ibn Saud's support to enter direct negotiations with a Jewish leader to reconcile Jewish and Arab differences, would have opted for the creation of a multinational state under the administration of Jewish, Muslim, and Christian leaders and placed in trusteeship status under the United Nations.[89]

Truman's decision to request the British to permit unlimited Jewish immigration to Palestine was a break from the "full consultation" formula and it set in motion a chain of events leading to American support for the creation of a Jewish state in Palestine. Truman acted as he did for the Jews because he believed that President Wilson had endorsed the Balfour pledge and that he (Truman) should fulfill this promise. Too, he believed that the American public wanted him to act on behalf of the Zionists. Truman also told oral biographer Merle Miller that his great familiarity with the Old Testament predisposed him to a definite pro-Jewish bias.[90]

In the final days of the war, the United States clearly departed from

Roosevelt's wartime policy of "full consultation." In so doing, it made it possible for Jewish immigrants to flow from Europe to Palestine. Arabs viewed this incidence of increased Jewish immigration as an example of European imperialism, a phenomenon made possible by policy emanating from the While House. By supporting the creation of Israel, Truman drew greatly from the large fund of good will that Arabs had for the United States.

Although the United States pursued a policy that aided the flow of Jews from Europe to Palestine and abetted the creation of Israel — a policy perceived by Arabs as imperialistic — it nevertheless pursued a wartime policy in Syria and Lebanon that called for an end to French imperialism in those two lands. However, to say that American policy in the Levant was simply anti-imperialistic is an oversimplification, for other considerations impinged on the shaping of policy for Syria and Lebanon.

Chapter 6

Military Considerations and Anti-imperialism in Syria and Lebanon

Following World War I Syria and Lebanon were detached from the moribund Ottoman Empire, and at the San Remo Conference in 1920 France accepted these two countries as mandates under the League of Nations. After the League Council's approval of the French mandates on July 24, 1922, lengthy negotiations led to the signing of the Franco-American Convention on Syria and Lebanon on April 4, 1924. This agreement recognized the rights of American citizens in the Levant to conduct schools and engage in commercial activities. The operation of these schools created a fund of goodwill among the Arabs of Syria and Lebanon.[1] Under the pressure of nationalism, the French had in 1936 promised Syrians and Lebanese their independence, but had not carried out this promise in June 1940 at which time France fell to German aggression. For a time the Vichy French regime exercised control, but when it became likely that Germany would occupy these two states, British and Free French forces occupied them in June and July 1941. Britain promptly recognized the independence of Syria and Lebanon, and General Georges Catroux, Free French commander in the Middle East, announced that he had come to terminate the mandate and proclaim the independence of Syria. Following the official British recognition of Syrian independence on October 28, 1941, the Foreign Office requested the State Department to follow suit. But the Department of State demurred on the grounds that recognition might well jeopardize American rights under the 1924 treaty and because the United States maintained relations with the Vichy government. But on November 19 the Department issued a statement expressing American sympathy with the political aspirations of the peoples of these two states.[2] American policy toward these two nations of the Levant was more complicated then opposing French imperial aspirations in the Middle East. Policymakers in the Department did not want to recognize the independence of Syria and Lebanon because to do so would antagonize the Vichy regime. Given the secret plan to invade North Africa in November 1942, officials in the Department hoped to gain advantages by dealing directly with officials in North Africa.[3]

But the United States was soon drawn into problems related to Syria and Lebanon that involved an Anglo-French dispute. It seems that the British hoped that Vichy would terminate the mandates, thus permitting the British to remove occupation troops from the Levant. But the Free French, under the leadership of General Charles de Gaulle, wanted to retain control over the two lands. The British hoped that independence would permit the Syrians and Lebanese the right to hold free elections, with a view to establishing sovereign independence. The French balked at this. Differences of opinion between British and French leaders brought on a crisis which the United States sought to mediate.

In the spring of 1942 relations deteriorated between General Sir Edward Spears, British minister to the Levant states and personal friend of Winston Churchill, and General Catroux, the Free French delegate. Because the Department of State did not wish to disturb relations with Vichy, Cornelius Van H. Engert, American counsul general at Beirut, counseled President Alfred Naccache of Lebanon that he did not feel that the present moment was the proper time to hold free elections. Postponing them until the end of the war would be more advisable, for then the Levant would no longer be threatened by enemy invasion.[4] On the 20th Engert suggested to President Naccache that holding elections would only encourage the Axis Powers to believe that the British and French were disunited, a hopeless situation that would only harm the war effort.[5] Because Anglo-French differences over the future status of Syria and Lebanon reached crisis proportions, Secretary of State Hull cabled Engert on April 24 that the United States would "be very pleased to assist in any way it may in bringing about a better understanding among the British, the Free French and the people of Syria and Lebanon."[6] But the British authorities in Beirut tried to inject the United States into the dispute by obtaining the Department of State's approval of holding free elections and American recognition of Syrian and Lebanese independence.[7] Matters between the British and French continued to deteriorate during the summer, but a silver lining appeared on the lowering diplomatic clouds when General Spears agreed to meet with General Catroux at a conference in Cairo in early August.[8] May and June meetings between the British and French officials were productive, for General Catroux announced the intention of permitting a return to democratic institutions in Syria and Lebanon, shortly thereafter to be followed by the holding of free elections.[9] From Cairo, Alexander Kirk, American ambassador, reported that the United States should establish a diplomatic representative for Syria and Lebanon in order to achieve Allied solidarity and to protect American interests in the region.[10]

At this juncture, a new factor entered the three-cornered Anglo-British-Arab dispute when General Charles de Gaulle arrived in Beirut, ostensibly to help solve the problem. But instead of spreading oil on troubled waters, the General further complicated the situation. In a conference with William M. Gwynn, American consul in Beirut, de Gaulle asserted that the French were determined to grant independence to the Syrians and Lebanese, "but that this can be done only when they are prepared for it, but that time has not come and may not for many years." In short, it would be dangerous to grant them independence prematurely.[11] To make matters worse, Gwynn reported to the Department that the General was determined "to force a show-down with the British, for he preceived that they had violated their promise to acknowledge Free French predominance in local affairs." Further, that the British were determined to supplant the Free French in the Levant.[12] Although the British Foreign Office denied having ulterior motives in Syria and Lebanon other than winning the war, and declared categorically that Britain did not wish to encroach in any way on the position of France, the situation continued to decline, and on September 1 Gwynn cabled Secretary Hull that "Franco-British relations here are at the breaking point."[13]

Aware that a serious breach could hurt the Allied war effort, Secretary Hull cabled John G. Winant, American ambassador in London, urging him to discuss the problem with the Foreign Office. He suggested that Winant state that the United States could support neither the Free French nor the British positions, but that it could not remain indifferent to the dispute. Hull asserted that General de Gaulle's statement that France might have to delay independence for many years was a bone of contention and that General Spears was probably overstepping the bounds of probity.[14] On that same day Hull cabled Gwynn to make clear to General de Gaulle the American concern that France fulfill her assurances of independence to the Levant states.[15] The British and Free French continued their quarrel during the autumn of 1942, with the British insisting that the French live up to the assurances that they had given the people of Lebanon and Syria with respect to independence. The climate became less strained following an exchange of correspondence between Prime Minister Churchill and General de Gaulle in the autumn. Finally, the French agreed in October to hold elections in the summer of 1943, and on October 21 Ambassador Winant so advised Secretary of State Hull.[16]

During 1942 American policy *vis-à-vis* Lebanon and Syria had slowly evolved. As late as August 19 the Department refrained from supporting the British policy of regarding Syria and Lebanon as independent and the calling for free elections in 1942. It refused to recognize Syria and Lebanon, because to do so would greatly complicate relations with

Vichy.[17] During the summer and autumn of 1942 the Department began to evolve its policy toward the Levant states. It backed off from the previously stated position of opposing free elections and from its stated opposition to recognition of the independence of the Levant states. Indicative of this new position was the appointment of George Wadsworth, former consul general for Palestine and Transjordan, as diplomatic agent for Syria and Lebanon, an event that signified limited recognition by the United States of the Levant states.[18] In appointing Wadsworth, the President gave encouragement to the peoples of Syria and Lebanon, for a diplomatic agent was a designation reserved to representatives dispatched to semi-sovereign states.[19]

Wadsworth, a former faculty member of the American University of Beirut, immediately presented his credentials. He had a difficult task to perform, for the British had agreed to recognize the "predominant position" of France in the two Levant states. The Department advised Wadsworth that the United States was not in agreement that France should enjoy a "preeminent and privileged position in Syria and Lebanon." Wadsworth repeatedly reassured the Syrian and Lebanese governments that Washington had not and would not recognize the French claim to a privileged position in the Levant.[20]

With the opening of the new year, the American position in regard to Syria and Lebanon continued to take shape. On January 30 Wadsworth reported from Beirut that the French were determined, despite the declaration of independence, to maintain the mandate in Syria and Lebanon. The French based this decision on the reality that most foreign states had not yet extended formal recognition to the two Levant states.[21] French obstinacy did not meet a kind reception at the Department of State. Foy Kohler of NEA recorded that members of the Division had an opportunity to meet with Richard G. Casey, British minister of state in the Middle East, and that they found themselves "in agreement with his views regarding the desirability of progressive implementation of the proclaimed independence of these states by the establishment of elective governments and the transfer of real power thereto." Concerning the continuation of the mandate, Kohler noted that "we shared his disapproval of the Fighting French regime's obvious efforts to retain complete mandatory control in denial of its promises of independence to the local populations." But concerning the British agreement to recognize a special relationship between the French and the Levant states, he recorded that "in view of our consistent policy regarding equality of opportunity, we are unable to agree with the British recognition of a 'preeminent and privileged position for France among European powers' in Syria and Lebanon, given in the Lyttleton-de Gaulle agreement of July 1941."[22]

That the French intended to maintain the status quo in the Levant became all the more evident from Wadsworth's cables from Beirut. On March 23, 1943, he advised that Arab leaders here "continued to nurse four fears — of French imperialism, British insincerity, American isolationism, and Zioinst expansionism." He related that General Catroux has reestablished the mandate regime and demands of Syria and Lebanon a special treaty of alliance as a quid pro quo for its termination. General Spears had indicated by a public speech that the British were quite willing to approve the special position for France in the Levant.[23] On May 24 he reported that French authorities were exercising undue pressure on the governments of Syria and Lebanon to postpone elections, all the while working behind the scenes to achieve electoral support for pro-French parliamentary candidates.[24]

But in the following month Wadsworth reported a change in French policy. He related that the achievement of French political unity in North Africa created the proper climate for the French to end pressure to postpone Syrian elections. Conversation with Jean Helleu, acting Free French delegate in Syria and Lebanon in the absence of General Catroux, on June 11 disclosed that plans for free elections were proceeding smoothly. The elections for Syria would be held in July.[25] However, in Lebanon a politico-religious crisis occurred, for the French increased the number of deputies to the Lebanese parliament in a manner that would give Christians a larger majority, thereby increasing French control over the parliament. A compromise solution was worked out by General Spears and Helleu eventually, and the date for Lebanese elections was set for September 1943. Although Maronite Christians hoped that Wadsworth would intervene, he refused, asserting that diplomatic practice precluded his interfering in an internal political affair.[26]

Thus the stage was set for the orderly progress from colonial status to that of independence for the Syrian and Lebanese peoples in the summer of 1943. Elections were held in Syria and the Syrian parliament opened in August. Sumner Welles, acting Secretary of State, advised Wadsworth that the United States officially welcomed the successful reestablishment of constitutional government in Syria and viewed this as an important step toward the fulfillment of sovereignty. But until there were an effective transfer of substantial authority and power to the new government, the United States could not extend formal recognition.[27] In early September Wadsworth related news of Lebanese parliamentary elections. While the French were making an effort to manipulate the elections in favor of the Christian element in order to maintain French control over the parliament, there nevertheless was a large voter turn out.[28] In response to news of elections in the Levant, Secretary Hull instructed Wadsworth to state to the leaders of Syria and Lebanon that the United States follows with enthusiasm the elections and is sympathetic with the successful reestablishment of constitutional government as a further step along the way to full sovereignty and independence under the banner of the United Nations.[29]

The Syrians were anxious to achieve full independence in order to win recognition from the United States. To that end, Syrian President Shukri el-Kuwatly requested Wadsworth to seek American assistance in achieving full independence. To this Wadsworth replied that the United States could not take any action until Syria had first acquired full possession of the machinery of government. Secretary Hull, when learning of Wadsworth's conversation with the Syrian President, replied that the Department approved his remarks concerning American policy in Syria.[30] But Hull did act in another direction to assist the Syrians, for he cabled Robert D. Murphy, personal representative of President Roosevelt, at Algiers on Noverber 9, 1943, to advise the French authorities that the United States Government took the position that the French should now take all practical steps to implement the independence promised to Syria and Lebanon. Failure to do so would create doubts in the minds of Americans about French adherence to the principles of the United Nations.[31]

It was at this juncture that the French created a political crisis in Lebanon. On November 5 Wadsworth reported that French authorities asserted that they could not recognize the power of the Lebanese government and parliament to unilaterally validate a new constitution. On the 9th he cabled that the French had clearly and publicly declared that they would not recognize the validity of the proposed constitutional amendments unless French consent had first been obtained. That same day he advised that Helleu had informed the Lebanese government that the mandate remained in effect and that constitutional modifications could not be accepted.[32] On the 11th Wadsworth shocked the Department with word that French Marines and Senegalese troops had arrested Sheik al-Khuri, president of Lebanon, and his cabinet. To compound the felony, Wadsworth observed that the French had installed a government of their own liking. Later in the day he cabled that French troops had established cordons around parliament and government buildings, in response to which angry crowds gathered. The troops fired at the demonstrators, killing five and wounding twelve.[33] The people of the country were in full-scale revolt against the newly appointed Emile Edde, the French-designated head of state. Wadsworth reported that the coup was brutally carried out, with Senegalese troops breaking into houses and carrying out all manner of brutal acts. Emile Edde, he described as "Chief French Stooge." During the riotous days of November a delegation of over one hundred doctors, lawyers, engineers, and journalists called on the American Legation, protested French use of force and requested American intervention.[34] The

Department immediately sent two cables, one to Wadsworth in Beirut, the other to Murphy in Algiers. Hull directed Wadsworth to have no official relations with the Edde Regime. He instructed Murphy to inform the French National Committee in Algiers that the United States government had learned with surprise of the repressive action of the French authorities in the Lebanese Republic. He asserted that "it is difficult to understand how the French, whose country is now groaning under the heel of the invader, can be unmindful of the aspirations toward independence of another people." Lebanon must cast the gravest doubt upon the sincerity of the avowed declarations of all the United Nations and this Government cannot permit itself to be associated in any way with such acts of repression." Hull directed that Wadsworth should advise the French that unless the Committee of National Liberation takes immediate steps to restore the duly elected government the United States would be compelled to publicly announce its complete disapproval of the acts of the French authorities in Lebanon.[35] Hull kept Roosevelt, then en route to the Cairo Conference, informed about the situation. At Cairo the President discussed the matter with Prime Minister Churchill, whose government had demanded that the French remove Helleu, liberate the imprisoned members of the Lebanese Government, and restore order in the republic.[36]

In this crisis the Department of State determined to follow the British lead, and Hull cabled Wadsworth that this decision was based on the British military presence in the area and on British commitments to which the United States was not a party. He instructed him to permit the British to take the initiative in any measures which might be called for by French reluctance to meet British demands.[37] The demands referred to in Hull's cable related to the ultimatum delivered by the British to General Catroux on November 18. The British memorandum declared that if the French did not release the president of the Republic and his ministers by November 22, they would be set free by British troops and that martial law would be declared in Lebanon for reasons of military necessity.[38] Catroux promptly communicated this British ultimatum to the French Committee of National Liberation at Algiers for a reply. Winant duly informed the Department of the British action, and he later related that the Foreign Office relayed to him word that the French had agreed to dismiss Helleu as a first step in solving the crisis.

News of French intention to give in reached Washington on the 23rd, when Wadsworth advised the Department that the French National Committee had consented to release President al-Khuri and his ministers, but that only the former was to be reinstated.[39] The British protested this intransigence, and on November 23 Hull cabled American Consul General Wiley at Algiers to inform the French Committee that "anything less that a restoration of the constitutional situation" would not be acceptable to the United States and that it would "not be willing to recognize an arbitrarily imposed or appointed successor in its stead."[40] These were harsh words. Given the combined pressures from Washington and London, the French had little alternative but to give in to their demands. On November 23 Wadsworth cabled that the French had abrogated the decrees setting aside the duly elected Lebanese government. On the following day he called on President Khuri, who received Wadsworth and expressed his thanks for American support during the crisis.[41] On November 26 the Department issued a press release, approving the action taken by the French National Committee and expressing the hope that negotiations could now go forward in a spirit of good will to bring about a solution to the outstanding problem of Lebanese and Syrian independence.[42] To bring the crisis to a conclusion, General Catroux met with representatives of the Lebanese and Syrian governments, and agreed to return to these governments the powers exercised in their name by French officials. This agreement provided that the services, jointly administered by the French and Syrian and Lebanese officials, would be handed over to the two states with the right to make laws and legislate beginning on January 1, 1944.[43]

During the following year there took place in Syria and Lebanon a gradual transfer to governmental powers, a process that had been in motion since November 1943. The Department of State was gratified that the French were dismantling their colonial regime and on September 5, 1944, Cordell Hull cabled Wadsworth that full recognition would be accorded Syria and Lebanon upon receipt of written assurances that the rights of American nationals as set forth in the Treaty of 1924 between the United States and France are fully recognized. He suggested that bilateral accords between the United States and the two Levant states could achieve this end. Finally, Hull informed Wadsworth that the President intended to appoint him as U.S. minister near the Syrian and Lebanese governments.[44] The agreement between the United States and Syria was effected by an exchange of notes signed on September 7 and 8, 1944, and a similar agreement between the U.S. and Lebanon was concluded on those same dates.[45]

But conditions in the Levant were not yet as they should be, for the French aimed to impose upon Syria and Lebanon treaties that would grant to France a special privileged position. Neither the Syrians nor the Lebanese desired this treaty relationship, which would permit the last vestiges of colonialism to remain intact. Indeed, the Syrian President cabled Wadsworth that "I would rather make Syria a Soviet Republic," and the Syrian minister of foreign affairs cabled Hull that such a condition of subservience was contrary to the Atlantic Charter.[46] Although the British initially supported such a position, they appeared to retreat from it on learning that the United States would not recognize any agreement that gave France a superior position in the Levant. Wallace Murray advised Michael Wright, counselor of the British Embassy in Washington, of the U.S. position on September 22. On the 28th Wright called at the State Department to present an *aide mémoire*, declaring that Britain favored an agreement between France and the Levant states which "would permit the conduct of their future relations on an ordinary diplomatic basis."[47]

What seems clear is that the United States, long committed to a policy of anti-imperialism that would permit the doctrine of self-determination of peoples full play in the Levant, faced an intransigent French government that desired to maintain the favored French position in the two states. The British, desiring to maintain a privileged position in Iraq, wanted the French to obtain the same footing, thereby buttressing the British imperial stance in the Middle East.[48]

By October the United States was prepared to move, and on the 10th Wallace Murray presented to the French delegation in Washington a memorandum, advising that the United States had concluded that both Syria and Lebanon could now be considered independent states and "is therefore according full recognition of this independence by accrediting to the local Governments at Beirut and Damascus an Envoy Extraordinary and Minister Plenipotentiary." But Murray's note cautioned that the U.S. would have no cause to object to treaties defining the relationship of France with Syria and Lebanon "which were freely and voluntarily agreed to between the interested parties and did not infringe on the rights and interests of others." In conclusion the United States "could therefore not agree that France or French nationals should enjoy discriminatory privileges in independent Syria and Lebanon."[49] In conversations with the French Delegate on the 10th, Wallace Murray pointed out that if the French demanded a special position in the Levant, they might compel the peoples of Syria and Lebanon to turn to the Soviets to find a counterweight. He asserted that he hoped the French would not press for the special realtionship.[50]

But the French were determined to obtain a special relationship, for on October 12 the American chargé in Damascus cabled that French colonial authorities had presented the Syrian government a request for the conclusion of a treaty giving France a privileged position in Syria. On the 14th Hull advised Wadsworth, the newly appointed minister to Syria and Lebanon, that the United States would refuse to approve a treaty giving "discriminatory privileges to France or to French nationals."[51]

Although the French continued to muddy the diplomatic waters in the Levant, Wadsworth presented his letter of credence to the Syrian and Lebanese presidents on November 16. He advised the Department of the presentation, relating that the French hoped to elicit a request from

Maronite clergy for French protection in the independent Lebanese state.[52] On December 7 President Roosevelt cabled the Syrian president that the U.S. Government had set forth its position on Syrian independence in notes to the French Delegation and to the Syrian Foreign Minister. That the United States would recognize no special French position in the Levant was implicit. Roosevelt added that "these documents speak for themselves...."[53]

Fearing that the French planned to undermine the independence of Syria and Lebanon by treaties that would give French nationals special privileges, officials at the Department of State were more than a little exercised. Wadsworth cabled from Beirut on January 9, 1945, that he had discussed the whole problem with President Kuwatly of Syria. The latter advised Wadsworth that Syria considered making "identic treaties of friendship, establishment, commerce, and consular relations" simultaneously with Britain, France, Russia and the United States. This would effectively undercut the French effort to obtain a preferred position in the Levant states.[54] Acting Secretary of State Grew replied to Wadsworth that the Department would be happy to be helpful in any way by advancing suggestions and giving informal support for the submission of treaty proposals simultaneously to France and the other major Allied Powers.[55]

So disturbing was the situation in the Levant that Grew cabled Jefferson Caffery, American ambassador in France, instructions to convey to the Quai d'Orsay the Department's concern about the situation in the Middle East. Grew urged that the Department would look with "disfavor on French use of military force in the present impasse, whether in the form of French troops or French controlled native levies." Simultaneously, Grew instructed Wadsworth to urge the Syrian and Lebanese officials to alter their present negative position and to enter into conversations with the French with a view to negotiating mutually acceptable agreements which would define their relations in such manner as would not infringe upon the rights and interests of other nations.[56] Wadsworth called upon the Syrian president on February 21. Kuwatly replied to Wadsworth's suggestion that Syria enter into treaty talks with France by saying tht the Syrian government had always been quite willing to give specific assurances that French interests would be protected. But he asserted that under no conditions would the so-called historic position of France warrant the granting of a preferred position to French nationals.[57]

From Paris the Department learned from Caffery that he had heard from Georges Bidault, French Minister of Foreign Affairs, that the French would soon put forward the treaties with Syria and Lebanon that would grant to France the same "position as the British have in Egypt and Iraq. They included permanent rights in naval and air bases and the turning over of the *Troupes Spéciales* at the end of the war." What is more, Bidault advised Caffery that the British were in agreement with the special position of France and would support that position.[58]

That relations between the United States and France were becoming even more tense was evident on March 2, 1945, when French Ambassador Henri Bonnet called on the Department and stated to Joseph Grew that the United States has assumed a position in opposition to the enjoyment of a privileged position by France, thereby creating a regrettable situation. Bonnet discussed at great length the historic position of France in the Levant, one based on tradition, culture, and economic ties.[59] To add to the problem, Ambassador Winant cabled from London that Prime Minister Churchill had discussed with the Syrian President at Cairo the French situation in the Levant. Churchill had declared himself to be in support of the special position of the French in the Levant.[60]

To clarify the U.S. position, Paul H. Alling and Foy Kohler, respectively the chief and assistant chief of NEA, discussed at length with Francis Lacoste, counselor of the French Embassy in Washington, the whole matter of the French position in the Levant. During the conversations, Alling advised that the United States had urged France to take those steps which would lead to the completion of treaties that would recognize the independence of Syria and Lebanon and at the same time protect French interests in a manner that would not discriminate against those of other powers. Lacoste replied that the French Government would be very disappointed at the American unwillingness to recognize the privileged position of France in the Levant.[61]

The situation deteriorated even further. The United States determined to send arms to Syria which had declared war on the Axis Powers, but it also opposed the French movement of additional troops to Syria and Lebanon. Not only did the French oppose the shipment of American arms but they also maintained the right to send French colonial troops from North Africa and France to the Levant.[62] The Department of State was adamantly opposed to the introduction of additional troops into the Levant. Grew instructed Caffery in Paris to advise the Quai d'Orsay that this act will only provoke a violent reaction among the Syrians and Lebanese and could only be interpreted as an effort to influence the course of treaty talks.[63]

In the spring of 1945 the United States was clearly moving on a collision course with its oldest ally. President Roosevelt, thoroughly disgusted with the French colonial record in North Africa and in French Indo-China, was determined that the intransigent de Gaulle would not work his will in the Levant. But the French were determined to maintain their position in the latter region. In fact, Foreign Minister Bidault had asserted on February 2 that "France is absolutely determined to preserve her preeminent position in these two countries, and to maintain order there by continuing to control the military forces at her disposal for this purpose."[64] In fact, Loy Henderson wrote a lengthy memorandum to the acting Secretary of State on May 16, advising that the current crisis in the Levant arises from the French determination to maintain a position of "preeminence and privilege" which they claim by virtue of "long historical association with the Levant States." The Lebanese and Syrian governments were both disturbed at the introduction of additional French troops, and Henderson warned that the popular reaction would be sharp and violent. Further, that the situation had now reached crisis proportions.[65]

That the French were determined to maintain a preferential position in the Levant is evident from the demands presented by the French to the Syrian and Lebanese governments. Wadsworth cabled the Department a list of these demands on May 19, 1945. He asserted that the French desired to protect their cultural, economic, and strategic interests in the two countries. The cultural interests referred to the French system of schools that had existed since the 19th century. The French also hoped to ensure that the French language was maintained as a second language. Economically, the French hoped to gain a treaty that would guarantee the flow of oil through the Syrian pipeline from Iraq. Strategically, the French wanted guarantees permitting the use of bases to preserve French lines of communication, two military bases, and port facilities for their ships.[66] In response to Wadsworth's cable, Grew advised Foreign Minister Bidault that the United States was "considerably disturbed" about the introduction of French troops into the Levant and the nature of the proposed French demands. Grew warned that disorders were likely to occur, as indeed they did.[67] On May 19 merchants in Damascus and Beirut closed their shops, thus proclaiming a strike. Looting broke out in both capital cities, and soon French troops were bringing in armored cars and automatic weapons to put down the violence.[68] The Syrian and Lebanese governments reacted by breaking off all negotiations, asserting that with the cessation of hostilities against the Axis, they would call for the evacuation of all foreign troops. Anti-French demonstrations brought more violence that resulted in the death of eight people and the wounding of twenty-five.[69] Loy Henderson warned William Phillips, special assistant to the Secretary of State, that the disturbances were likely to spread and this would give the French good cause to bring in more troops, battleships, and perhaps aircraft. He suggested that the Department should contact the British, with a view to holding a conference in London that might help to reconcile the French and the peoples of Syria and Lebanon.[70]

Reaction on the diplomatic front to the French employment of force was soon forthcoming. Whitehall proposed that the United States and Britain engage in a joint effort to prevail upon the French to join them and the Levant states in a conference with regard to the whole question covering the presence of French and British troops in the Levant.[71] The Syrian Foreign Office requested President Truman to use his good offices to pressure the French to withdraw all troops, thereby respecting the sovereignty of Syria.[72] The State Department approached the French with a view to holding multipartite discussions in Paris. The King of Saudi Arabia requested the United States to intervene to put an end to the violence and to pressure the French to withdraw all demands that infringed on the sovereignty of Syria and Lebanon.[73]

So serious did President Truman consider the issue in the Levant that on May 26 he called for a meeting with Acting Secretary Grew and with Dean Acheson, the Assistant Secretary of State. Grew urged that the United States assert its opposition to the course of French policy in the Levant. The President, unsympathetic to French colonial aspirations, approved, and on that date Grew instructed Ambassador Caffery to deliver to the French government a note, advising that Washington placed great value upon its traditional and historic friendship with France but urged the French to review their policy toward Syria and Lebanon, with a view to finding a means of settling peacefully the outstanding dispute.[74] Two days later the Department cabled Whitehall that the U.S. Government would be happy to send representatives to a conference in either London or Paris to settle the outstanding crisis in the Levant.[75]

Unfortunately, the diplomats were losing control of the situation, for on the 29th Wadsworth cabled from Beirut that the Syrian government was fearful that widespread hatred of the French would undoubtedly result in additional violence.[76] Later that day Wadsworth advised that heavy fighting had broken out in Damascus and that the French forces were using heavy machine-guns, artillery, and aircraft. The State Department responded immediately by considering the draft of a note to be sent over the President's signature to General de Gaulle, calling for a truce. But Prime Minister Churchill, not sanguine about settling the matter diplomatically, informed President Truman that he intended to order the commander-in-chief of British forces in the Middle East to intervene immediately to put a stop to the fighting.[77]

The course of events moved rapidly on May 31st. That morning Loy Henderson sent a memorandum to the President, relating the extent of violence and the resultant loss of life in Syria. Realizing the urgency of the situation, the President met in conference with Acting Secretary Grew, Admiral Leahy, William Phillips, and Captain J.K. Vardaman, his naval aide. The President agreed with the British proposal to intervene to prevent further bloodshed in the Levant.[78] In addition, the White House released to the press a statement that the United States had issued Lend-Lease aid to the French for defense against the Axis forces in this war and "this Government does not intend to provide military equipment for any other purpose. This government has not assigned any material for use in Syria."[79] Later in the day, Grew cabled a message to de Gaulle, with the approval of the President, calling on the French to refrain from further violence in order that peace might be restored. He informed him that the Syrian and Lebanese governments had been requested to refrain from any action that would aggravate the situation.[80]

With the green light from Washington, Churchill cabled de Gaulle, noting that British forces would "intervene to prevent the further effusion of blood in the interests of security of the whole Middle East, which involves communications for war against Japan."[81] British intention to intervene came just in time, for Wadsworth reported that the French had bombarded Homs, Hama, and Aleppo. They subjected Damascus, one of the oldest cities in the world, to savage bombardment by planes, artillery, and tanks. Whole sections of the city had been ravaged. Several thousand persons had been killed or wounded.[82]

Pressured by Washington and London, de Gaulle had no alternative but to give in. On June 2 Caffery wired from Paris that de Gaulle had ordered General Beynet, general delegate and French plenipotentiary, to order French forces to cease fire on the 31st. That same day the Department received word from Wadsworth at Damascus that British troops and armored cars had moved into the Syrian capital. The French, he advised, were complying with the order to cease fire.[83] That de Gaulle felt humiliated by the diplomatic pressure causing him to put an end to hostilities is evident from Cafferey's June 3 cable from Paris. The Ambassador observed that British intervention in the Syrian crisis has seriously damaged the General's prestige both in France and abroad. Moreover, his anti-British public statements indicated that he would seek to save face and to embarrass the British. But de Gaulle's cable to President Truman was conciliatory. He thanked him for urging a moderate attitude in Damascus and Beirut, and advised that he had ordered a cease fire on the 31st.[84]

With the cessation of hostilities in the Levant, there remained the need for the French to negotiate treaties with the Levant states recognizing their independence. Whitehall suggested a conference in London between British, American, and French representatives who would meet officials from Syria and Lebanon. Washington agreed with this plan, but the French, not to be outdone, suggested a five-power conference that would include delegates from the Soviet and Chinese governments to consider the broad range of problems covering the presence of European troops in the Middle East. This move was designed to remove the spotlight from Syria and bring it to bear on the British presence in Egypt, Palestine, and Iraq.[85] On June 8 Grew informed the French ambassador that the United States did not consider an international conference on Middle Eastern questions to be appropriate, but it would meet the French to work toward an orderly settlement in Syria and Lebanon.[86] The British reply to the French proposal was equally negative.

But the French were not deterred. Paranoid about British intentions of ousting them from the Middle East, the head of the French Delegation at the United Nations Conference on International Organization submitted to E.R. Stettinius, the chairman of the conference, an *aide-mémoire* on June 24, 1945. He requested that Stettinius appoint three neutral, impartial commissioners who would investigate the origin of the dispute and promote a friendly settlement between the parties to the conflict.[87] Stettinius replied that he did not believe the Levant crisis called for the Preparatory Commission to deal with the problem. Rather, he believed that the matter should be settled through normal diplomatic channels by the United States, Great Britain, France, and officials from the Levant states.[88] Having successfully avoided attending an international conference that would place France in an embarrassing position, de Gaulle adopted a different solution to the problem.

The General chose to enter direct discussions with Beirut and Damascus to bring about a settlement. Count Stanislas Ostrorog, French minister plenipotentiary, went to Beirut in late June to begin discussions with Syrian and Lebanese officials. The Frenchman proposed the orderly transfer of the *Troupes Spéciales* to the Levant governments and the simultaneous withdrawal of all French and British troops. Wadsworth reported from Beirut that the French had moved quickly, thereby hoping to "by-pass British proposal for London conference with American participation."[89]

As an epilog to the American wartime effort to use diplomatic means to bring about an orderly transition in the Levant states from colonial to independent status, the French turned over command of the *Troupes Spéciales* to the Levant governments. In December 1945 the British and French negotiated an agreement, with assistance from Washington, that called for the simultaneous evacuation of British and French troops from Syrian territory. Indeed, British Foreign Secretary Ernest Bevin thanked Loy Henderson for his support.[90]

The American policy of ensuring that the subject peoples of the Levant enjoy the right of self-determination was temporarily interrupted during the early days of the war by reasons of military expediency. Delaying recognition of Syrian and Lebanese independence was based on the need to maintain ties with Vichy in order to facilitate the landings in North Africa. Once assured of a successful military settlement in North Africa, the Department of State began an orderly transition in its policy toward the Levant states. Supported by President Roosevelt whose distrust of French colonial pretensions was intense, the Department of State pursued a policy that encouraged the orderly process from colonial status to that of independence. It is now necessary to follow the course of events in the Maghreb, where American policy also had to consider the independence of the peoples of Algeria, Morocco, and Tunisia. While the peoples of the Maghreb were not so far advanced on the road to self-determination as were the peoples of the Levant, American policy was no less anti-colonial in nature in wartime North Africa. But as was the case in the Levant, military considerations took precedence over support for anti-colonial policy.

Chapter 7

Military Considerations
and Anti-imperialism in
Algeria, Morocco and Tunisia

America's earliest diplomatic intercourse in the Middle East was with the peoples of North Africa. The Barbary pirates, operating out of ports in Morocco, Algeria, and Tunisia, preyed on American merchant shipping in the Mediterranean in the years following the American Revolution. The establishment of diplomatic ties with Morocco, Algeria, and Tunisia was a high priority objective in order that American merchants might engage in the lucrative Mediterranean and Middle Eastern trade. The Department of State, aided by ships of the U.S. Navy, early made treaties and established diplomatic relations with Morocco, Algeria, and Tunisia. But during the nineteenth and early twentieth centuries France added these states of the Maghreb to the expanding French Empire. A French expedition acquired Algeria in 1830. French occupation of Tunisia in 1881 led to the establishment of a French protectorate in that land. By virtue of the Entente Cordiale with Great Britain, and the act of Algeciras of 1906, France obtained a preferred position in Morocco, and the Treaty of Fez in 1912 gave France a protectorate. Because of French control there the United States lost its vital interests in North Africa until the outbreak of World War II.

Following the fall of France in 1940 the United States maintained ties with the Vichy French regime which governed North Africa. Strategic considerations motivated this policy. The successful landings in North Africa in November 1942 vindicated the American policy in regard to Vichy. After the successful conclusion of Operation TORCH, military considerations continued to dominate American policy toward North Africa, even though opposition to French imperialism was a central theme of American diplomacy in the Middle East throughout most of the war. However, Cordell Hull made it clear that the United States regarded the entire North African situation from the "military point of view, and con-

100

sequently civil questions were subordinate except as they contributed to military effectiveness."[1] Thus during the early war years the United States could not concern itself with more than planning abstractly for the future self-determination of the peoples of Morocco, Algeria, and Tunisia.

To accomplish its military objectives, the United States effected an agreement with Admiral Darlan to bring about a ceasefire in North Africa. Following Darlan's assassination, General Giraud, previously selected by Washington to command French troops in North Africa was promoted to Darlan's position. Because General Charles de Gaulle, claiming to represent French democratic interests, criticized Giraud, and made a radio broadcast in early January 1943 attacking the United States, the President intensely disliked him. From a reading of dispatches to Prime Minister Churchill and Cordell Hull's memoirs, one can deduce that the President thought de Gaulle a pompous posturer.[2] Because of his distrust for de Gaulle and his belief in Giraud, President Roosevelt and General Giraud agreed to a memorandum on January 24, 1943, whereby Roosevelt acknowledged that Giraud should be regarded as a kind of trustee for French interests in North Africa. Because Churchill was absent from the Anfa Conference at which the Franco-American accord was drafted, it was subsequently amended on February 6. Somewhat changed, the accord reaffirmed the view that Giraud had the "right and duty of acting as a trustee for French interests, military, economic and financial, in French territories...." Further, that because the "French Motherland could not assert its will in establishing a government, France does not now possess a recognizable government and the question of the future government of France in not capable now of final solution."[3]

American policy, as expressed in the Anfa Accord, affirmed the belief that Giraud was a temporary caretaker for French colonial and military interests for the duration of the war and that since the French people could not chose their own government, France did not possess a recognizable government. But this policy was soon to be questioned by de Gaulle who began his bid for complete power over all French interests in North Africa and for recognition as the head of a provisional French government. To complicate matters further, Great Britain had supported de Gaulle and continued to do so, thus creating Anglo-American difficulties in addition to political problems in North Africa that threatened to impede the Allied military effort.

In the spring of 1943 Prime Minister Churchill, accompanied by Anthony Eden, his Foreign Secretary, traveled to Washington to discuss outstanding Anglo-American diplomatic questions. The French North African problem received much attention. On March 22 Hull advised Eden and British Ambassador Lord Halifax that the United States viewed de Gaulle as then making a bid for supreme political power in North Africa.

Hull argued that "our own policy and attitude toward the French situation had always been that we did not feel that there should be any supreme political power set up now to exercise control over the French people." Further, "we felt that the primary purpose in any French organization should be the prosecution of the war for the liberation of France, and we felt that there should be no form of provisional government set up or recognized, and that any political activities should be kept to a minimum dictated by necessity."[4] Hull knew whereof he spoke, for Robert Murphy, American diplomatic agent in Algiers, had conferred with General Giraud on March 4, and he learned that Giraud favored the French people's determining their own political destiny. Giraud's main task was "to get on with the war and liberate the French people at the earliest moment possible." Further, Giraud disavowed any political ambitions.[5] On March 14 Murphy advised Roosevelt and Hull that de Gaulle expected to come to Algiers to "establish his leadership of any united French movement." While he would leave Giraud in military command of all French forces, his main purpose "would then be the establishment under his direction of a provisional government of France, probably in Algiers."[6]

The British had made a commitment to de Gaulle, one justified by the assistance that he had given Britain during the war. Eden did not believe that de Gaulle desired to establish a provisional government in North Africa, with himself head. But to Hull, it was apparent that de Gaulle was so inspired and was thereby driving a wedge between the American and British policy-makers and was creating a political climate in North Africa that could only have adverse results on the Allied war effort. During the course of the high-level talks, Lord Halifax raised the possibility that de Gaulle and Giraud would make a pact, one that envisaged the formation of a French National Committee that would provide leadership for the duration of the war. Hull of course did not object to greater unity among the French factions, just so long as this unity was for military purposes with no political foundation, for the duration of war. No provisional government could exist except to prosecute the war effort.[7]

There the matter rested until May 1943, at which time Churchill returned to the United States. It was an auspicious time, for the Allies were bringing to an end Axis resistance in North Africa. But the French North African situation was growing more complicated. Murphy cabled on May 8, 1943, that de Gaulle intended to fly to Algiers for the express purpose of reducing Giraud's power in this area, thereby enabling him to seize power. Murphy argued that the time had come for the United States to thrash out the problem in North Africa in order that a common Anglo-American policy might be realized.[8] Roosevelt acted immediately, dispatching a memorandum to the State Department about de Gaulle's political aspirations in Algeria. He warned that de Gaulle's "course and attitude is well nigh intolerable" and that he was "taking his vicious propaganda staff down to Algiers to stir up strife between the various elements. He is expanding his present group of agitators who are working up counter demonstrations and even riots." Continuing, he cautioned that "de Gaulle may be an honest fellow but he has the Messianic complex." With respect to the French Committee acting as a provisional government, Roosevelt added that he did not think it should be so regarded by the United States.[9] On the 10th Hull replied to the President, asserting agreement with Murphy in not allowing the French problem to disturb Anglo-American relations. De Gaulle, he pointed out, threatened the military success against the Axis Powers. To remedy the problem presented by de Gaulle, Hull declared that it was imperative that the United States and Britain reach an agreement on the fundamental question of the future of France.[10]

Roosevelt discussed Hull's points with Churchill but was unable to reach an agreement, and he requested the Secretary of State to call upon the Prime Minister to find common ground. Churchill told Hull that de Gaulle had proven difficult for the British, but that Britain was not attempting to build de Gaulle up. Hull asserted that de Gaulle was using propaganda in North Africa to destroy the reputation of Giraud and that his purpose was to assume political power that later would allow him to take control of Metropolitan France. Further, the General's activities were creating friction between the United States and Britain. The conversation with the Prime Minister was barren of results and no accord was reached.[11]

That de Gaulle was bent on undermining the American relationship with Britain and with General Giraud was evident from a dispatch forwarded to the President from Murphy in Algiers. Murphy advised that de Gaulle had a well designed plan to place Giraud in a secondary position — this from General Catroux, one of de Gaulle's closest supporters. Catroux, Murphy advised, recommended that Washington and London issue a joint statement supporting French unity but opposing de Gaulle's drive for supreme powers.[12]

Roosevelt was unable to win Churchill over to the full realization that some definite agreement should be made, and, given the lack of concert, de Gaulle moved ahead with his plan. The General flew to Algiers at the end of May and began his drive for power. He was responsible for the resignation of Marcel Peyrouton, governor general of Algeria. On June 3 de Gaulle and Giraud announced the formation of the French Committee of National Liberation, with each man acting as co-president. They proclaimed that this body was the central power of France, was empowered to conduct the French war effort, exercise sovereignty over French territories, would relinquish power to the provisional government that was to be constituted after the liberation of Metropolitan France, and would reestablish all liberties and laws of the Republic of France.[13] Hull recorded that de Gaulle used immoral tactics to gain this end but that the President and the Prime Minister agreed to accept this committee, hoping that it would end the bitter infighting between the two French factions and accomplish unity of purpose. At a meeting with Henry Hoppenot, chief ad interim of the French Military Purchasing Commission, and Philippe Baudet, delegate ad interim of the French National Committee in the United States, Hull advised that the United States appreciated the unity of action and hoped that the French Committee of National Liberation would contribute to the war effort and to the liberation of continental France.[14]

While Washington accepted the formation of the French Committee of National Liberation, both the President and the Secretary of State had reservations about its status. The President questioned whether France could be included in the roster of United Nations, and the Secretary was concerned that General Giraud might be removed as French commander and the French Committee be considered as a provisional government.[15] The French assured Washington that General Giraud would remain in supreme military command, and at length the Department of State worked out a formula for the future relationship between the British, the United States and the French Committee of National Liberation. This formula asserted that Britain and the United States would agree to treat with the committee as the administrative agent of French overseas territories, thereby acknowledging it as a trustee. Further, the committee would be given military and economic facilities for the prosecution of the war effort.[16] The President forwarded the American formula to Churchill on July 22, adding that he wished to avoid recognition of the French Committee as a provisional government. Unfortunately, the Prime Minister's reply indicated British willingness to employ the word "recognition."[17] On August 3 the President cabled Churchill, saying "I earnestly hope that nothing will be done in the matter of recognition of the Committee of National Liberation until we have an opportunity to talk it over together."[18]

It was becoming increasingly apparent to Hull and the Department that de Gaulle was involved in an effort to make himself the supreme figure in the committee and assume Giraud's power as commander of French North African forces. On August 5, Hull sent a memorandum to the President, advising that the United States had agreed to equip a French army of 300,000 men under the command of General Giraud. Further, that the French Committee of National Liberation had issued a decree creating a Committee of National Defense under the chairmanship of General de Gaulle. He declared that "it is our view that General Giraud has lost further ground...." He concluded with the admonition that the "United States and Britain must make a clear-cut distinction between military and other questions."[19]

While the diplomatic exchanges between Washington and London continued during August, the President and Prime Minister were preparing for the Quebec Conference which opened on August 11. One of the major topics of discussion at Quebec was the matter of recognition of the French Committee of National Liberation. Churchill asserted that all liberal political elements in the world favored granting full recognition to the committee. The President declared that he opposed giving control of the French liberation movement to the group of men that comprised the present committee. The discussion went on rather strongly until the 24th of August, when it became evident that no agreement could be reached. The British opted for recognition of the French committee, while the American representatives opposed, with the President declaring that he refused to give de Gaulle a white horse on which he could ride into France to assume complete mastery of the French government. At length it was agreed to issue two separate statements. Roosevelt issued the American statement on August 26. It instructed Murphy in Algiers to inform the French Committee of National Liberation that the United States welcomed its formation and expected the committee to work for the active prosecution of the war; but the relationship with the committee "must continue to be subject to the military requirements of the Allied commanders." The statement added that the U.S. recognized the committee as the administrative agency over those French overseas territories that acknowledge its authority. Finally, it recognized the committee as "functioning within specified limitations during the war."[20] The British issued a statement on that same day which granted the committee recognition.

Unable to achieve an agreement on future relations with the French National Committee, Hull began working on a new project following the Quebec Conference. It was his intention to obtain the French Committee's adherence to the principles of the United Nations Declaration. Hull's initiative was not successful, for the French Committee wanted to be considered as a government or a nation or member of the United Nations. Neither the President nor Hull would agree to this enhanced status.[21] That the French Committee responded as it did is indicative of the control that de Gaulle had gained over it.

During the late summer and autumn of 1943 de Gaulle continued to gain power in Algiers. In the autumn and winter of 1943 Franco-American relations centered on the controversy regarding the role of the French Committee in North Africa and on the struggle for power between de Gaulle and Giraud. The latter's position weakened steadily with the passage of time. On November 8 Giraud resigned from the French Committee, but retained his command of French military forces. En route to the

Tehran Conference, the President cabled Hull from Cairo on November 27 that de Gaulle's power had increased. Roosevelt related that "the latter now claims the right to speak for all France and talks openly of plans to set up his Government in France as soon as the Allies get in."[22] The contest for power between de Gaulle and Giraud was resolved by the spring of 1944 when the former received full authority over the French military forces.

On May 12, 1944, President Roosevelt grudgingly found himself having to deal with de Gaulle. He advised Churchill that he had no objection to discussions with de Gaulle on military or political matters and that General Eisenhower had full authority to engage in talks with the committee on military matters. But the President admitted that "I am unable at this time to recognize any government of France until the French people have an opportunity for a free choice of government."[23]

But by mid-September, the State Department changed its position on the French Committee. Secretary Hull wrote a memorandum to the President on September 17, urging the extension of de facto recognition of the French Committee as the Provisional Government of France. He stated that General de Gaulle had been accepted as the national leader in liberated France, that there was no chance that he could become a personal dictator, and that the withholding of recognition will make "it more difficult for the committee to maintain the internal stability necessary for the prosecution of the war and orderly rehabilitation of the country."[24] On October 21 the President decided to recognize the Provisional Government of France; on October 23 Jefferson Caffery, diplomatic representative of the United States at Paris, informed Bidault, the French Foreign Minister, that the United States accorded de facto recognition to the Provisional Government and desired to accredit him as American ambassador to France.[25]

Thus, in Europe as in North Africa, the American relationship with Vichy and the French Committee of National Liberation was determined by military considerations. That is not to say that the State Department did not take into account the future self-determination of the Algerian people. Although this ideal and the desire to allow the French the right of free election of a government were part of the reason for American nonrecognition of the provisional government, these ideals were set aside when fighting the war suffered because of nonrecognition.[26] Both the President and his Secretary of State clearly stated on more than one occasion that the primary American aim in North Africa was the successful prosecution of the war effort. Hull defined policy objectives to the Consul General at Algiers very succinctly on May 8, 1943, writing: "Our one primary consideration and concern in the African campaign is the waging of battle until the continent is conquered, and we see no reason, therefore, why political or other considerations should be allowed to interfere with the military effort."[27]

Nevertheless, the President had little respect for the French imperial position and was determined to effect changes in the French Empire. For example, he commented to Robert Murphy at Casablanca in early 1943: "You overdid things a bit in one of the letters you wrote to Giraud before the landings, pledging the United States Government to guarantee the return to France of every part of her empire. Your letter may make trouble for me after the war." Murphy concluded that this was the President's initial intention to reduce the size of the French Empire, writing later that the President had discussed with him the transfer of control of Dakar, Indo-China, and other French possessions.[28] Further indication of the President's views on French imperialism can be gleaned from his memorandum to Hull on January 24, 1944: "Each case must stand on its feet, but the case of Indo-China is perfectly clear. France has milked it for one hundred years. The people of Indo-China are entitled to something better than that."[29]

During the last months of the war, when North Africa was securely in Allied hands and removed from the immediate theater of war in the Mediterranean, the State Department began to plan for implementing the right of self-determination for the peoples of the Maghreb. On January 39, 1945, Jefferson Caffery, newly accredited U.S. ambassador to France, cabled that he had met with Georges Bidault, French Foreign Minister, to discuss postwar plans for the overseas territories of France. Caffery observed that "There was a very frank discussion on both sides about colonies.... The Ministers were obviously very interested, especially [René] Pleven who was Minister of Colonies until recently. They declared that the fundamental French colonial policy is ... to go forward with the integration of the colonies into an Empire system; that is to say, as fast as their education ... allows, they will advance towards complete equality with Metropolitan France — politically and otherwise."[30]

However, French imperial aspirations and plans in North Africa ran counter to the development of nationalism in that area. At the outset of World War II there was very little nationalistic political activity in Algeria. But following the liberation of Algeria by the Anglo-American allies in November 1942, the yeast of nationalism began to work. In 1943 Ferhat Abbas, an Algerian nationalist, issued a manifesto to the Algerian people, calling on them to support the end of colonialism and the right of the Algerian people to practice self-determination and direct their own political destiny. Although the French made reforms in Algeria, they were too little and too late. Algerians demonstrated their intense opposition to French colonialism in May 1945. On May-Day and during the V-E Day celebration, Algerians marched with green and white nationalist flags. The police fired on the populace and the demonstrations soon became riots, with many deaths and many wounded. The French employed artillery and airplanes to quell the rioters.[31]

French reprisals caused a sharp reaction. Summerville P. Tuck, U.S minister to Egypt, reported to the Secretary of State on June 21, 1945, that Abdul Rahman Azzam Bey, secretary general of the League of Arab States, had come to him for advice as to what action should be taken in obtaining the intervention of the U.S. Government with the French "in connection with the serious situation now obtaining in North Africa." Tuck relayed word that Azzam Bey felt that the United States was largely responsible for the course of events in North Africa because "it was the military force of the United States which had saved the North African possessions for France and had re-established French domination over them." Tuck conveyed Azzam Bey's wish that the United States would intervene with the French Government and counsel moderation.[32] The Department acted promptly, and on July 30 sent a despatch to Caffery at Paris, instructing him to inform Bidault that the riots and violence in Algeria were "a source of anxiety ... to the Government of the United States but also to public opinion in this country, which is deeply conscious of the sacrifices in American lives and equipment expended in the liberation of North Africa, and the economic aid subsequently made available to that area and envisaged for the future."[33] On October 5 Dean Acheson, acting Secretary of State, directed Minister Tuck to relate to Azzam Bey that the United States had taken a clear interest in the situation in Algeria. But he urged him to tell the Arab leaders that under no circumstances should an American "interest in the North African situation ... be interpreted as acceptance on our part of his contention that the United States has acquired responsibility for developments in North Africa because of our military assistance in liberating the area."[34] On November 13 Alexander Lyon, American chargé in Cairo, advised the Department that he had communicated to Azzam Bey the Department's concern about the situation in Algeria. Lyon reported that Azzam Bey was profoundly impressed with the American attitude and expressed his gratitude for this concern. Lyon also stressed the caveat that American assistance in the liberation of North Africa should in no case be construed as acceptance of responsibility for the ultimate independence of the states in that area.[35]

The American reaction to Azzam Bey's request for assistance is important, for it indicates a departure from past policy. With the conclusion of the hostilities in the European-North African theater, and the military imperative no longer a factor in American relations with North Africa, it was possible for the Department to express sympathy and concern for the peoples of that region who aspired to practice self-determination.[36]

American wartime policy in Morocco was no less governed by the military imperative than it was in Algeria. But an American expression of concern for the future self-determination of the people of Morocco came much earlier in the war. While attending the Casablanca Conference in

early 1943, President Roosevelt gave a dinner party for Sultan Muhammad V on the evening of January 22. Others in attendance were the
Sultan's Grand Vizier and Chief of Protocol, Harry Hopkins, Prime
Minister Churchill, General Auguste Nogues, Elliott Roosevelt, and Mulai
Hassan, the Sultan's son. While Churchill sat glumly at this Muslim meal
served without alcohol, the convivial Roosevelt conversed with the Sultan
in French. They discussed the natural resources in Morocco and the
possible development in that country in the aftermath of the war. The
President commented about Morocco's "sovereign government" and
alluded to possible American economic assistance in the future. Subsequently, the President sent two letters to the Sultan, promising to "act
personally at the end of the war to hasten the coming of Morocco's independence." This promise did not yet constitute official American policy,
but the Sultan and Moroccan nationalists construed it as such, and this
assurance from Roosevelt gave teeth to their assertion of independence in
the face of French intentions to maintain the North African empire.[37]

Moroccan nationalists were indeed encouraged by the President's
promise to help end the French protectorate after the war. While a
national sentiment began to germinate in the middle of the nineteenth century in Morocco, it did not take form until the 1920's.[38] Moroccan
nationalism lagged behind that of the other countries in the Maghreb. One
of the leading nationalists was Ahmed Balafrej, who during 1943 spent his
time working with members of the National Party to form the Istiqlal, the
independence party. Balafrej became its secretary general.[39] But the
Moroccan nationalists had to contend with the French, for during 1943 the
power of General de Gaulle grew rapidly. He had initiated the process of
gaining supreme power by purging Vichyites and slowly removing
General Giraud from power. While not actually one of de Gualle's
lieutenants, Gabriel Puaux, the resident general of Morocco until March
1946, seemed to have had the confidence of the General. He worked to
strengthen French authority in Morocco by arresting prominent
nationalists, removing power from the sultan, and promising reforms.[40] In
the face of French determination to hold on to the protectorate,
nationalists moved ahead in 1944 with the launching of the Istiqlal Party
in January. It issued a manifesto stating party aims.[41] In addition to
denouncing the French protectorate, the Manifesto called for the independence of Morocco. It recalled Moroccan contributions in both world wars.
It called upon the Allies to fulfill the promises of the Atlantic Charter and
admit Morocco to the United Nations.

In spite of the growth of French authority in Morocco, nationalists
and the Sultan maintained an undaunted optimism about the future. In
February 1943 Vice Consul Bagby at Tangier learned from a Moroccan that
the Sultan was much gratified by Roosevelt's reception and was certain

that his support would have good results for Morocco's future.[42] In June 1943 Robert Murphy attended a ceremonial visit of Sultan Muhammad to Adja, where the Moroccan leader was the guest of General Mark Clark and the American military forces. As an aside, it might be noted that General Clark desired to fete the Sultan, for the Sultan had previously entertained Clark. Clark records in his memoirs that the Sultan's interpreter told Clark that "His Majesty wants me to tell you that this has been one of the happiest moments of his life." Clarke recalled that "I grinned and said, 'tell him that for a fellow who has a hundred and twenty wives that is saying something.'" At all events, Murphy reported that at the General's fete the Sultan expressed the desire to cooperate with the Americans and that he hoped the United States would intervene on behalf of the Moroccans to relieve them from the French protectorate.[43]

But at the outset, American reaction to Moraccan nationalism was not very supportive, for official U.S. policy continued to recognize the French protectorate, and the military imperative imposed by the war continued to dominate policymaking. For that matter, there did not seem to be a fund of sympathy in the Department for Morocco. For example, Robert E. Sherwood visited Morocco in April 1943 and found much discussion about the establishment of an American university, modeled after the American University of Beirut, to be built at Fez, the cultural center of Morocco. Sherwood relayed this information to the President, suggesting that it might be built by private subscription and serve as a monument to the American landings in North Africa. On hearing of it, Secretary Hull would not give the suggestion his support, for he advised that it would be considered as an American propaganda effort and that the French would not permit such an institution to be founded by foreign nationalists in their protectorate.[44]

The French were making it clear that they had every intention of holding on to Morocco. At the Conference of Brazzaville, opened on January 30, 1944, General de Gaulle announced the pledge that France would bring all of the sixty million colonials into integration with the French community. He closed with the warning that "the objectives of the civilizing work accomplished by France in the colonies reject all idea of autonomy, all possibility of an evolution outside the French block of the Empire. An eventual constitution, even in the distant future, of self-government in the colonies is rejected."[45]

Even this declaration did not arouse American foreign service officers to announce support for the aims set forth in the manifesto of the Istiqlal Party. For example, Muhammad Lyazzid and Ahmed Balafrej, prominent Moroccan nationalists, discussed the goals and aspirations contained in the manifesto with American Consul Fred Mayer at Rabat on January 4, 1944. They desired American assistance in revising the French protectorate in Morocco. Mayer replied that he did not think that the American public and the State Department would favor any political movement in Morocco that would detract from the war effort.[45] On January 11 Moroccan nationalists presented to the Sultan a memorial calling for Moroccan independence under the Sultan, adherence to the Altantic Charter, and representation at the Peace Conference. J. Rives Childs, American chargé at Tangier, cabled the memorial when one of the Sultan's representatives called on him advising of the content of the memorial. Childs reported that he had recently dined with Puaux, the French resident general, and told him that he did not think it "in our common interest when winning the war was a paramount consideration that disorder should occur in French Morocco hampering the military effort." Further, he cabled the Department that "I do not consider it in our interest to provoke political activity in French Morocco at this time, or to give least opportunity to Moors to play us off against French as they are only too ready to do."[46]

While American foreign service officers in Morocco were reporting their negative reaction to Moroccan nationalism, a position based on the American commitment to the French protectorate and to the military imperative taking precedence over support for local political aspirations, the truth of the matter is that the United States had not yet formulated a policy on Morocco. On December 1, 1943, E.R. Stettinius addressed an inquiry to H. Earle Russell, consul general at Casablanca. In view of United States adherence to the broad principles of the Atlantic Charter, and in view of the close relationship between the "native question" in French North Africa and Arab problems elsewhere in the Middle East, Stettinius requested Russell to report on political and social developments in North Africa. In addition, he was to advise the Department on all aspects of the French colonial administration.[47] Russell replied that the Moroccans bore resentment against the French authorities who administered the protectorate. Because the nationalists were not in accord as to their ultimate goals, Russell declared that the possibility of Moroccan independence was out of the question. Morocco would require some sort of protectorate following the war, and the nationalists were not yet settled on which state should hold the protectorate or mandate. He concluded that the French had made no change in administraton in the last two and a half years.[48] Concerning the American policy in North Africa, Wallace Murray wrote Edmund C. Wilson, American representative to the French Committee of National Liberation at Algiers, that there was "at that time no well-defined policy on American relations with the indigenous inhabitants of North Africa." However, Luella Hall concludes that Stettinius' directive of December 1 served as the starting point for the formulation of a policy *vis-à-vis* North Africa.[49]

While Moroccan nationalists were not settled on a given policy, there were those who did have a goal in view. Thami al Glaoui, one of the Great Kaids of the South, gave an interview to C.B. Elbrick, American chargé at Tangier, in which he expressed the goals of Moroccan nationalism. The Moroccan dignitary said he looked forward to the elimination of protectorates or zones of influence and the creation of a unified Moroccan state. He declared that he had been authorized to speak for the Sultan who was of the opinion that the United States would want to restore Morocco in accordance with the Atlantic Charter. He asserted that Morocco desired political and economic aid from the United States in exchange for granting the United States air communications facilities and bases for hemispheric defense. He asserted that Morocco should be placed under an inter-allied mandate, with the United States as principal mandatory power.[50] Early in 1944 Mulai Larbi, another of the Sultan's officials, called on J. Rives Childs to explain the Sultan's position on the French plan to unite Morocco with Algeria and Tunisia as an entity in the French empire. He asserted that Morocco wanted an international mandate established in lieu of the then existing ties to France or inclusion in the empire envisaged by the French.[51] Larbi called on Childs in the following month of February, presented a list of grievances against the French, and related that the Sultan desired an official diplomatic relationship with the Allied Powers in order to ensure his freedom of action, with a view to proving Morocco worthy of national liberation. Childs replied that an international mandate was feasible, but not one that would place France in an inferior position. The Americans, he declared, might render assistance in the fields of education, agriculture, health and sanitation, but France would have primary responsibility for the security of Morocco.[52]

But, as the year progressed nationalists became more firmly convinced that the Istiqlal program had merit. Larbi called on Childs in the summer of 1944, to report that he and other Moroccan nationalists now espoused the cause of the Istiqlal. The French arrest of nationalist Balafrej, French violence in putting down the strikes and riots at Fez and Rabat in January, and the French position in the Lebanese crisis were responsible for this change of position. He related that Larbi admitted widespread Moroccan disappointment that the American landings in 1942 had brought no change in the relationship between Morocco and France. He concluded with the comment that Larbi was of the impression that the Americans had armed the French against the Moroccans.[53]

Throughout the month of January and for some months thereafter, foreign service officers sent the Department dispatches dealing with the hardening of relations between Morocco and France following the January outbreaks. But ever mindful of the military imperative of prosecuting the war, Hull advised in response that this was not the time "to argue the question of political independence, but ... broad changes in the concept of colonial or protectorate administration may be anticipated after the war...." The Secretary warned that "an open dispute with the French at the present could only harm Morocco and work to the advantage of Axis agents and propaganda."[54]

As the war drew to a close, giving Moroccan nationalists hope that the United States would eventually espouse their cause, communists in French Morocco, directed by those in Algiers, endorsed the nationalists' drive for independence. This new turn of events gave the Americans reason for concern in Morocco. The Moroccan Communist Party's open endorsement and encouragement of Arab hopes and desires for a free and independent state tainted the nationalist cause and gave the French good justification for opposing the nationalist movement on ideological grounds. As the war in Europe closed in 1945, Moroccan nationalists had little to cheer about, for Morocco had not been admitted to the United Nations, and the end of the war saw no independent Morocco emerge. Following V-E Day in May 1945, American troops began to depart and Moroccans were angry that the American liberators were leaving them under French rule. But with the formation of the Arab League they now could look to the future with some hope.

The winning of Moroccan independence is beyond the scope of this work. Suffice it to say that although President Roosevelt led Moroccan nationalists to believe that the United States would work for the independence and uplifting of the standard of living in Morocco following the war, that official American policy during the remainder of the conflict continued to rest on the military imperative of winning the war and maintaining the French Protectorate intact.

Before leaving the subject of Morocco, a few words need to be said about U.S. participation in the change in the status of the Tangier enclave, an entity established by the Treaty of Fez which stated that no one power would possess this strategic port alone. In 1923 a regime was established by Britain, France, and Spain. In 1928 Italy and Portugal joined. During World War II Spain illegally occupied the International Zone of Tangier, and Spanish authorities permitted Axis espionage agents to operate in Tangier. The United States used its diplomatic good offices to effect the expulsion of Axis agents from Tangier in 1944.[55] In the following year, the Department participated in the diplomatic exchange which led to the recreation of the International Zone of Tangier. A Conference of Experts on Tangier met in Paris during August 1945, and on the 21st representatives of the United States, the Soviet Union, Britain, and the French Provisional Government signed the final act which provided for the reestablishment of the Tangier Zone in accordance with the Statute of 1923. This instrument directed that France, Spain, and Britain should govern the Tangier Zone, with permission for the signatories to invite the United States and the Soviet Union to participate in the regime.[56]

As the fighting in French North Africa stimulated the movement for independence in Morocco and Algeria, so did it also speed up the nationalist movement in Tunisia and eventually resulted in the independence of that country in 1957. A French protectorate since 1881, Tunisia was the first of the three states of the Maghreb to develop a modern nationalist movement. The Wilsonian principle of self-determination stimulated the course of nationalism following World War I, with Habib Bourguiba providing leadership for an independent Tunisia. World War II interrupted the nationalist movement, and it proved no problem to the French until 1943.[57] Operation TORCH was carried out in November 1942, but because of a change in Allied plans no landing was effected in Tunisia, an error that permitted the Germans to occupy the strategic Tunisian airports and prolong the fighting in North Africa. After the German collapse in May of 1943, the French reoccupied Tunisia,and on May 14 General Giraud announced the ouster of Bey Musin from the throne, despite his impeccable anti-German credentials based on unwillingness to collaborate with the Nazis. Shortly thereafter the Dustur Party issued a manifesto calling for the institution of self-government in Tunisia.[58] The documentary record of the State Department's reaction to this bid for independence is not contained in papers in *Foreign Relations*, although they do indicate that the Department was considerably exercised at the German taxation of Tunisia's Jewish community during the period when Rommel's "Desert Rats" occupied Tunisia.

The granting of independence to Algeria, Morocco, and Tunisia is beyond the scope of this work. In the immediate aftermath of the war communists gave their allegiance to the nationalist movements in the countries of the Maghreb. While the United States was concerned that communists might take over the nationalist movements, it is apparent that there were differing views in the Department about the best defense against a communist thrust. On the one hand, there was the solution presented by Paul Alling, diplomatic agent at Tangier. Writing on January 30, 1947, he asserted: "Although Arabs here are naturally friendly to our country, I do not entirely discount possibility that if French hold them in check too tightly or too long, nationalists may reluctantly accept aid from Communist sources in mistaken idea that course would give them real freedom." In conclusion, Alling suggested that "in my opinion it is in interest France and U.S. that progress toward self-government be quickened."[59] On the other hand, the international situation in which Communists posed a distinct threat in Metropolitan France and North Africa caused a cautious reaction to nationalist movements in North Africa. In a conversation with Habib Bourguiba on

December 19, 1946, Andrew G. Lynch told the Tunisian nationalist that he was unable to make a statement in support of Tunisian independence, asserting that the "international situation imposes apparently an attitude of silence on our part."[60] Indeed, L. Carl Brown writes that

> the United States was officially very circumspect in pushing for decolonization, buffeted as it was by the conflicting aims of rebuilding Western Europe and developing the NATO system on the one hand and developing new ties with what was later to be called the Third World on the other. In the process the more conservative policy of going for the bird in hand, of lining up with existing power to meet immediate needs rather than putting too many chips on future power (the nationalist movements destined eventually to independence), often won the day.[61]

While the United States faced a difficult situation in the states of the Maghreb, complicated by the needs of war and by the growing movements of national liberation, it found a situation more manageable in Iraq, where Britain held on to the last vestiges of empire in a country well advanced toward the ending of all ties with a European state.

Chapter 8

New Prospects in Iraq

Of all the countries in the Middle East, Iraq seems to have been of less concern to the State Department than any of the others. The Department's diplomatic record, as preserved in *Foreign Relations*, shows that Iraq was something of a diplomatic backwater for Washington. This was not always the case, for during the interwar period Iraq gave the Department of State greater cause for concern than any of the other countries in the Middle East, with perhaps the exception of Turkey. The reason for this concern was of course oil. American participation in the international oil consortium that developed the rich Kirkuk oil field in Iraq resulted from continuous and unrelenting pressure by the Department of State upon the British Foreign Office. Britain was awarded a mandate for Iraq at the San Remo Conference in April 1920, but gave the country nominal independence in 1922. Iraq joined the League of Nations in 1932, but Iraqi nationalists maintained a steady pressure to remove the remaining British influence so well documented in the Anglo-Iraqi Treaty of Alliance of 1930. Because of the new status of Iraq, the State Department initiated talks with Whitehall in 1925 to establish a convention protecting the rights of American nationals in Iraq. The Anglo-American Convention on Iraq was signed in January 1930. It recognized the British mandate while guaranteeing American philanthropic and property rights. But, as with the situation in Egypt and Palestine, the United States recognized the superior British position in Iraq.[1]

At the outbreak of hostilities in 1939 the Iraqi government fulfilled the terms of its treaty with Britain. While British troops heavily garrisoned Syria, Palestine, and Egypt, their military presence in Iraq was small by comparison. Only a limited number of British soldiers were stationed in Iraq at Habbaniyah and Shuaiba airfields. During the early years of the war Arab nationalism in Iraq gave vent to strong Anglophobia, which threatened the British military position. Rommel's victories over the British in Egypt, the rise of Pan-Arab sentiment, bitterness over the growth of Jewish influence in Palestine, and the arrival in Iraq of Ham Amin al-Husseini, the grand mufti of Jerusalem, all were factors that

116

turned Iraq in the direction of Germany. Iraqi nationalists began to explore possible ties with Germany that might reduce the British presence in Iraq as defined in the 1930 Anglo-Iraqi Treaty. In 1940 the "Golden Square," a conspiratorial group of four colonels, and Rashid Ali al-Gaylani, a lawyer, politician, avowed nationalist, and enemy of Britain, joined forces to develop a connection with the Axis. Sir Basil Newton, British ambassador in Baghdad, urged the United States and Turkey to intercede with Rashid Ali to deter him from his pro-Axis course.[2] American and Turkish representations to that end were unsuccessful, for Rashid Ali was bent on a pro-Axis orientation. Nevertheless, his initial effort failed because of a turn in Iraqi internal political affairs. His second try was successful.

But the British were fearful lest the Rashid Ali cabal undermine Britain's predominance in Iraq. The British Embassy in Washington dispatched a note to the Department of State on January 6, 1941, urging that the United States government prevent an American arms firm from selling arms and ammunition to the Iraqi government. In making this suggestion, the British warned that Prime Minister Rashid Ali was even then engaging in intrigues with the Axis Powers and that he would probably hand over the arms secured from his American suppliers to the Palestinian insurgents in order to enable them to foment strife in Palestine, thereby disrupting the British war effort in the Middle East.[3] Hull duly advised the British that export licenses for the war material were being denied.[4]

But the crisis was not over, for on April 2, 1941, Paul Knabenshue, American minister resident in Baghdad, cabled the Department that Abdul-Ilah, the regent, came to seek refuge in the American Legation, disguised in native woman's clothing covering a dressing gown and pajamas. He related that the "Golden Square" had initiated a coup to force the resignation of the new Prime Minister al-Hashimi and reinstate the pro-German Rashid Ali in his place. Knabenshue took the Regent to Habbaniyah Air Base where he emplaned for safer quarters at Basrah. Knabenshue warned that the military cabal had established Rashid Ali as head of government and that civil war was likely to ensue. He related that Sir Kinahan Cornwallis, the new British ambassador and an expert on Iraqi affairs, had arrived in Baghdad, and refused to have any diplomatic relations with Rashid Ali's government, for the British regarded it as unconstitutionally established.[5]

On April, 5, 1941, the British Embassy in Washington forwarded to the Department of State an *aide-mémoire*, advising that the British government was not prepared to recognize Rashid Ali's government on the basis that it was born of a military coup d'état and was therefore illegal. The British hoped that the United States would withhold recognition of the regime.[6] In response to the British request, Secretary Hull advised Knabenshue that it was not yet decided to take a position on the question of the recognition of the Rashid Ali regime. He requested Knabenshue to interview Rashid Ali and obtain information as to his actual intentions. He might use the growing anxiety over the protection of American interests in Iraq as a basis for the visit.[7] Knabenshue promptly reported on April 10 that Rashid Ali has a political history "which reveals him as intriguer, unreliable, unscrupulous, ruthless, backed at first and now dominated by group with same characteristics." He related that the British had provided him with evidence of Rashid Ali's pro-German orientation, thereby making an interview unnecessary.[8]

The situation was growing more tense in Baghdad, for on the 9th of April Knabenshue reported that the Iraqi Army posed a threat to British forces at two air bases and thus provided a situation for British occupation to head off a German infiltration and preserve the British position in Iraq. He relayed word that the Iraqi Parliament dismissed the Regent and appointed a new one, who called on Rashid Ali to form a new government as chief of national defense. That the British took seriously the developments in Iraq is apparent by the decision to dispatch one battalion of troops from India for service at Shuaiba Air Base near Basrah, with about one division of troops to follow, in company with elements of the Royal Navy.[9] The coup d'état was complete, and events took an even more ominous turn. On April 11 Rashid Ali appointed his cabinet ministers, and Knabenshue cabled that these men were predominantly pro-German. On April 12 he related that chiefs of diplomatic missions were to call at the Iraqi Ministry of Foreign Affairs to offer congratulations on the appointment of the new government. He pointed out that British, Turkish, Egyptian, Iranian, French, and American chiefs would not do so.[10] In not paying the official call, Knabenshue was giving tacit approval to the British policy of withholding recognition.

The crisis was taking on serious overtones, for on April 18 additional British troops arrived by ship at Basrah and by plane at Shuaiba. The arrival of these forces caused Rashid Ali to call for their earliest evacuation from Iraq. He issued a warning not to bring in more troops. Knabenshue reported that Rashid Ali wanted to hold the number of British troops in Iraq to 8,000, thus giving him military superiority until the Germans could send in forces.[11]

That the Iraqi were acting in tandem with the Germans is evident from intelligence gathered by the British military. The British could not permit a German occupation of Iraq that would deny them a vital source of fuel and major transportation and communication facilities. Given recent German victories in the desert, Iraq offered the Germans an excellent opportunity to strike a blow at the British position in the Middle

East.¹² But George Kirk wrote that while it would appear that the Rashid Ali movement was but part of a larger German pincer-movement against the British in the Middle East, with the southern arm being Rommel's desert army in North Africa, the Germans were concentrating their forces for the invasion of Russia.¹³ Even so, the rapid spread of news throughout the Arab world that Rashid Ali's coup was successful gave the British great cause for concern. King Farouk of Egypt dispatched his congratulations to Sharif, the newly appointed Iraqi regent, thus extending recognition to the new government and indicating an anti-British sentiment.¹⁴

While Egyptians recognized Rashid Ali's government, Knabenshue advised that he discussed the matter of recognition with the Iraqi Foreign Minister. He declared that he had only been authorized to establish "informal contact," which was not to be construed as recognition.¹⁵

Matters were coming to a head in the waning days of April 1941, for on the 29th Knabenshue advised Washington that with the increase of British troops it was obvious that Britain intended to crush the revolt, restore the legal Iraqi government, return the Regent Abdul Ilah, and thus remove an obstacle to the British war effort. That the British intended to use force was evident from the evacuation of all British women and children. On the following day he cabled that there were some six thousand British civilians at Habbaniyah Air Base who were besieged by a division of Iraqi troops. He related that a mixed lot of Americans and other foreign nationals had taken refuge in the American Legation.¹⁶ On May 5 the British military commander sent an ultimatum to the Iraqi government demanding the withdrawal of the Iraqi Army from the heights overlooking Habbaniyah Air Base within four hours. The Iraqi countered with an ultimatum of their own, asserting that if the British bombed public buildings in Baghdad that the Iraqi would bomb the civilians at Habbaniyah. Hostilties commenced on May 2 when the Iraqi ineffectually shelled Habbaniyah, and Knabenshue was compelled to destroy all of his codes and confidential files.¹⁷ One glimmer of hope came from John Van Antwerp MacMurray, American ambassador in Turkey, who related that the Iraqi War Minister sought American mediation in the Anglo-Iraqi dispute. He cabled that London had requested that Washington discontinue any effort toward mediation with Rashid Ali, a known pro-Nazi sympathizer who had been intriguing with the Germans for some time.¹⁸

British General Sir Henry Maitland Wilson, commander of British forces in Egypt, put together a relief force of some 7,500 men, consisting of clerks, cooks, stewards, and Bedouin mercenaries, and sufficient vehicles to carry them to Habbaniyah. The "Habforce" departed Palestine for its 500-mile trek to the relief of Habbaniyah Air Base. The Iraqi had subjected the base to bombings and artillery attacks between May 2nd and 30th, when Habforce arrived on the scene. The British force relieved the Air

Base and then proceeded to Baghdad. The Iraqi Army put up a poor resistance, believing the British force to be much larger than it was. On May 31 Rashid Ali and his pro-Axis cabinet ministers fled Baghdad, some going to Iran and others to Turkey.[19] The Rashid Ali putsch, with its threat to the British war effort, was thus brought to a close. An armistice was declared on May 31, the Regent returned to Baghdad on June 1, and on the 3rd a new governement was formed. The British suppressed all rioting in Baghdad and imposed martial law.[20]

American policy-makers approved British action in this instance; it was viewed not as a measure to crush a genuine nationalistic movement, but as a necessary means of scotching a pro-German movement that would hinder the British war effort. Approval of imperial tactics was merited by the imperatives of war.

While the British could count on American support in suppressing the Rashid Ali coup, they did have to contend with a real problem in Iraq. Knabenshue reported that the Iraqi people and Army were pro-German and that they would rise as one if the German Army made a thrust into Iraq. The British were planning to station four divisions in Iraq to maintain Britain's vital interests in that country.[21]

Matters took a turn for the better in the fall of 1941, for when General Nuri as-Said was appointed Prime Minister of Iraq on October 9, 1941, the British and Americans could rest assured about Iraq's role in the war. Knabenshue reported that Nuri wanted to establish an Iraqi legation in the United States and desired that American teachers come to Iraq. Further, he hoped the United States would send mechanized equipment to Iraq that a volunteer mechanized division could be formed with American machines and American instructors.[22] With assurances that the turn of events in Iraq would have salutary benefits for the British, the way was now open for Iraq to play a positive role in the war.[23] Nuri as-Said would prove a devoted ally of the British and Americans. During the war he worked to restore the ties between Britain and Iraq, but at the same time struggled to help build the Arab League. But with a new regime in power, the opportunity had arrived for Iraq to receive American Lend-Lease aid in 1942.[24]

Iraqi willingness to accept American advisers and Lend-Lease aid leads one to conclude that the Iraqi, like their Iranian neighbors, were attempting to use the United States as a make-weight against the British to reduce their influence in Iraq.[25] But as yet the United States had developed no well defined policy toward Iraq.

On January 9, 1942, Knabenshue cabled the Department that Prime Minister Nuri as-Said requested that Lend-Lease aid be extended to Iraq. Inasmuch as aid had been given to Turkey and Egypt, he desired the same privilege for Iraq "Because of its moral effect and prestige value." The British ambassador, Sir Kinahan Cornwallis, gave the request his stamp of approval and recommended that London accord its affirmation.[25] Secretary Hull replied on May 1 that President Roosevelt would announce on the 2nd that Iraq was eligible to receive Lend-Lease aid. He instructed Knabenshue to so advise the Iraqi Foreign Minister.[26]

But Iraqi reception of Lend-Lease aid was delayed. On the 6th of May Hull related to Knabenshue that the United States had decided to participate in the Middle East Supply Center, the British-directed operation designed to bring about efficient use of economic resources in the Middle East. To promote coordination of the use of resources for civilians in the region, the Department had appointed individual Foreign Service officers in the several countries in the region to act as controlling officers to ensure that supplies were distributed equitably. The Department appointed Knabenshue to coordinate economic activities in Iraq and to serve as representative on the Central Supplies Committee in Baghdad.[27] Delays in receipt of Lend-Lease resulted from British disapproval of the Iraqi government's application for Lend-Lease, the reason being that London desired to maintain control over the dispatch of certain kinds of military supplies to Iraq. The American chargé in Baghdad cabled this news to Washington and requested instructions to direct him in answering the Iraqi Foreign Minister's request for Lend-Lease. Hull instructed him to approach Frederick Winant, recently appointed United States representative on the Middle East Supply Center. Hull advised that the Department approved the policy to sell Lend-Lease food supplies to the Iraqi for cash in order to prevent the outbreak of runaway inflation in that country.[28] Discussion on procedure for the extension of Lend-Lease to Iraq dragged on through the remainder of 1942 and into 1943, with little being accomplished. Finally, on August 9, 1943, the State Department explained to Ali Jawdat, Iraqi minister in Washington, that the United States had entered into formal Lend-Lease agreements with those countries that had been declared eligible. All agreements followed the British master Lend-Lease agreement. The Department provided the Minister with a copy of the British model for his study and consultation. The Minister was handed an *aide-mémoire* explaining the text of the proposed agreement, indicating that it was a copy of the British model and that it provided for payments of goods and services rendered under the 1941 Act.[29] Iraq took no further action toward signing the Lend-Lease Agreement during 1943, but it was signed on July 31, 1945.

Although Iraq did not sign the Lend-Lease agreement until 1945, she agreed to declare war on the Axis Powers on January 16, 1943. The ostensible reason offered for this move was that the Axis, specifically the

Germans, had fomented rebellion in Iraq and promoted the coup d'état in 1941. But as Thomas M. Wilson, now the American minister resident in Iraq, cabled Hull, the Iraqi's declaration was motivated by a desire to join the United Nations in order to protect its own postwar interests and to promote those of the other Arab states.[30] Phillip Baram concluded that Prime Minister Nuri's ulterior motive was to reduce British influence in Iraq by playing off Washington against London and to promote his bid for leadership in the Pan-Arab movement.[31]

In spite of the Iraqi declaration of war, relations with the United States were fraught with difficulties, for the Iraqi insisted on taxing American war materials that passed through Iraq bound for Iran, withholding fiscal and judicial privileges from the personnel of the U.S. Army similar to those received by the British under the Treaty of 1930, discriminating against American petroleum interests that participated in the Iraq Petroleum Company, and failing to compensate those Americans who made claims against Iraq for damages suffered during the violence that accompanied the abortive coup d'état in 1941. Finally, the Iraqi were quite exercised at what they perceived to be American support for Zionist goals in Palestine.

In 1942 the outstanding problem was the Iraqi practice of imposing customs and other dues on American military materials destined for the Iranian military mission. American Chargé Farrell cabled the Department on June 22, 1942, that he had discussed with the Iraqi Ministry of Finance the taxing of goods in transit through Iraq. He declared that the Iraqi desired that the Department should send a note through the Ministry of Foreign Affairs, requesting those immunities and privileges then enjoyed by British forces in Iraq in accordance with the Anglo-Iraqi Treaty of 1930.[32] Farrell subsequently reported that customs authorities at the port of Basrah demanded cash payment of goods imported by Pan American Airways. Hull replied that both Pan American and Douglas Aircraft were working under contract with the War Department, and he hoped that Farrell would be able to obtain a satisfactory arrangement with Iraq for free passage of such goods.[33]

An impasse was reached, for Iraq demanded that the United States negotiate a convention to authorize the free transit of Lend-Lease goods. But the War Department was insistent on an immediate arrangement that would permit the passage of American goods duty free through Iraq. The Department of State insisted that Iraq could grant this privilege through existing legislation. Hull instructed Farrell to inform Iraqi authorities that the United States was engaged in activities to provide security for the Middle East, including Iraq, and the goods in question were not of a commercial character. Farrell replied that Prime Minister Nuri informed him that existing Iraqi legislation did not provide for exemption for the goods in question. Hull was eager to reconcile the differences and he directed Farrell to propose to the Iraqi the signing of a formal agreement. Minister Resident Wilson responded that such a move would most likely prove unproductive.[34] There matters stood, for Wilson advised the Secretary in December 1942 that he had not pressed the matter for a settlement of the question, since it would not be fruitful.

The question of exemption of customs duty on passage of Lend-Lease goods was resolved early in 1943. With a large number of U.S. Army troops in Iraq to assist with the passage of Lend-Lease supplies to Iran, it is understandable that the Army authorities and the State Department desired an agreement that would give the Army jurisdiction over cases involving American military and civilian personnel who were involved in disputes with Iraqi citizens. Wilson advised the Department that the Iraqi government planned to declare war on the Axis Powers and sign the United Nations Declaration, thereby becoming an ally of the United States. When this was effected, he advised that Americans would automatically enjoy all privileges and immunities which the British enjoyed under the Anglo-Iraqi Treaty of Alliance of 1930.[35] On March 17 Wilson cabled the Department that the Iraqi Parliament had passed a law granting to the forces of the United Nations the rights and immunities that the British enjoyed. This act of course applied to American jurisdiction over cases involving American military and civilian personnel in litigation. Concerning the exemption of Lend-Lease supplies in transit, he observed that the "problem would be solved by the application of the present grant of immunities and privileges but the question of goods passed in transit prior to the effectiveness of the law remains open." However, he added that the Anglo-Iraqi Treaty of 1930 mentioned specifically that the immunities and privileges include "freedom from taxation."[36]

While the problems of exemption for Lend-Lease goods in transit and the exclusive jurisdiction of American judicial authorities over U.S. personnel in Iraq were cleared up, another matter was outstanding that cast a shadow on American-Iraqi releations. This involved the question of an American oil concession in Iraq. The Near East Development Corporation (NEDC), an American corporation which participated in the international consortium known as the Iraq Petroleum Company (IPC), had difficulties related to its concession in Iraq. The NEDC owned stock in the Basrah Petroleum Company (BPC), a subsidiary of the IPC, and the Iraqi government asserted that BPC's concession was considered null and void as of November 29, 1941, because BPC had not lived up to its bargain in carrying out certain tasks related to the concession. But the Iraqi government called on BPC to pay 200,000 gold pounds as rent for the concession for the year 1942. It received its payment and then required BPC to make an additional payment for 1943. The company claimed that *force majeure* prevented it from carrying out its developmental tasks per the concessionary agreement. The State Department became involved in the question, and Secretary Hull advised Minister Wilson on February 12, 1943, that "it is our considered view that Iraq's continued demand for an acceptance of substantial ground rent payments for a concession which Iraq alleges to be void is warranted neither in law nor in equity." He added that by accepting the rent, Iraq was admitting to the validity of the concession. But Hull directed Wilson to assist the company to have the terms of the concession altered in order to reflect the conditions imposed by the war. He advised that Mr. Skliros, managing director of the Iraqi Petroleum Company, was on his way to Baghdad to negotiate for revision of the terms of the concession. Wilson was to give Skliros all possible assistance by stating to Prime Minister Nuri Pasha the position of the American government.[37] Wilson replied on February 24 that he had conferred with Nuri Pasha and learned that the Prime Minister opposed revision of the concession, desired continued payment of 200,000 gold pounds to keep the concession in force, denied the *force majeure* claim because the British government had brought development to a halt, but was amenable to arbitration proceedings.[38] Sumner Welles, acting Secretary of State, responded on March 11 that the United States regarded the Basrah concession as important, favored its development, but was doubtful that the Iraqi government could demand full rent for a concession that it did not deem valid. He instructed Wilson to put the Department's view to Nuri Pasha, making it absolutely clear that the United States was interested in the concession and its ultimate development.[39] Wilson discussed the matter with Nuri Pasha on March 14, and he related that the Prime Minister adhered to his interpretaton of *force majeure* but did agree to a settlement by friendly agreement on the outstanding issues. Wilson concluded that "I feel perfectly certain the Iraqi government does not want to invalidate this concession and very likely never did want to do so." He declared that Skliros had had his initial talks with Nuri Pasha a week earlier and had submitted his proposals for consideration.[40]

That Nuri Pasha wanted an agreement was apparent from Wilson's cable of March 23. He disclosed that Skliros had signed two agreements with Nuri, one calling for settlement of the BPC concession by a moratorium of rent in exchange for a loan of a million gold pounds to be recovered by oil royalties, and a second covering the BPC and Mosul concession, with a moratorium being declared on rents in exchange for a loan of a million and a half gold pounds to be recovered by oil royalties.[41] On April 2 Wilson cabled that the oil companies had signed the second agreement and that Nuri Pasha's government had presented to the Iraqi Parliament a bill for the necessary enabling legislation which would be promulgated prior to May 20, 1943.[42]

While it would appear at first blush that Nuri Pasha was driving a hard bargain, a second look at the situation discloses that he wanted the American company involved in Iraqi oil development. Wilson's cable of March 14 indicates this latter interpretation. Phillip Baram asserts that Nuri did desire closer diplomatic ties with the United States, because Britain was touting Egypt for leadership of the Pan-Arab movement. He claims that Nuri sought American assistance to develop both the Mosul and Basrah concessions. Oil development would give him the royalties needed to vie with Syria and Egypt for Arab world leadership.

Two other problems obstructed closer ties between Iraq and the United States. The first involved American claims for damages to property suffered during the abortive Rashid Ali putsch in 1941. Wilson cabled the Department on May 12, 1943, declaring that after two years of correspondence between the Legation and the Ministry for Foreign Affairs there had been little success in reaching a solution to the claim of American citizens for compensation for property damages suffered in 1941.[44] Hull instructed Wilson that he should not press the Iraqi government to pay the claims unless it could be proven that the government was negligent during the time of upheaval. But that if the government was negligent then he should by all means press for compensation.[45] A settlement was made in September of 1944. Loy W. Henderson, newly appointed minister in Iraq, cabled that as a result of his representations to the Iraqi Ministry for Foreign Affairs, the Ministry had sent the Legation a check to cover claims of American nationals. He advised that claims of American commerical firms would be paid in full.[46]

Settlement of the claims for damages and of the Basrah concession dispute was indicative of Nuri Pasha's intention to turn toward the United States. He hoped that American money and influence would serve to counter Great Britain. To further solidify relations with the United States, Nuri Pasha invited President Roosevelt to meet Abdul Ila, the Iraqi regent, following the Yalta Conference. The President declined, but on his return to the United States, Roosevelt in March 1945 extended an invitation to the Regent. The invitation was accepted, but almost immediately postponed because of the President's death on April 12. President Harry S Truman invited the Regent to visit him at the White House in May. The Regent accepted and brought along a large entourage headed by Nuri Pasha. The latter engaged in lengthy talks at the Department of State. A memorandum of conversation prepared by Acting Secretary of State

Grew disclosed that the United States desired "closer relations with Iraq ... to develop a free flow of traffic and communications between our two countries." To achieve this end, the Department urged the negotiation of agreements that would permit the "free and direct access of American civil aviation to Iraq and also the setting up of a direct radio-telephone and telegraph circuit with the United States.[47] Nuri Pasha, former Prime Minister of Iraq, but still a leader in postwar Iraq, discussed the development of Iraqi petroleum. In conversation with Acting Secretary Grew and other officials at the Department, Nuri Pasha stated that he hoped the United States would do all possible to bring about "an increase in the extraction of pertroleum in Iraq." The Iraqi leader pointed out that Iraq had three great oil fields — Mosul, Kirkuk, and Basrah — and of the three only Kirkuk was being fully exploited. He said that the United States, which held 23.75 per cent of the IPC, could push the consortium to develop the Mosul and Basrah fields. Nuri urged the American officials to consider that Iraq needed a 24-inch pipeline from Kirkuk which could only be constructed from steel manufactured in the United States. He related that several officials of Socony Vacuum and Standard Oil Company, American shareholders in IPC, advised him that they could raise the funds to build the pipeline. The officers present replied that the matter would be referred to the appropriate governmental agency. Nuri Pasha told the officials that he was also anxious to strengthen economic ties with the United States and he hoped that the government would show more interest than in the past years in industrial development of Iraq and in an increase in trade. Grew replied that the United States shared Nuri Pasha's hope for closer economic ties and he hoped that the Iraqi government would approve direct radio-telegraphic communications between the United States and Iraq and also license American airlines to fly to and through Iraq. Nuri Pasha asserted that he was certain that such arrangements could be made at some time in the near future.[48]

It is apparent that Nuri Pasha was trying to create closer economic ties with the United States to offset the long-standing British preferred position in Iraq. In this respect, he was following the same line as that pursued by the Iranians, who desired the United States to serve as a balance against British and Russian influence. He was only partially successful, for American oil companies seemed reluctant to proceed with development in Iraq. Perhaps they perceived greater opportunity to earn greater profits elsewhere, with Saudi Arabia being the primary target for postwar oil development.[49] However, the fact that the United States and Iraq signed a Lend-Lease agreement at Washington on July 31, 1945, is indication of closer economic relations.[50]

While American relations with and interest in the economic prospects in Iraq were only minimal, the reverse was true regarding Egypt.

The Department of State exhibited a much greater interest in Egypt much earlier in the war for reasons that will be disclosed.

Chapter 9

The Military and Economic
Influences on Diplomacy
with Wartime Egypt

The United States had few interests in Egypt during the interwar years, because Britain remained supreme in the Land of the Nile. A British protectorate since 1882, Egypt had received nominal independence in 1922. American interests in Egypt were chiefly cultural, with missionary schools, the American University of Cairo, archaeological expeditions, and tourists constituting the main concerns. Indeed, William M. Jardine, American minister to Egypt, wrote the chief of the Near Eastern Division in 1932: "Egypt is a charming post at which to be stationed.... As I see it there is not much going on here of tremendous consequence to my Government. The facts are, it appears to me to be quite a side show...."[1] British primacy, the lack of oil, little opportunity for commercial expansion, and a greater traditional concern for the Far East were all factors militating against an enhanced interest in Egypt. Not even the Suez Canal proved a major factor in American communication and transportation routes. But with the growth of Egyptian nationalism accompanying the granting of independence in 1922, American missionaries requested the Department of State to negotiate a treaty that would guarantee their rights in Egypt. Accordingly, treaties of arbitration and conciliation were signed on August 7, 1929, with an agreement signed on May 24, 1930, that accorded to American merchants unconditional most-favored-nation treatment. At the Montreux Conference in 1937 Americans supported the Egyptian bid to end all capitulations.[2]

But in 1937, Phillip Baram concludes, a basic change occurred in American relations with Egypt that had a bearing on this country's wartime relations with that land. In that year the Department of State embarked on a policy that became more competitive with Britain in Egypt, progressing steadily on a course to undermine the British system of imperial privileges and replacing it with an enhanced American position that would result in greater profits and increased prestige.[3]

With the outbreak of war in 1939, Egypt's ties to Britain became strained due to strong nationalist feeling, anti-British sentiment, and pro-Axis sympathy. With German and Italian armies posing a threat to the British position in Egypt, American interest in Egypt grew stronger. On March 31, 1940, the Axis forces attacked the British in Cyrenaica, advancing to a point about eighty miles south of Benghazi. By April 11 the Axis had pushed the British back to the Egyptian frontier, and surrounded the fortress city of Tobruk.[4] The situation in Egypt was crucial, for there was unrest among the people and the government was compelled to issue reassuring statements to a populace that had mixed feelings about the British imperial position in Egypt and the approach of a German army. U.S. Minister Alexander Kirk cabled from Cairo on April 13, 1941, that the situation had stabilized but that there was considerable doubt that the British would be able to contain the Axis thrust toward Egypt.[5] Although the British repulsed the Italo-German attack on Tobruk on April 14 and 15, there was extensive unrest and fear among Americans in Egypt. Kirk had advised the leaders of the American community in late April that they should avail themselves immediately of the transportation facilities and evacuate the country.[6] The precarious position of the British Eighth Army became a reality to Washington in late May when Kirk cabled the Department on the 23rd that the Army, which would earn its laurels at El Alamein in late 1942, lacked sufficient tanks, artillery, and airplanes. To make matters worse, there was a lack of spare parts for vehicles in the field and a dearth of communications equipment. That the British political position in Egypt was also precarious is evident from Kirk's cable on May 29. He warned that there was considerable fifth-column activity in Egypt, much defeatist talk, and a great deal of pro-Axis propaganda.[7]

In the following month Kirk dispatched a warning to the Department that a feeling of defeatism had penetrated segments of the British Army. He reported that the Commonwealth forces from New Zealand and Australia had low morale and that there was a deterioration of morale among both British and Egyptians. But he offered a glimmer of hope, writing that this decline in morale could be "counteracted by a more open participation in the war on the part of the United States and the capacity to resist would be immeasurably increased by the speedy development of more inspired and courageous leadership here and by the immediate arrival of needed war material."[8] On June 7 Kirk cabled that the greatest contribution that the United States could make to the desert war would be the immediate delivery of bomber and fighter aircraft to the west coast of Africa, there to be assembled and flown to the British Army.[9]

This last reference refers to the Takoradi route, an airway

pioneered by the Royal Air Force in the 1920s. Merchant ships delivered American planes at Takoradi, a port on the west coast of Africa (in what is today Ghana). They were assembled by British mechanics, assisted by American technicians, and then flown via Nigeria and Chad to Khartoum in the Anglo-Egyptian Sudan, then north to Cairo.[10] President Roosevelt, apprised of the British plight in North Africa, was determined that planes could be flown to Takoradi and then ferried via the overland route to the British Army. He and Prime Minister Churchill had engaged in a lengthy exchange on this matter, which was supervised by Harry Hopkins, with Averell Harriman, the American official in London expediting the shipment of Lend-Lease. During the following year, the Takoradi air route handled an enormous traffic in American aircraft being flown to the British by pilots of Pan American Air.[11] By the month of July Kirk could relate that morale was high and that the British forces could "give a good account of themselves if provided with proper equipment under properly coordinated command." Further, more American Army and Navy officers and men were hard at work receiving, erecting, and maintaining American Lend-Lease equipment and instructing the British in its use. Tanks were being unloaded and a tank school functioned to train the British in the use of the Sherman tank. By mid-July the German threat in Egypt had been substantially reduced by the German invasion of Russia which channeled elsewhere material that could have been used in the desert. Kirk related that the sense of urgency had been relieved.[12]

Although the war situation had improved, there were problems related to the delivery of American Lend-Lease to the British. Kirk related the dismal news that American material was pouring into Egypt, but that defective organization in the British Army resulted in wastage and serious loss of time in the employment of the material.[13] In reply to a request from the Department for details relative to wastage of American supplies, Kirk asserted that numerous factors entered into the problem and his special telegram to the Department delineated the improper use of American supplies.[14] While there was improper use of American supplies by the British Army, nevertheless the record indicates that the performance of American tanks in the desert was satisfactory, and historians later credited the British victory over the Germans to air superiority, a fact attributed to the arrival of American aircraft viá the Takoradi route.[15]

To be sure, the supply of Lend-Lease material to the British to stave off the Italo-German attack on the Allied forces in Egypt was uppermost on the list of American priorities during the hectic days of 1941. But the diplomatic record indicates that the Department of State and Foreign Service were vitally concerned with expanding trade with Egypt during the critical days of 1941 when the Germans threatened the British position in Egypt. Phillip Baram writes that Department officers hoped that the large

American presence in Egypt, based on having personnel to assist the Middle East Supply Center and carry out orders of American military missions in Egypt and Iran, was sufficient to increase the American political-economic position in a land where British prestige was on the wane due to the adversities of war. He argues that American foreign policy objectives were in order of priority to halt the Axis advance, expand American power, and ultimately displace the British presence.[16] While his conclusion might be somewhat overstated, there is sufficient evidence to suggest that there is certainly a modicum of truth in his argument. During 1941, when the British were hard pressed by the Axis forces on the battlefield and in need of all available cargo space on ships to bring them vitally needed supplies, the Egyptians became more dependent upon American exports. Alexander Kirk advised the Department of the plight of the Egyptians on April 12. He argued that regular sailings of American flag vessels between New York and Egyptian ports could put an end to the severe shortages in Egypt and immediately step up the rate of American trade. In a manner reminiscent of William Brown Hodgson's mission to Egypt in 1834 to drum up trade for the United States,[17] Kirk listed numerous items such as automobiles, tires, lubricating oils, tobacco, radios, office appliances, steel, tin plate, cotton goods, fertilizers and paper that Egyptians needed from the United States. He also supplied the Department with a list of goods that the Egyptians could sell to the United States. This included essential raw materials such as phosphates, manganese, tungsten, wolfram, and raw cotton.[18]

Kirk's calling attention to the possibilities of an increased trade between the United States and Egypt aroused the curiosity of the Department of State. Hull cabled that Herbert Feis, adviser on international economic affairs, was intrigued by the possibilities of such trade. Hull's reaction was positive: "Much interested and will follow matter through vigorously. An arrangement might be facilitated if estimates were transmitted at once of immediately available supplies particularly of manganese, tungsten, and wolfram, with particulars as to grades."[19] On May 8 Kirk suggested that increased trade would depend upon a routine number of sailings of American ships from east coast ports to the Red Sea. This would enable American exporters to obtain the required letters of credit payable against ocean bills of lading to facilitate payment of exported goods. In the following week Kirk cabled that Egyptian railways urgently required rolling stock and engines to handle the expected increase in trade from the United States. Kirk suggested that the Lend-Lease Act should serve to facilitate the immediate dispatch of the required railroad equipment to Egypt.[20]

Kirk's pleas for expanded trade and additional shipping bore fruit, for on May 15 Secretary Hull advised him that there would be an increased amount of shipping tonnage for supplying the needs of Egypt. While priority would be given to shipments required for British military effort, space would be found for shipment of commodities for Egyptian consumption. He wrote that the Department had urged the Egyptian Legation in Washington to take up with the British Purchasing Commission space needs for commodities and other required supplies.[21]

On May 23 Kirk sent to the Department a long list of supplies required by the Egyptians for import from the United States. It included drugs and medicines, industrial and agricultural chemicals, cable, rope, wire, nails, spare parts for automobiles, rubber, paper, machine bolts, motorcars and trucks, iron and sheet metal, tractors, generators, and numerous other metal goods. His report also included a list of goods that Egypt could ship to the United States. It included onions, cotton seed oils, rice, beans, lentils, garlic, phosphates, manganese and epsom.[22]

Hull replied on the 26th that the Arab tendency to generalize was a bar to expediting shipment of needed materials. If the Egyptian government desired imports from the United States, Hull said, it must dispatch to the United States a mission having full and detailed knowledge of the required items. The mission must specify precisely what sizes, kinds, and technical description of items required. The matter must be taken up with the British Purchasing Commission, which evinced an interest in approving Egyptian needs.[23]

To remedy matters, the Egyptian Minister in Washington, along with his Commercial Counselor, called on Dr. Feis, Department of State Economic Adviser, to inquire about obtaining exports from the United States. Feis told them that the Egyptians must supply specific detail about their needs. He again stressed the necessity for the Egyptians to work closely with the British Purchasing Commission which was concerned about Egyptian requirements.[24]

In spite of Department advice on the procedures for acquiring American goods, A.A. Berle could only advise Kirk on September 5 that little progress had been made in solving the problem of sending supplies to Egypt. The crux of the matter was that the Egyptians could not supply specific details about their needs. Too, the British had presented complications in the form of a letter from the British Supply Council, arguing that direct trade with Egypt would involve withdrawal of dollars from the Sterling Area. The British suggested the possibility that Lend-Lease aid would reduce the drain on British dollar resources.[25] Kirk responded on October 15 with the suggestion that Egypt was in the area of military operations, and "I can see large benefits from the political, economic and financial standpoints of developing American-Egyptian relations on those bases not only for the purpose of the actual war effort but also as a possible impetus to a larger postwar trade in this entire area."[26]

This response is important for two reasons. First, it indicates the need of Egyptians for expanded trade with the United States to fulfill shortages necessitated by the British military effort which required the utilization of the bulk of all shipping space slated for the Middle East. But second, it does give credence to revisionist historians such as Phillip Baram who argue that American Foreign Service Officers in the Middle East were of a mind to establish expanded commercial ties with Egypt that would enable the United States to supplant Britain economically in the postwar era.

That Kirk's entreaties were not entirely futile is evidenced by Hull's cable of October 25. The Secretary related to Kirk that the War Department was dispatching two military missions to the Middle East on November 1. One would be stationed in Iran, but the second, headed by General R.L. Maxwell, would be located in Egypt. Three railroad experts would accompany the two missions and they were to be available for railroad work both in Egypt and the Persian Gulf area. Hull advised in another cable that the Department had explored the possibility of extending Lend-Lease aid to Egypt, but he added that it had been decided to make no commitment at this time, for all available shipping and material were badly needed by the British, the Russians, and the Chinese.[27] Not to be denied, Kirk cabled on December 4, asserting that the extension of Lend-Lease to Turkey should serve as a precedent for according to Egyptians like treatment. On December 10 Hull informed Kirk that the President had written to E.R. Stettinius, Lend-Lease Administrator, that he found that the defense of a number of countries, including Egypt, was necessary to the security of the United States; therefore, Lend-Lease should be extended to them. On December 24 Hull instructed Kirk to inform the Egyptian authorities that Egypt was now eligible for any type of Lend-Lease aid that might be rendered through the United States government or indirectly through the British government.[28]

Of the economic relationship between the United States and Egypt, Phillip Baram concludes that the expansion of American trade with that country during a time when Britain could not supply that country's needs for consumables was a primary goal.[29] But the British could and did place obstacles in the way of this trade. On September 8 Kirk advised the Secretary of State that the Egyptian Prime Minster issued a proclamation that whoever held American dollars or stocks or other negotiable securities in dollars must declare them to the Ministry of Finance. On the following day Kirk cabled the Secretary that the British Embassy was responsible for the proclamation. In giving British motives for this move Kirk related that the increased demand for dollars to purchase American goods was causing an enlarged drain on the British dollar pool. This situation was brought about because the Egyptians did not generate dollar exchange by selling goods to the United States. The Bank of England is thus trying to curtail dollar expenditures in Egypt.[30] Several days later Kirk cabled that several American businessmen had complained that the Egyptian proclamation was forcing them to liquidate their affairs in Egypt rather than comply with the onerous regulation. On September 12 Hull cabled Kirk that the British government had granted broad exemptions in favor of American nationals in Egypt.[31]

With the removal of restrictions on American nationals in Egypt, one obstacle to trade was removed. To further stimulate trade between the United States and Egypt, Kirk worked actively throughout 1942 to induce the Egyptian government to dispatch a trade delegation to Washington. There were already considerable American interests in Egypt that included oil, films and insurance, and involved outlays of millions of dollars. Kirk reported that the Egyptian press was pro-American, wanted the United States to play a larger role in Egypt, and that it was the British who blocked augmented commerce between the two countries.[32]

In addition to placing restrictions on the expenditure of dollars in Egypt for American goods, the British also tried to control direct trade between Egypt and the United States in another area. In February 1943, Kirk advised Hull that the Egyptian government desired to purchase for cash two Lockheed Lodestar passenger planes. These aircraft would be employed by the Misr Airwork, an Egyptian government company, to replace the current fleet of eight planes which were no longer capable of flying. The British had sent out two planes on a merchant ship which was sunk in transit. Kirk suggested that sale of the planes would enhance American prestige and build up good will in Egypt. He was depressed to hear from Adolf Berle that the War Department could not release two aircraft for the Egyptians because military needs precluded such a sale.[33] Kirk pressed ahead with the project, only to be told by the British Embassy that Egyptian orders for "warlike and other stores" should be placed through the British Military Mission of the Egyptian Army. Kirk reported that this British agency would not meet the Egyptian needs.[34] He later cabled the Department that the British considered the aircraft in question to fall within the category of "warlike and other stores" and that in his opinion they would not permit the sale of the planes. At this juncture the Secretary of State instructed Kirk to inform the British Embassy that it was the intention and policy "of this Government to receive direct inquiries from the appropriate Egyptian officials regarding the availability of American military supplies to meet their needs and that such supplies will be furnished to them if it is feasible to do so."[35] Hull's instruction carried a note of rancor and evinced a tone of displeasure at what he considered British obstruction. Kirk approached American Army Service Forces about the procurement of the planes and learned that the War Department would give the matter further consideration. He advised the Department that he had made it possible for the controller general of the Egyptian Ministry of National Defense to consult with the appropriate person in Army Service Forces with a view to obtaining the aircraft.[36]

In addition to making direct sales to the Egyptians through private channels, the Department of State moved ahead on another front. It tried to induce the Egyptians to sign a Lend-Lease agreement. In an *aide-mémoire* dated August 9, 1943, and delivered to the Egyptian Legation in Washington, the Egyptians learned that the implementation of a Lend-Lease agreement would "assure the greatest possible degree of cooperation in the task of post-war economic reconstruction...."[37] The Department furnished the Egyptians with a draft Lend-Lease agreement with appropriate instructional notes. The tone of this document implies that the United States would be in a position to supply Egyptian needs during the postwar period. But there was considerable delay in perfecting the instrument. On December 28, 1943, Secretary Hull sent a curt note to Minister Kirk, instructing him to ascertain the reason for the Egyptian delay in signing the agreement.[38] The year 1944 witnessed considerable haggling between the Department of State and the Egyptian government over principles and wording of the draft agreement. At year's end, the American Minister cabled the Department that differing views among Egyptian agencies continued to delay action on the agreement.[39]

In the meantime the Egyptians did receive Lend-Lease through the British in 1942, and Lend-Lease was one means of exerting American political pressure on the Egyptians and on the British preferential position in Egypt. For example, in early 1944 the Department of State expressed concern that a 78-mile long pipeline built between Shell Company storage tanks at Suez and Cairo, with pipe supplied by the Lend-Lease Administration for the British Army's use in Libya, might possibly be transferred in the postwar era. The Department registered concern that transfer of this property to the Shell Company or to the Egyptian government might be made without due authorization of the Lend-Lease Administration. The Department was also worried that the Shell Company carried petroleum for civilian as well as military use. Apparently the Department of State did not desire to make a division of ownership between the United States and Great Britain at the time, but merely wanted to adopt some plan for future operation of the pipeline. James Landis prompted the Department to realize that an understanding should be reached with the British about the future disposition of the pipeline.[40] The Department would evidently settle for an agreement that would place control of the pipeline in Anglo-American hands, with limited Egyptian participation.[41]

The pipeline question demonstrates the Department of State's increasingly aggressive attitude toward the British position in Egypt. But there were several other problems hindering economic intercourse between the United States and Egypt, involving taxes on American petroleum shipped from Egyptian ports, the sale of Egyptian cotton in the United States, and the unresolved matter of the Lend-Lease agreement.

On February 2, 1944, Minister Kirk relayed news from Cairo of an Egyptian government plan to levy a 15 percent export duty on oil exported from Egypt by American petroleum companies. This duty was considered onerous by American oil men because the Egyptians already exacted a 15 percent royalty. American oil men would thus operate at a considerable disadvantage. In a subsequent cable Kirk implied that the British petroleum interests in Egypt were operating at an advantage and it was British government pressure that resulted in the 15 percent export duty.[42] Pursuant to instructions from E.R. Stettinius, acting Secretary of State, Kirk inquired at the Egyptian Foreign Office about the export duty. He learned that it was a revenue raising measure. He obtained from the Commissioner for Customs the opinion that it was not in Egypt's best interests to impose this tax. That official promised Kirk to urge the Finance Minister to repeal the tax. Kirk informed the Department that the matter was satisfactorily settled, as indeed it was as noted in one of Kirk's subsequent cables to the Department on March 24, 1944.[43]

But Egyptian failure to sign the Lend-Lease Agreement with the United States was continuing to irritate the Depatment of State. That the Department desired to complete the agreement is all too evident. Talks on the proposed agreement were resumed by the Legation in Egypt and the Egyptian Ministry for Foreign Affairs in January 1945. The agreement was signed on April 17 by Secretary of State Hull and Egyptian Minister Hassan. On that date, Hull handed the Minister a note, setting forth Hull's understanding of certain clauses in the agreement. One of them concerned American installations in Egypt. Hull must have had in mind the oil pipeline mentioned earlier and the large American air base at Cairo. The Secretary observed that in any future provision for ownership of the American installations, the U.S. government must have a voice. The year ended and the treaty was still unsigned. A note to the Egyptian Ministry of Foreign Affairs determined that the Egyptian Parliament had not approved the agreement, and in the summer of 1946 the United States discontinued the Lend-Lease program. The agreement was considered to be unperfected.[44]

Perhaps one reason for the Egyptian Parliament's failure to approve the treaty was the Egyptian government's anger at the sale of American cotton on the world market at prices below the American domestic price. Egyptian Minister Hassan queried the Department about this, asserting that this large sale would damage the price of Egyptian cotton. He said that the American sale had the benefit of a subsidy, and this practice was against the provisions of the Atlantic Charter. The Department replied that the United States maintained a domestic price support program which boosted domestic prices considerably above those on the world market. In lowering its prices for export to a level below the domestic price, the U.S. was still selling cotton at competitive prices.[45]

That the United States government urgently wished to extend its influence and economic prospects in Egypt is apparent. But in early 1942, there occurred in Egypt a political crisis that could have prejudiced the American economic future. The political crisis was set off on January 6 when the Egyptian government announced that diplomatic relations with Vichy France were terminated. This policy was in keeping with the precedent of breaking off all ties with countries at war with Egypt's British ally. The Vichy minister then successfully brought about a reversal of this policy. He caused the twenty-two-year-old King Farouk to act. The King, greatly angered at not being properly consulted on the break with Vichy, castigated the Foreign Minister, who subsequently resigned his office. Hussein Sirry Pasha, Egyptian Prime Minister, supported his cabinet colleague, and there appeared to be a compromise in the offing. At that point, Ali Mahir, a pro-Axis Egyptian leader, took advantage of the situation to bring about a demonstration of extremist students on February 1. The Prime Minister argued with the King that his government was merely carrying out a legitimate act of policy in rupturing with Vichy, because it was in compliance with British wishes. The King, not notably pro-British, was outraged. On February 1, Minister Kirk, who had reported in detail on the course of developments in Egypt, cabled that the Egyptian Prime Minister advised Sir Miles Lampson, British ambassador, that his position had become untenable and that he intended to resign on February 2.[46]

The British position in Egypt was becoming untenable, for the Axis force were advancing in Cyrenaica and students had demonstrated in favor of Rommel. The British ambassador called on the King on February 3 and announced that the Embassy did not like to interfere in internal politics, but that the situation called for him to recommend that the new Egyptian government should be willing to carry out the terms of the Anglo-Egyptian treaty and be prepared to maintain absolute control over internal affairs. Ambassador Lampson asserted that such a government could be formed only with the leadership of Nahas Pasha, the leader of the Wafd Party. When the Ambassador insisted that the King must consult with Nahas Pasha by the following day, the King proved difficult, replying that he would consult with all of his leaders.[47] The King did indeed consult with his leaders and decided that Egypt required a coalition government, whereupon the British ambassador insisted that the King call upon Nahas Pasha to form a government. George Kirk concludes that certain Egyptian leaders wanted sufficient access to power to treat with the Axis in the event that Rommel broke through to Egypt.[48] His temper frayed, Sir Miles delivered an ultimatum to the King at 3 o'clock on February 4, asserting that unless the King instructed Nahas Pasha to form a cabinet by 6 o'clock, he, the King, must accept the consequences of such a refusal. The King consulted his immediate advisors and they disapproved the King's acting in compliance with the British demand.[49]

During the crisis Minister Kirk met with the King and impressed upon him the great danger presented by Hitler's desert army. Kirk asserted that Hitler was the great enemy, that all measures must be taken to assist in his defeat, and that he was sure that Egypt would join Britain and the United States in effecting that end. Kirk concluded his conversation by stating that although he was prevented from interfering with Egyptian internal politics, he "profoundly hoped that he [the King] would be guided solely by the practical consideration of what contributed the maximum effort to win the war."[50]

The King granted an audience to Sir Miles for 9 o'clock in the evening, but at 7 p.m. three British tanks, accompanied by infantry, surrounded the palace. Promptly at 9 p.m. the Ambassador, escorted by Lieutenant General R. G. W. Stone, commander of British troops in Egypt, called upon the King and insisted on his sending for Nahas Pasha to form a government. At 10 p.m. the King called Nahas and instructed him to form a cabinet. On the following day, Nahas conferred with Sir Miles and agreed that his government would not act in any way that would impair the Anglo-Egyptian treaty.[51]

Thus Britain had overcome a very powerful pro-Axis political cabal in Egypt that could have obstructed the British effort to win the war. Britain acted as she did with the compliance of the United States. Minister Kirk's statement to the King that winning the war must override all other considerations was tantamount to an endorsement of the British action. In so doing, the Minister was supporting the privileged position that Britain enjoyed in Egypt per the clauses of the Anglo-Egyptian treaty of alliance. But American endorsement was not without opposition in the Department. Wallace Murray, chief of NEA, sent a memorandum to Under Secretary of State Welles, declaring that the British ambassador had exhibited lack of tact in handling the King, that the King should be retained on the throne, and that the British high-handed method had "served effective notice that Egyptian independence is not only a fiction but one which has worn completely through...." Murray concluded that a protest should be tendered to Sir Oliver Lyttelton, the British Minister of State who exercised general political supervision in the Middle East.[52] Phillip Baram writes that the upper echelons of the Department vetoed such a protest, suggesting that a protest of that nature would have reduced the British influence in Egypt and made that country an American responsibility.[53] In vetoing Murray's suggestion, the Department cabled Kirk that the United States "has a legitimate present interest in political developments in the Egyptian area in connection with the war effort and in view of the presence of General Maxwell's mission in Egypt[54] [Major General R.L. Maxwell was chief of the United States Military Mission in North Africa, with headquarers in Cairo, and was responsible for assisting Britain in the use of American Lend-Lease supplies sent to Egypt], and of the large quantities of ordnance which have been sent to that area from the United States," the Department instructed Kirk to advise the Egyptian government that the United States desired an accommodation that would permit the King to remain in power and allow Nahas Pasha to assume the premiership "under conditions enabling the latter to retain the support of the great body of Egyptians which he has enjoyed in the past."[55]

Wallace Murray voiced his disapproval of the American support of the British action in Egypt to Under Secretary Welles, whereupon Welles replied that in view of the importance of the Middle East as a combat area, one in which vast quantities of American supplies have been committed to Britain, the United States "cannot remain wholly inactive when any country in that area shows definite possibilities of going to pieces, either politically or economically."[56]

Although the British used strongarm tactics on King Farouk, that monarch was not popular in the United States. His pro-German posture brought about open criticism of him. In fact, in the January 1941 issue of *Foreign Affairs* there appeared an article critical of the King and Egypt. The writer referred to King Farouk as a "Quisling." Sirry Pasha, the Prime Minister, called Raymond Hare, American chargé d'affaires in Cairo, to come to the Ministry of Foreign Affairs, where Sirry registered a protest against the article. Hare replied that there were no laws governing censorship of the press in the United States, and writers were free to state their own ideas. Hare advised Secretary Hull of the incident, and a reply was soon forthcoming from Acting Secretary Sumner Welles. Welles instructed Hare to say that the Department supported his statements concerning the operation of a free press in the United States but regarded the incident as regrettable. Further, that the Department of State would declare its views on the matter to the editor of the journal. Prime Minister Sirry Pasha was mollified on learning from Hare of the Department's sympathetic views, and there the matter rested until a second incident occurred.[57] On June 30, 1941, Mahmoud Hassan Bey, Egyptian minister in Washington, called on Assistant Secretary Breckinridge Long, asserting that an article had appeared in *PM* magazine which was critical of the Egyptian royal family. Long replied that the Department had no control over the press, but added that the magazine had also been very critical of officers at the Department of State. This answer seems to have satisfied the Minister.[58] In early 1942 an article appeared in *Time* magazine, entitled

"Farouk the Foolish." The Egyptian Minister again called at the Department on February 16 and aired his views to Wallace Murray. Murray advised Hassan Bey that it would be wiser to drop the matter, for there was little that the State Department could do except to express its regrets over the incident. Murray passed the Minister's complaint along to Sumner Welles, who advised the Minister that the United States government regretted incidents of this character, but that he well knew that there was no rule of censorship governing such magazines. There the matter ended.[59]

Just as much of the diplomatic intercourse between the United States and Iran concerned the presence of American military personnel in Iran to further the flow of Lend-Lease aid to the Soviet Union, so, too, did an American military presence in Egypt give rise to a lengthy exchange between Washington and Cairo. The War Department had designated Major General Russell L. Maxwell as commanding general of the United States Army Forces in the Middle East. The first troops under his command to arrive consisted of a small group of officers and technicians to assist the British Army in Cairo in the operation, maintenance and repair of airplanes, tanks, cars, and other military equipment being delivered under Lend-Lease. Since these men were attached to the British Army no permission was necessary for them to be in Egypt. Following American entry into the war in December 1941, no thought was given to the presence of American troops in Egypt because of the pressing nature of the war. However, during 1942 incidents involving American personnel and Egyptians gave rise to the need for some kind of agreement that would regularize the presence of military and civilian personnel in Egypt.[60] Minister Kirk cabled the Department on June 18, 1942, that the location of American troops in Egypt would cause a diplomatic problem because there was no treaty between the United States and Egypt similar to the Anglo-Egyptian treaty of 1936, which permitted the British to retain troops in Egypt. Kirk urged that steps be taken to specify the status of these U.S. troops.[61] Several months later Kirk related that General Maxwell had suggested making a "gentleman's agreement" which would permit U.S. Army authorities to punish violations of Egyptian law by American military personnel. Kirk urged that Americans should be amenable to jurisdiction of American military courts, but that the Department must use care in raising the matter with the Egyptians, for it would arouse memories of the capitulations. Kirk requested instructions about the initiation of negotiations.[62] On October 6, 1942, Acting Secretary Welles instructed Kirk to undertake talks with the Egyptians on the matter of jurisdiction. Welles informed him that the War Department wanted exclusive jurisdiction over military personnel. He urged Kirk to try to obtain jurisdiction by means of an informal agreement. Welles stated that the Egyptians had accorded jurisdiction to the Australian government without a formal agreement.[63] Kirk complied with his instructions, and on December 12 he cabled the Department that the Egyptian government proposed to concede to American military authorities jurisdiction over Army and Navy personnel over crimes and misdemeanors, but reserved the right when an aggrieved party was a civilian to determine whether the crime was committed in line of duty and whether it should be tried by Mixed Court or handed over to American military authorities for trial.[64] During early 1943 Kirk reported that the Egyptians still had the matter of civilian cases under advisement. Subsequently, he cabled that the Egyptian government was holding up the agreement over the question of payment of damages by Americans guilty of crimes. But on February 3 Kirk reported that some sort of an agreement concerning jurisdiction must be reached, for a drunken American soldier had killed an Egyptian at Port Said. The Egyptian Prime Minister insisted that the soldier be turned over to a Mixed Court for trial.[65] Secretary Hull informed Kirk that the War Department wanted exclusive jurisdiction over the aforementioned case and all other crimes involving American personnel. The Department did not consider that the question of claims should hinder the making of an agreement. But the Department, Hull related to Kirk, could not admit to claims questions being referred to mixed claims commissions.[66] At length, Hull instructed Kirk to make an agreement gaining exclusive jurisdiction over military personnel involved in crimes and allowing the Egyptian government to decide in each case where a civilian was charged with a criminal case whether he should be tried by mixed court or military tribunal. Accordingly, on March 2 Kirk made an exchange of notes regarding the question of jurisdiction over American military and civilian personnel in Egypt.[67]

The American diplomatic problems in Egypt were unlike those in any other country in the Middle East, with the possible exception of relations with countries in the Maghreb, for Egypt was actually in the war zone and following the fall of Tobruk when a German invasion looked likely, Minister Kirk had to consider the evacuation of American civilians from Egypt. The months of June and July 1942 were grim for the Americans and British. With Rommel knocking at the door of Egypt, Americans assumed that the Axis forces might sweep into Alexandria and Cairo and continue their move eastward to link up with the Japanese moving west from India. But Rommel was unable to maintain his drive to the east, for Allied air superiority was the decisive factor in halting the Italo-German forces. Control of the air was due to the planes of Major General Lewis H. Brereton's Tenth Air Force heavy bombers which struck at German and Italian forces. Too, the Royal Air Force was supplied with American aircraft flown in by the Takoradi air route and this also proved a decisive factor.[68]

American relations with Egypt during the war years of World War II were complicated by the desire of American Foreign Service officers to obtain a portion of the markets normally enjoyed by Britain in Egypt and by the need to supply Britain with Lend-Lease aid to stem the Italo-German tide of invasion that threatened to overrun the Land of the Nile. But because Egypt was actually involved in the war, the problems presented to the United States in that country differed from those faced in Turkey. It now remains to discuss the lengthy diplomatic intercourse between the United States and Great Britain concerning the Turkish role in the war.

Chapter 10

The Economic and Diplomatic Problems Related to the Turkish Role in the War

Following the American Senate's rejection of the Versailles Treaty and its subsequent refusal to accept President Woodrow Wilson's bid for consent to accept an American mandate for Armenia, the United States withdrew from the political dynamics that led to a postwar settlement of the Ottoman Empire. Although American diplomatic ties with Turkey were severed during the war, the American postwar relationship with Turkey continued to rest largely on the two pillars of missionary activity and commercial enterprise in the Anatolian peninsula. The missionary element, working in tandem with the philanthropists who dispatched aid to Turkey in the aftermath of the war, bequeathed a dual legacy to American-Turkish relations. On the one hand, the missionaries and philanthropists deposited a fund of good will in Turkey because of their charitable and educational activities. On the other hand, they also created bad feeling, stemming from their propaganda on behalf of the Armenians that projected the "terrible Turk" image in the minds of Americans. Ultimately, enlightened missionaries and American diplomats corrected this image. Too, the American good will investment in Turkey amounted to millions of dollars to provide direct aid and support schools, orphanages, hospitals, colleges, and clinics.[1]

But during the interwar years, American economic investment and trade with Turkey grew, with exports increasing from $25 million in 1919 to $42 million in 1920. Rear Admiral Mark L. Bristol, the U.S. high commissioner to Turkey from 1919 to 1927, worked diligently to expand American commerce in Turkey via the Open door policy. In so doing, he sought to achieve a better climate between the United States and Turkey by correcting the bad image of the Turkish people that existed in the minds of many of his countrymen. Although the U.S. Senate rejected the 1924

Turco-American Treaty, Bristol effected a *modus vivendi* between the United States and Turkey to make possible the continuation of commercial relations between the two countries. Ultimately, normal treaty relations were restored in 1927.[2]

In the 1930s diplomats and enlightened missionaries, aware of new Turkish aspirations following the rise of Mustapha Kemal, worked to heal the breach between the United States and Turkey. This effort created a Turco-American rapprochement. That relations between the two countries were amicable at the outbreak of World War II is a tribute to American diplomatists who refused to permit the missionary-philanthropic lobby to solidify the "terrible Turk" image in the minds of Americans and to force the Department of State to pursue diplomatic goals in Turkey at variance with the American national interests.

At the outbreak of World War II, the United States recognized the preeminent British position in Turkey based on the Anglo-Turkish treaty of alliance of 1939. Anglo-Turkish military conversations gave evidence that Turkey would live up to her obligations and would fight if Germany should attack her. That the United States supported the British effort to bolster Turkey is evident from Secretary of State Hull's instruction to John Van Antwerp MacMurray, American ambassador at Ankara, to assure the Turks that the United States supported Britain's war effort and that Americans were confident of a British victory.[3] MacMurray did so, and reported that the Turks were committed "to the purposes and ideals with which both Great Britain and the United States are identified." Further, he reported that Turkey feared involvement in the war and desired to remain neutral. But he inquired about the possibility of Turkey's receiving American military materials.[4] The Turkish position was understandably vulnerable. She feared German occupation of Bulgaria and a simultaneous German-Soviet attack. While Turkey was prepared to act in British interest and in her own defense to prevent the German invasion of Turkey to gain access to Asia, she could not count on Great Britain to supply her with the necessary arms to blunt a German attack.[5] To complicate matters further, the German Foreign Office advised the Turkish ambassador in Berlin that Germany was prepared to take immediate military action if Turkey let "so much as one British plane to base upon her territory."[6]

Understandably, Britain desired the United States to extend military aid to Turkey to bolster that country's effort to check a German advance through the Straits of the Dardanelles and the Bosporus. Lord Halifax, British ambassador in Washington, inquired of Cordell Hull on March 3, 1941, to determine if the United States would supply Turkey with war materials directly or through Great Britain. Before giving an answer Hull learned from MacMurry in Ankara that the Turkish Minister of

Foreign Affairs stated to him that Turkey was firm in her intent to resist a German effort to control the Straits. Further, that Turkey planned to place barriers in both the Bosporus and the Dardanelles to deny German submarines the use of those vital waterways. On March 7 Hull replied to Lord Halifax's inquiry, declaring that the United States would prefer to aid Turkey by the retransfer of material from Britain.[7]

While the Turks were adamant in their intention to oppose German aggression, the Turkish Army was poorly equipped to fight a modern war. Although allied to Britain, the fall of France in 1940 and the subsequent evacuation of British forces from Dunkirk had left the British Army stripped of modern weapons. Britain had been unable to deliver to the Turks such vital defense equipment as antitank guns, machine guns, and antiaircraft guns. In order to keep her fences mended with Turkey, maintain the defense alliance, and prevent Turkey from falling into the German fold, the British maintained steady pressure on Washington to extend Lend-Lease aid to Turkey. With the passage of the Lend-Lease Act in March 1941, Major General James H. Burns, of the British Army and Navy Munitions Board, telephoned Sumner Welles at the Department to inquire if the United States would make available to Turkey under the terms of the Lend-Lease Act fifty 155-millimeter howitzers and 18,500 rounds of ammunition.[8] In a conversation with Mehmet Munir Ertegun, Turkish ambassador in Washington, Welles first assured himself that Turkey would safeguard her rights against German aggression and carry out her defensive alliance with Britain. Welles expressed confidence in the intent of the Turkish government and so advised Wallace Murray. Murray interviewed the Turkish ambassador, who called on him on March 26 and expressed interest in the receipt of the 155-millimeter howitzers and the accompanying ammunition. Turkey, he said, desired to qualify for Lend-Lease aid. Accordingly, Murray advised Under Secretary Welles that Lend-Lease assistance should be dispatched to the Turks as a part of the aid extended to Great Britain.[9]

While the Turks would use American aid to bolster her defensive posture against possible German aggression, the British could not persuade them to send a few divisions to Greece as a symbol of unity with the British, Greeks, and Yugoslavs. As MacMurray cabled the Department, "Turkey is desparately anxious to avoid hostilities but will fight ... if attacked." While closely identified with the British position, Turkey would not be persuaded by the British to enter the Balkan campaign. A big factor in this decision was the British inability to supply the Turks with adequate military assistance. The vulnerability of the Turkish position became increasingly apparent with the German victory in the Balkans, a reality that permitted the Germans to exercise negative control over the Straits, blockade Turkey's entire Aegean coast, and deny regular supply lines from the United States and Britain. Turkey, as Ambassador MacMurray cabled the Department on May 6, had little alternative but to "appease the Germans."[10]

With the German domination of the Balkans, Turkey now felt isolated, with little prospect for receiving adequate aid from Britain. With her Balkan flank tied down, the Germans now felt secure in launching an invasion of Russia, but before doing so, the German Foreign Office desired to negotiate a nonaggression pact with the Turks. Lord Halifax advised Sumner Welles of the Turkish intention to sign such a part, and he urged the Department to use its good offices to "indicate to the Turkish government what a disastrous effect upon American public opinion this step would involve." In compliance with this request, Cordell Hull instructed MacMurray to make it clear to the Turks that the United States opposed the negotiation of such a pact. Further, that he was to use Lend-Lease aid as a lever to sway the Turks. MacMurray agreed, but demurred in using Lend-Lease as a lever, since it would only irritate the Turks. Hull heeded the judgment of the Ambassador and urged him to use his own discretion.[11]

The Turkish-German nonaggression pact was signed on June 18 and MacMurray promptly forwarded to the Department a translation of the treaty on the 19th. While he could assure the Department that the Turco-British alliance remained unimpaired, he did forward the bad news that Turkey would now negotiate a commercial agreement with Germany whereby Turkish raw materials such as copper and chrome would be bartered for German weapons and spare parts. Germany was trying to pressure the Turks to soften their ties with the Allies. To counter these German efforts, MacMurray suggested that Lend-Lease should be extended to Turkey in order that the Turks would not lose confidence in the Anglo-American allies. To reassure the Turks, Sumner Welles instructed MacMurray to inform them that Turkey was the only neutral country outside the Western Hemisphere to receive direct Lend-Lease aid. At the time some fifty 155-millimeter howitzers valued at $1.2 million were en route to Turkey. In addition to ammunition for these weapons, no fewer than 200 two-and-a-half ton trucks, 50 tractors for the howitzers, and 1,500 sledge hammers have recently been set aside for Turkey without cost under the act. In addition, some 35 applications for additional Lend-Lease aid, covering ammunition, entrenching tools, 406 heavy duty trucks, 108 75-millimeter guns, 300 one-half ton trucks, 50 water tank trucks, 7,000 field telephones, 6,500 miles of heavy field cable, 900 truck and car tires, and 1200 pack saddles with mounts and ammunition were being processed. In addition Turkey had been accorded a favored position to purchase commodities, chemicals, and other strategic materials. Welles suggested that Turkey must indicate her intention to remain in the Allied camp and that the withholding of chrome from Germany was a good opportunity to show this steadfastness.[12]

That the United States was firmly committed to supporting the Anglo-Turkish alliance and to employ economic warfare to keep Turkey in a defensive posture *vis-à-vis* the Germans is obvious. But hardpressed in Africa, Britain could not supply Turkey with an adequate supply of weapons, and she desired that the United States meet Turkey's weapons needs and extend assurances to Turkey that the U.S. supported Ankara's decision to renew the commercial agreement with Britain in January 1942 whereby Turkey would guarantee to deliver to Britain her entire output of chrome, which would subsequently be forwarded to the United States. On July 1, 1941, the British Embassy in Washington forwarded an *aide-mémoire* to the State Department, urging the Department to continue to extend supplies to the Turks, asserting that this course was most necessary to neutralize Turkey in the great power struggle then being fought by Germany and Russia.[13]

By mid-1941 it was a facet of U.S. policy toward Ankara that the extension of Lend-Lease aid was dependent upon Turkish willingness to supply chrome. An exchange of notes between Dean Acheson, Assistant Secretary of State, and a British Embassy official indicates the linkage between aid and chrome and U.S. opposition to the completion of a Turco-German trade agreement. But the British were opposed to withholding aid from Turkey, and Ambassador MacMurray in Ankara also voiced opposition to denial of supplies due to the Turco-German pact. In addition, the British urged the Department to accord to Turkey special priority in Lend-Lease aid. While willing to continue such shipments to Turkey, officials at the Department reasoned that Turkey was not at war and that she should not be given special consideration because her attitude toward the Germans was too uncertain. Secretary Hull so informed Mac-Murray of the Department's decision.[14] That the United States would continue its aid to Turkey was evident, for fifty 155-millimeter howitzers arrived in Turkey in September. This gratified the Turks, but they continued to have cause for complaint about the Lend-Lease program.

In September 1941 the President issued a report covering Lend-Lease operations and listing nations that received aid. Turkey was not listed. Paul Alling, acting chief of NEA, advised Sumner Welles that this was cause for discontent in Turkey. He revealed that the British Supply Council had vetoed extension of Lend-Lease items to the Turks, and the Turks blamed the United States and not Britain for this hold-up. When queried about this matter, the British Purchasing Commission in Washington admitted that it made applications for Lend-Lease goods in excess of the amount needed in order to make allocations of goods to the

Turks. The difficulty caused an exchange of notes between the State Department and the British Foreign Office.[15] Ultimately, the matter was settled when the Lend-Lease Administration, working in conjunction with the State Department and the British Foreign Office, arrived at an agreement whereby Turkey obtained much of her Lend-Lease aid by the process of retransfer from the British. But the agreement also provided that the Turks could obtain direct Lend-Lease materials from the United States.[16] Matters were greatly improved when the President on November 7 announced that the defense of Turkey was vital to the United States and that Turkey was eligible for Lend-Lease aid. The Turkish ambassador in Washington expressed his apreciation, but the Turkish press did not give the fact extended coverage in order not to arouse the ire of the Germans.[17]

Following American entry into World War II, the United States and Britain prosecuted the war on the basis of a Europe First policy. Accordingly, the President seems to have been anxious to step up the war effort in the Middle East. Persuaded by Churchill at the first Washington conference that the Allies needed to give Turkey aid, the President in early 1942 evinced a desire to fulfill Turkish requests for Lend-Lease materials. On February 11 Sumner Welles advised E. R. Stettinius, Lend-Lease administrator, of the Department's decision to increase Lend-Lease shipments to Turkey "as soon as possible, not only for the purpose of strengthening the Turkish government in its announced determination to resist aggression but also in order to enable that resistance to be effective." Welles declared that the Turks desired immediate delivery of 950 trucks, for which a cash payment of $1 million had already been made.[18] But from Britain came word on February 14, 1942, from John G. Winant, American ambassador to Great Britain, that the British were supplying large amounts of food and other supplies to Turkey and were convinced that they should coordinate the delivery of all supplies to Turkey. The British reasoned that the shortage of shipping made a coordinated policy mandatory. Winant concurred in the wisdom of the British argument.[19] To assure the Turks of American intentions, Ambassador Steinhardt informed Turkish Minister of Foreign Affairs Sukru Saracoglu that the United States was making every effort to transport Lend-Lease aid to Turkey and that American ships were then lying to in various Mediterranean ports with goods awaiting transportation to Turkish ports. He suggested that Turkish vessels carry chrome to these ports, transship the chrome to Allied vessels, and pick up the Lend-Lease materials for delivery to Turkey.[20]

But delivery of Lend-Lease supplies to Turkey was fraught with complications, because the British asserted that all aid should be extended to Turkey by retransfer through British agencies. Given the U.S. willingness to recognize British dominance in Turkey, this demand seemed reasonable to Ambassador Winant, who advised the Department on March 9 to accept the British position. But the Turks urgently desired direct transfer of Lend-Lease materials from the United States, and Steinhardt reported from Turkey that the Ankara government had little confidence in Britain, given her military defeats in the Libyan campaign and in the Far East.[21] Steinhardt warned that the Turks disapproved the British diversion of shipments from Turkey to Egypt to support the British war effort in North Africa. He urged that "steps be taken at the earliest possible moment to forward the American Lend-Lease material which I understand had been awaiting shipment.... I cannot emphasize too strongly that the actual physical arrival in Turkey of even a few hundred tons of war material in the immediate future is likely to have an effect on the morale of the Turkish government out of all proportion to the tonnage involved...."[22] Sumner Welles informed Dean Acheson that "prompt action should now be taken to give some concrete evidence to the Turkish government that we are doing something for it." But the British continued to argue that Turkish requests should be processed through the Coodinating Committee at Ankara, a committee that should be supplemented with the addition of an American representative. In addition, the British urged that the Middle East Supply Center process all Turkish requirements for commodities. British arguments were effective, for Dean Acheson had advised Lord Halifax that the United States recognized the primacy of British interests and responsibility in Turkey but that efforts should be made to meet Turkish needs. He recommended that American and British officials in Ankara process all requests emanating from Turkey. From London came word from Averell Harriman, Lend-Lease expediter, that the British wanted the Ankara Coordinating Committee enlarged and that he (Harriman) concurred in the soundness of this plan. The Department forwarded an aide-mémoire to the British Embassy on March 30, 1942, agreeing that the Ankara Coordinating Committee should be enlarged to include an American representative and that this committee would process all Turkish requests for Lend-Lease aid. The committee would then facilitate the direct transfer of supplies to the Turks. Welles instructed Steinhardt that all transfers of materials to Turkey were for repayment in money or in property. Transfers would be processed through the Ankara Coordinating Committee, with the exception of shipments of cereals and similar commodities, which would be processed through the Middle East Supply Center (MESC).[23]

Steinhardt informed the Department that the Turks agreed to collaborate with the British-American Coordinating Committee which would process requests for hard goods, while MESC would take responsibility for commodities. But on June 11 he cabled that the Turks desired to negotiate a Lend-Lease agreement with the United States, similar to that made with the British. He related that the Turks were disappointed in British delivery of weapons and desired an agreement. In Washington the Turkish Ambassador advised George V. Allen of NEA on July 29 that Turkey expected to be included in the Lend-Lease program. The wheels of government began to turn. In December the Turkish Ambassador received from the Department a master Lend-Lease agreement between Turkey and the United States. George Allen advised O. H. Erol, counselor of the Turkish Embassy, that the United States now proposed to negotiate an agreement with Turkey.[24]

Although American officials had drawn up a comprehensive plan for the handling of Lend-Lease shipments to Turkey, the Combined Chiefs of Staff informed the State Department that Anglo-American agreements reached at the Casablanca Conference in early 1943 decreed that Turkey was to be regarded as falling within the British sphere of military responsibility. Therefore, all Lend-Lease applications would henceforth be screened by British officials. Sumner Welles instructed Ambassador Steinhardt to inform the Turkish government of the new procedure for handling Lend-Lease applications.[25]

Nevertheless, the Department was anxious that Turkey complete a Lend-Lease agreement. But the Turks were reluctant to perfect the agreement because they questioned the provisions dealing with postwar economic arrangements such as tariffs. Steinhardt conversed with the Turkish Minister for Foreign Affairs in late December, urging him to complete the agreement. He stressed the American desirability of implementing it as soon as possible.[26] But negotiations between the United States and Turkey continued during early 1944 with little results, because Anglo-Turkish political differences and constitutional questions obstructed the completion of an agreement. There matters lay until September when Ambassador Steinhardt queried the Prime Minister about the status of the agreement. He learned that Turkish failure to complete it was due to the fact that the British claimed that all Lend-Lease deliveries to Turkey had been made under their auspices. The Turks were unwilling to acknowledge receipt of supplies from two governments. In subsequent conversations with officials at the Turkish Ministry of Foreign Affairs, he learned that the Turks objected to terminology and interpretation of the agreement and to the necessity of concluding a mutual aid agreement with the United States.[27]

Negotiations over the Lend-Lease agreement continued into the final year of the war. The Turks were reluctant to conclude the agreement because they were afraid that signing it would require them to pay twice for those items of United States Lend-Lease goods that were retransferred to them through the British. Even though the British gave the Turks assurances that they would not be required to pay for goods retransferred to them through British officials, the Turks refused to sign. The war ended and the agreement was still unperfected.[28]

As has been alluded to previously, Lend-Lease aid to Turkey was related to other economic problems. The United States and Britain engaged in making preemptive purchases of Turkish raw materials such as chrome, copper, hides, tobacco, mohair, oils, and other materials in order to deny them to the Germans. Germany had brought Turkey into close economic ties with the Third Reich prior to the war. To ween her from the German bloc Britain began to make large purchases of Turkish chrome. The Turks also required Britain to take large quantities of Turkey's perishable raw products as well. The Turks astutely played the British off against the Germans. They hoped to trade chrome and other raw materials in return for trucks, spare parts, guns, machinery, railway equipment, and other goods related to an industrial economy.[29] The United States supported the British program of preemptive purchases. On May 17, 1941, Secretary of State Hull instructed Ambassador MacMurray to urge the Turkish government to ship chrome to Haifa, Port Said or to ports on the Red Sea, emphasizing that the United States urgently needed this raw material. Further, Hull directed him to link deliveries of Lend-Lease aid to Turkish shipments of chrome.[30] Hull directed MacMurray on June 28 to urge the Turkish government to resist the German effort to purchase chrome. MacMurray replied that Numan Bey, secretary general of the Foreign Office, stated that Turkey "will positively refuse in the future ... to sell chrome to Germany."[31] On July 18 MacMurray reported that Britain was negotiating for next year's entire supply of Turkish chrome. He also cabled the bad news that he had heard rumors of German intentions to negotiate for future purchases of Turkish chrome. The rumors proved well founded, for on September 17 MacMurray cabled that Germany intended to strike a barter agreement with Turkey, whereby Turkish chrome would be exchanged for German military equipment.[32] The Department urged MacMurray on September 19 to confer with the British Ambassador Sir Knatchbull-Hugessen and to assist in the negotiation for the 1942 production of Turkish chrome. He was further directed to state to the Turks that the United States was prepared to purchase wool, olive oil, mohair, and valonia in the amount of £4 million.[33] In spite of Anglo-American efforts to purchase the entire Turkish chrome output, it was inevitable that Turkey would negotiate the so-called "Clodius Agreement" with Germany on October 9, 1941. The Turks agreed to ship 45,000 tons of chrome to Germany between January 15 and March 31, 1943, 40,000 tons of chrome in 1943, and 90,000 tons in 1944. The Germans agreed to ship military supplies in exchange.[34]

American and British officials were displeased, and the British Ministry of Economic Warfare planned to purchase every ton of chrome from Turkey so as to leave no chrome in Turkish ownership at the beginning of 1943, thereby denying chrome delivery to Germany. The Department maintained its accord with the British preemptive purchase program, and Secretary Hull directed MacMurray to cooperate in this project with the British ambassador. Further, he informed MacMurray that the United States was perpared to meet Turkish needs for foodstuffs.[35]

Some time passed before Turkish Prime Minister Sukru Saracoglu related to Ambassador Steinhardt that Turkey had a serious wheat shortage. He said he gave priority to shipments of wheat over any military supplies. Steinhardt recommended to the Department on July 17 that shipments of wheat be dispatched to Turkey to strengthen the American and British position in that country.[36] Secretary Hull realized the urgency of Steinhardt's recommendation, and he replied on July 22 that the Department had requested the Lend-Lease Administration and the War Shipping Administration to issue instructions that wheat be loaded as a filler on all ships assigned to carry supplies to Turkey. The War Shipping Administration informed the Department that the Middle East Supply Center was considering the immediate shipment to Turkey of 5,000 tons of wheat from its stocks. On August 8 Steinhardt learned from Hull that MESC had shipped 12,000 tons of wheat to Turkey and had dispatched by rail from Iraq 3,800 tons of barley.[37] That shipment of American wheat was related to Turkish dispatch of strategic materials to the United States is evident from Hull's cable to the American Embassy on December 5. Hull related: "Turkey may be able to offer such inducements in connection with strategic materials. We want to accommodate Turkey in this matter, but can do so only on the basis of a distinct *quid pro quo*."[38]

The United States had joined Britain in 1942 in a preemptive purchase program. The purpose of this was to buy up such materials as hides, wool, tobacco, opium, antimony, mohair, copper, woolen rags, cotton clips, molybdenum, flax, and hemp. On August 6 Ambassador Winant cabled from London that British authorities agreed with the inauguration of the American preemptive purchase plan in Turkey. On August 17 Hull informed Steinhardt in Turkey that the United States had joined Britain in an effort to buy up materials that might possibly have gone to Germany. The Department anticipated that the program would run for twelve months. According to the stipulations in the Anglo-American agreement on preemptive purchases, the United States assumed responsibility for buying antimony, copper, wollen rags, molybdeum, and linseed. The British would bear responsibility for the other raw materials.[39]

But of the above raw materials, none was so vital as chrome, for this ore was needed in the manufacture of steel. Germany needed Turkish chrome and was willing to exchange war materials for this vital mineral. There was every possibility that Turkey would begin to sell chrome to

Germany after January 8, 1943, the date when the Anglo-Turkish agreement expired. Secretary Hull instructed Steinhardt on June 20, 1942, to assist Britain in making a new chrome agreement with the Turks. Further, he must endeavor to purchase the maximum tonnage of chrome now mined in order to deny chrome to the Germans after January 8.[40] But the Turks had contracted to deliver to the Germans 90,000 tons of chrome in 1943 under the Clodius Agreement. In return the Germans agreed to deliver weapons. Steinhardt and the British ambassador conferred with Sukru Saracoglu on September 25. The Turk agreed to a contract for 1943 and 1944 that called for Turkey to deliver to Britain the entire chrome output over the commitment to Germany of 90,000 tons. Hull authorized Steinhardt to share with the British the necessity of meeting the price of 270 shillings per ton. In December the British completed negotiations with the Turks for delivery of chrome for 1943 and 1944. All chrome in excess of obligatory deliveries to Germany would go to the British during these years. Turkey agreed to make no agreement with either Britain or Germany for deliveries after January 1, 1945.[41]

Shipments of Turkish chrome to ports in Egypt and the United States for the year 1942 totaled 122,210 long tons. But during the year 1943 it was necessary for British and American officials to maintain surveillance and inspection of chrome dumps to ensure that chrome was not diverted to Germany. Secretary Hull put it succinctly when he wrote Ambassador Winant in London that "the day-to-day problem of keeping Turkish chrome out of German hands is one in which we are prepared and anxious to take a full and active part.... Not only do we consume the Turkish chrome ourselves, but we have an equal interest with the British in its preclusive and financial aspects."[42] But during 1943 it was inevitable that the Turks would begin to make chrome available to the Germans in exchange for weapons. Although the Turkish Foreign Minister assured the American chargé in Ankara that he could "rely upon him to delay and reduce the deliveries of chrome to Germany," nevertheless, the Turks did ship substantial quantities to the Germans. In fact, on September 18, 1944, Ambassador Steinhardt reported that Turkish deliveries of chrome to Germany actually increased during the previous three months.[43] The reaction at the Department of State was immediate, and for a time British and American officials considered the possibility of applying economic sanctions against the Turks. But on second thought, this expedient was set aside, for as Secretary Hull cabled Steinhardt, "Having cut off military supplies, our arsenal for further economic reprisals is pitifully bare. It is doubted that Turkey's standard of living is such that it is economically vulnerable to blockade action."[44] Steinhardt had protested on several occasions the Turkish decision to increase deliveries of chrome to the Germans, but received little satisfaction. But on April 14 he called on the

Foreign Minister and handed him a note similar in nature to one presented by the British ambassador. The notes called for an end to Turkish sales of chrome to Germany and an end to trade with that country. Steinhardt reported that the Minister received him "in a friendly spirit indicating a cooperative state of mind." He announced that he was not disposed to continued trading with Germany and he expressed concern that "the United States and Britain had not long since taken action to relieve him from his dilemma by destroying means of transportation between Turkey and Germany. Steinhardt reported that the Minister would give careful consideration to his note protesting continued Turkish chrome deliveries to Germany.[45] On the 15th Steinhardt reported that the Foreign Minister had agreed to reduce deliveries to Germany to 4,000 tons per month. On April 20 the Foreign Minister announced to the Turkish Parliament the government's intention to cease all shipments of chrome to Germany and other Axis nations as of that date. Finally, on May 26 the Turkish government submitted to Anglo-American protests and consented to a draft agreement that prohibited Turkey from exporting chrome to Germany and her allies for the duration of the war.[46]

What can be said of the Anglo-American program of economic warfare in Turkey? Edward Weisband sums it up very well. He concludes that the Turks were determined to sell chrome to both sides and to charge a price that would guarantee a high profit. He asserts, however, that Germany's failure to deliver war materials to Turkey in exchange for her chrome and other raw materials had a greater effect on Turkey than the Anglo-American preemptive purchases.[47] In other words, Germany's failure to deliver weapons caused the Turks to reduce shipments of chrome. Indeed, the American chargé in Britain cabled the Department on March 4, 1943, declaring that German failure to deliver weapons to Turkey, as prescribed by the Clodius Agreement, would no doubt reduce the amount of Turkish commodities that Germany could purchase during 1943.[48] Nevertheless, the program of economic warfare had a salutary effect on the Turkish economy, kept Turkey from falling completely under the sway of Germany, made it possible for the Americans and British to maintain relations with Turkey during the war, and caused the British to believe that Turkey could be brought into the war as an ally.

Roosevelt and Churchill discussed at some length the problem of Turkish entry into the war at their Casablanca conference during the period January 17-27, 1943.[49] Prior to attending the meeting, Churchill tipped his hand on his plans for Turkey. In a memorandum dated December 2, 1942, Churchill asserted that "If we could get Turkey into the war we could not only proceed with operations to open the shipping route to your left flank on the Black Sea, but we could also bomb heavily from Turkish bases the Roumanian oil fields which are of such vital importance to the Axis...."[50] At a conference of the Combined Chiefs of Staff on January 14 at Anfa Camp, General Alan Brooke, chief of the Imperial General Staff, argued that a concerted effort should be made to defeat Italy and then bring Turkey into the conflict on the side of the Allies. On the following day Brooke returned to repeat the same argument, connecting Italian defeat with Turkish entry into the war. Brooke reiterated his argument at a subsequent meeting of the Combined Chiefs on the 16th.[51] General Marshall was adamantly opposed to efforts to bring Turkey into the war, for he reasoned that it would only withdraw material badly needed to support the cross-Channel operation. He grew weary of the lengthy arguments presented by Brooke.[52] But the British Prime Minister was determined to have his way. At a meeting of the Combined Chiefs of Staff with Roosevelt and Churchill on January 18, the latter asserted that Turkey should be given tanks, antiaircraft weapons, and other mechanized vehicles, reinforced with British troops, and encouraged to enter the war. He asked of the President "that the British be allowed to play the Turkish hand, just as the United States is now handling the situation with reference to China." The President concurred with this request.[53] On the following day, Harry Hopkins conferred with Churchill, who informed him that he wanted to meet President Ismet Inönü of Turkey "and push him pretty hard on the business of getting Turkey into the war."[54] At the conclusion of the conference the Anglo-Americans agreed to take steps to hasten Turkey's entry into the war. The Allies would supply defensive weapons that would bolster her militarily.[55]

Following the Casablanca conference, Prime Minister Churchill, accompanied by his military advisers, went to Adana, Turkey in late January 1943 to meet with President Inönü of Turkey. Prior to meeting with the Turkish head of state, Churchill addressed a statement to the Turks, suggesting that Turkey must be prepared to meet German aggression and to that end the British would "increase the supply of modern munitions which the Turkish Army unhappily lacks." Churchill wrote that the President had authorized him to act for the Anglo-Americans in this matter. At the Adana conference, Churchill committed the British to increase Turkish supplies of arms and to build up air protection in the event Turkey entered the war.[56] But the Prime Minister was unable to obtain a commitment from the Turks to enter the war. Edward Weisband concludes that the Turks made no commitment because fear of Russia was a strong factor influencing the decision.[57] Their reasoning is simple to follow. Turkish belligerence would likely result in a German invasion of Turkey which would result in the entry of Soviet troops into Turkey. The latter would likely remain or be used as pawns to extract postwar concessions from the Turks, a reasoning not far wrong, given the postwar turn of events in Iran.

But Churchill was undeterred, and three months later at the Washington conference in May 1943, he again broached the possibility of Turkey's entering the war. President Roosevelt expressed optimism at the idea of Turkish involvement in the war at a meeting of the Combined Chiefs of Staff at the White House on May 12. This encouraged Churchill. On May 13 General Sir Alan Brooke read a memorandum prepared by the British Chiefs of Staff at a meeting of the Combined Chiefs, stressing the importance of defeating Italy, thereby creating a situation in which Turkey could be induced to enter the conflict.[58] Although the record would indicate that Churchill had now persuaded the Americans to engage in planning for operations in Turkey, there is every indication that this was far from true.[59]

Although the British were prepared to implement Operation HARD-IHOOD (the operation for supplying Turkey with arms preparatory to her entry into the war), the Turks were hesitant about proceeding with all speed to accommodate the British. The Turks wanted to remain neutral at all costs and did not desire that Britain supply them with an adequate supply of arms that would enable them to engage the Germans.[60]

The British Prime Minister had another opportunity at the Quebec summit conference in August 1943 to set forth his case for Turkish entry into the conflict. He again faced opposition from the American Chiefs of Staff, whose August 7 memorandum asserted that "Turkey is not apt to make an early departure from her position of neutrality."[61] This memorandum could not have encouraged Churchill, but even so the Prime Minister had presented to the President an argument, asserting that Turkey "must be drawn into the war" at which time the Allies could utilize Turkish airfields to launch operations against Rumanian oil fields.[62] In spite of his well-reasoned arguments, the Combined Chiefs of Staff concluded that "the time is not ripe for Turkey to enter the war on our side."[63]

After the Quebec conference on September 3 came word of the Italian surrender, an event Churchill considered as a green light to push for Turkish entry into the war. But he had not counted on unremitting American opposition to Turkish entry, a position based on the conviction that Britain would need to funnel war materiel and shipping to Turkey as a prerequisite to her entry and this would draw off materiel and shipping badly needed to support the cross-Channel operation. Forrest Pogue wrote that "the Prime Minister's enthusiasm for new possibilities opened up by recent developments in Italy got no takers. The Americans remained set on preparations for the cross-Channel attack."[64]

Support for Turkish declaration of war came from a new quarter, when the Allied foreign ministers met at Moscow in October 1943. Cordell Hull recorded that Soviet Foreign Minister Vyacheslav Molotov proposed on the 25th to Anthony Eden, British Foreign Secretary, and himself that the three governments should exert concerted pressure on Turkey to come into the war. Hull noted that he felt Turkey should assume belligerent status as soon as "militarily feasible."[65] The following day the President conveyed to Hull that this was a military problem which came within the jurisdiction of the Joint Chiefs of Staff. He related, "It would not be deemed advisable to push Turkey at this moment into a declaration of war on the side of the allies since the necessary compensation to the Turks in war materiel and war supplies including armed forces and ships would divert too much from the Italian front and the proposed OVERLORD operation."[66]

Anthony Eden returned home via Cairo, where he met with Turkish Foreign Minister Numan Menemencioglu to broach the question of Turkey entering the war. Eden indicated that Britain desired the use of Turkish air bases, but the Turk replied that this was tantamount to assuming the status of a belligerent. He argued that neither the Turkish public nor Allied logistics was adequately prepared to support this status.[67]

When the Allied heads of state came to Tehran for their summit conference in November 1943, the way seemed prepared for the Allies to support Turkish entry into the war. On the 28th Roosevelt met with his Joint Chiefs of Staff and questioned them about British plans for the Turks. General Marshall replied that Turkish belligerency would divert supplies from Operation OVERLORD. The President was convinced that he must oppose Turkish entry into the conflict.[68] Churchill remained adamant in his support of Turkish entry, and he recorded: "I said I was prepared, on behalf of His Majesty's Government, to give an assurance that Great Britain would go a long way towards bringing Turkey into war. From the military point of view, the entry of Turkey into the war would not mean the diversion of more than two or three Allied divisions at most."[69] Anglo-American tensions ran high over the Turkish question. Stalin now joined Roosevelt in asserting the view that it would be a mistake to bring the Turks in, thus diverting supplies from operations in northern France. Churchill continued to plod on with his idea. Stalin and Churchill lunched with Roosevelt on November 30. The British Prime Minister argued that Russia deserved logistical support through the warm water ports. He discussed the Turkish problem again at a luncheon on December 1. The three heads of state agreed that President İnönü would meet with Roosevelt and Churchill at Cairo following the Tehran conference.[70] Churchill got his way, for on December 1 the heads of state agreed that "it was most desirable that Turkey should come into the war on the side of the Allies before the end of the year." February 14, 1944, was the date set aside on which Turkey should be requested to assume the status of belligerent.[71]

Following the Tehran conference, arrangements were rapidly concluded to transport President Inönü and his Turkish delegation to Cairo, there to confer with the Anglo-American leaders in "free and unprejudged discussion as to the best method by which Turkey could serve the common cause...."[72] Inönü came to the conference convinced that the United States was becoming more interested in the war in the Pacific and less determined to bring Turkey into the war.[73] Churchill pressed his case hard. On the evening of December 5 he entertained the Turkish President to dinner. Inönü was most cautious and evinced continued concern about the danger the German military machine posed to Turkey. Churchill argued that with Italy knocked out of the war, there was little danger to Turkey from the Germans. On December 6 he drafted a memorandum delineating policy in the event that Turkey came into the conflict.[74] Roosevelt displayed a "considerable amount of sympathy for the Turkish point of view" and on one occasion stated "that it was quite understandable that these distinguished and amiable gentlemen should 'not want to be caught with their pants down.'"[75] In this regard, the President, in siding with the Turks, told Churchill on December 4 that "if he was a Turk, he would demand more materiel than Britain had supplied before he would bring Turkey into the war."[76] At the conference the Turks continued to take a cautious attitude, emphasizing all the while their inability to mobilize an army well equipped with modern weapons. While admitting that Germany posed a threat to Turkey, the Turks were all the time more concerned about the probable necessity of Russia's extending assistance to a Turkish state threatened by the Germans. This could well result in Russian occupation of Turkish territory.[77] At length, the Turks nevertheless agreed to enter the war, provided that the deficiencies in Turkish military equipment could be met by the British.[78]

Pursuant to the Cairo agreement, the British dispatched a military mission to Ankara to discuss with the Turks the need to fulfill Turkish military requirements. The Turks began to drag their feet. They overestimated the strength of German forces capable of attacking Turkey, demanded great amounts of materiel, and objected to British plans to ready the Turkish airbases.[79] On February 4, 1944, Secretary of State Hull advised the President that Anglo-Turkish conversations had reached a stalemate. He declared that the British were prepared to withdraw their mission, to suspend further shipments of military supplies, and to direct their ambassador to have no further contact with members of the Turkish government. He reported that the British had requested the cooperation of the United States in taking a distant attitude toward the Turks. The President approved this tack and Hull instructed Steinhardt to "cool off" his relations with the Turks. British and American arms shipments to

Turkey ceased almost immediately. Lend-Lease deliveries were also halted.[80]

With relations between Turkey and the Anglo-American allies at a low ebb, the Turks approached the Soviets, with a view to developing better relations. But the Russians turned a deaf ear to this initiative.[81]

Turkey was isolated, for her relations with Britain and the United States were strained, her initiative in the direction of the Soviets rebuffed, the Germans definitely on the defensive, and the Allies now enjoyed greater prospects for victory in the European theater of war. The Turks were faced with the need to mend their diplomatic fences with the Anglo-Americans. The Turks now sought to appease the Allies by resorting to alternatives other than immediate entry into the conflict.

To satisfy the British and Americans the Turks repealed a wealth tax which had offended the free enterprise theories so prevalent among many English and American leaders. Ambassador Steinhardt reported on July 18, 1943, that the tax, assessed against those who were amassing fortunes as a result of the war, did in fact discriminate against minority groups.[82] It seems that the law was most often applied to Jews, Armenians and Greeks who were frequently jailed for violation of the law. Repeal of the tax on March 17, 1944, satisfied the British and the Americans.[83]

To appease the Soviets, the Turks ended the Pan-Turanian movement which had the effect of losening the ties of Turkic ethnic groups in the Soviet Union to the central government in Moscow.[84] In addition, the Turks took other steps in 1944 in order to more closely identify Turkey with the Allies. As was mentioned, the Turks responded positively to American and British pleas to cease the sale of chrome to Germany. Next the Turks closed the Straits to German warships, which had been allowed to transit the Straits. According to the Montreux Convention, during a war in which Turkey is neutral, warships of belligerent powers are prohibited from passing through the Straits. In January and February 1944 the British ambassador lodged a protest with the Turkish Foreign Office, asserting that German auxiliary vessels of war were permitted to pass through the Straits. The British ambassador presented another protest in June. The Turks then protested to Germany that she was violating the Montreux Convention and then prohibited further passage of German warships through the Straits.[85]

In order to further align Turkey with the Allies, the Turkish government dismissed Foreign Minister Numan Menemencioglu, generally associated with the Turkish connection with Germany. His removal from office paved the way for stronger relations with the Americans and the British.[86]

But perhaps no Turkish act proved as satisfactory to the British and

Americans as Turkey's severance of relations with the Axis Powers. On June 23, 1944, Anthony Eden, British Foreign Secretary, proposed to Secretary Hull that the United States join Britain in a joint effort to compell the Turks to break all ties with the Axis.[87] On June 13 the British Ambassador submitted to Foreign Minister Sukru Saracoglu a request that Turkey break off diplomatic relations with Germany. The Turk promptly broached the possibility of an Anglo-American military operation in the Balkans. The British ambassador replied that no such operation was being contemplated by the Combined Chiefs of Staff.[88] The United States supported the British effort, intimating to the Turks that a severance of diplomatic relations "was regarded as only a first step toward active belligerence."[89] At this juncture General Marshall warned that the United States must state emphatically to the Turks that the United States was not committed to any military operation in the Balkans.[90] The Turks complied with the Anglo-American request and announced the break in diplomatic relations with the Axis Powers on August 2, 1944.

Ultimately, Turkey followed through and declared war against Germany and Japan on February 23, 1945. This declaration did not result from Allied pressure, but was motivated by Turkish desire to participate in the opening meeting of the United Nations at San Francisco. The Turks also wished to assuage the Allies. Turkey no longer had to fear attack from the Germans, but she now had great reason to fear the Soviet Union.

Before discussing the Soviet threat to the Turks, a final word needs to be said about Turkish entry into the war. Historian Harry Howard claims that "with the possible exception of the period when Italy entered the war in June 1940 and the winter of 1943-44, despite Churchill's position, the evidence would seem to indicate that neither the United Kingdom nor the United States nor even the Soviet Union actually desired Turkey's entry into the 'shooting war.'"[91] The British Chiefs of Staff were not in favor of this tack, and it seems that it was more Churchill's plan — one that he anticipated could strike at the "soft underbelly" of the German fortress in Europe. The Turks were of course loath to enter the conflict because they had a constant fear of the Soviet Union, one that was well founded given the turn of events in early 1945.

On March 19, 1945, the Soviet Union initiated an effort to subordinate Turkey and make of her a client state, for on that date the Soviet Foreign Office denounced the Turco-Soviet Treaty of Neutrality and Nonaggression which dated from December 17, 1925.[92] This early move gave the British and Americans no cause for real alarm. But in June 1945 the Soviets presented the Turks with another demand. The Kremlin now demanded a base on the Straits and changes in the Soviet-Turkish border to favor Russia. Inasmuch as American leaders were then planning to attend the Potsdam summit conference, they rejected Turkish pleas to tar the Soviets with the brush of aggression. This rebuff caused the Turks to become all the more determined to obtain U.S. support against Soviet demands.[93]

During the remainder of 1945 the Turkish government continued to consult with the Department of State about Soviet demands on Turkey. In addition to revision of the regime governing the Straits and a base in the Straits, the Soviets also demanded territorial concessions. In December 1945 Acting Secretary of State Dean Acheson gave the Turks assurances that the Soviet demands were cause for alarm as they constituted a threat to peace and good order, and the United States now took the "deepest interest" in this Soviet effort to subordinate Turkey to the aims of the Soviet Union.[94]

Thus in the closing days of the war Turkey aligned herself closely with the United States and Great Britain. Soviet intentions of aggrandizing Russian territorial aspirations caused the Turks to seek the active protection of the Western Allies. Thus the stage was set for the Cold War era when the United States would begin to respond to Soviet aggression in the Middle East. The dispatch of elements of the U.S. Navy to eastern Mediterranean waters — the forerunners of the Sixth Fleet — the extension of economic aid, the making of mutual assistance pacts all became part of the American policy to contain a Soviet bid to achieve hegemony in Turkey.

Chapter 11

The Middle East Supply Center

During World War II the United States joined with Britain in codirecting the affairs of the Middle East Supply Center (MESC). This was a British-founded office established in 1941 to centralize Middle East trade control in order to reduce Allied shipping space for ocean-borne imports of civilian goods, thus freeing space needed for military supplies.[1] The Supply Center served an area that included the Maghreb, Libya, Egypt, the Sudan, Ethiopia, the Arab states of Palestine, Syria, Lebanon, Transjordan, and Iraq, Turkey, Iran, Afghanistan, and India. The exigencies of war demanded the formation of MESC, for Britain lost control of Mediterranean shipping routes in 1940 with the fall of France and Italy's entry into the war. Shipping space became extremely important to Britain, for it was now necessary to bring cargoes around the Cape of Good Hope to Red Sea and Persian Gulf ports. The British military forces had first call on shipping space, and this priority made it necessary to curtail the import of civilian goods into the Middle East. But the peoples of the region required some five million tons of goods imported into their lands from the outside world each year. Given the Axis military threat to the British strategic position in the Middle East, a curtailment of imports could give rise to discontent and political unrest, eventualities that would threaten the rear of the British Desert Army. British Middle East Command realized the need to develop an economic office that could exercise control over civilian imports in order to provide the needed shipping space for the military, and yet at the same time stimulate production of goods within the area to make up for the shortfall brought on by lack of shipping space. On April 1, 1941, the Middle East Supply Center opened its doors. Its director was Commander Robert Jackson, a hardboiled officer of the Royal Australian Navy, who quickly realized that a strict licensing system of imports and stimulation of food production in the region were necessary to aid the war effort to achieve victory. Jackson started up the machinery which expanded the jurisdiction of MESC to an area larger than the continent of Europe, with a population of some 100 milion people.[2]

With American entry into the war in December 1941, it was not long before the British desired that the United States have a representative in MESC. On February 24 G.F. Thorold, first secretary of the British Embassy, called on Herbert Feis, economic adviser at the State Department, to express the view that the British "would be glad to have such American membership on the [MESC] Council." He told Feis that the American Embassy in Cairo and General Maxwell's staff both maintained liaison with MESC.[3] Within the month, Sumner Welles cabled Alexander Kirk in Cairo that the Lend-Lease Administration viewed with favor American representation on MESC, with one military representative from General Maxwell's mission and a civilian representative from the legation. Further, all requests for goods in the Middle East should be processed by MESC before transmittal to the Lend-Lease Administration. Welles requested Kirk's views on future American representation on MESC.[4] Kirk replied that both the legation and General Maxwell's mission maintained close contact with MESC. He recommended that Norris B. Chipman, second secretary of the legation, be designated American civilian representative on MESC, and he stated that General Maxwell would designate a Captain Jones of his staff.[5]

The first real experience that the Department and the Lend-Lease Administration had with the operation of MESC came on March 21, when Kirk cabled the Department that MESC desired that all cargoes of grain and other bulk materials being imported into the area from Lend-Lease stocks should be processed by the MESC office in Cairo. Full consultation with MESC would permit the redistribution of bulk materials to those people most in need. Kirk reported that both he and General Maxwell approved this procedure.[6]

That American Lend-Lease shipments would be subject to review by a British-founded agency gave some cause for worry in the Department. Frederick Winant of the division of Exports and Defense Aid wrote a memorandum on April 17 to Dean Acheson, Assistant Secretary of State, setting forth the arguments for the subordination of American Lend-Lease shipments to MESC control. Winant asserted that there were two different systems of control governing the influx of civilian supplies into the Middle East. The British used MESC to control civilian imports, thus establishing broad control over the entire Middle Eastern region. The Americans utilized a country-by-country control system. Thus there were two systems of control, with inevitable complications. Indeed, with dual authority, there were frequent collisions in the area of supplies. Winant pointed out that MESC "performs a very constructive service for the war effort and the civilian population in the Near East area." He declared that the United States could either collaborate with the Center's local supply committees or else join MESC itself. The British, he asserted, desired American membership in MESC, and "self-interest" would seem to dictate that "the United States should consider the possibility of playing a more important role in Near Eastern affairs." The United States, if it desired to join, should send "a representative of the very highest type" to serve in the organization. Winant closed his memorandum with a list of advantages and disadvantages surrounding American participation in MESC, with the former clearly outweighing the latter.[7]

Winant's arguments were well received at the Department, and on April 30, 1942, Secretary of State Hull cabled Minister Kirk that the Department had decided to formally participate in MESC, with one representative for military supplies and one for civilian supplies. Kirk learned that the American Legation in Tehran had been apprised of this decision and that the Department had instructed the minister in Tehran to assign a member of his staff to sit on the local supply committee. Legations in other countries of the Middle East also received similar instructions. The Department directed Kirk to assign a member of his staff to sit on the MESC Council and consult with General Maxwell that he might assign a military representative.[8] A subsequent instruction from Hull to Kirk describes in detail the procedure employed by MESC to process civilian requirements of each country in the Middle East. First, the requirement was submitted to the local supply committee of the individual country which would then forward its findings to MESC in Cairo. The Center would examine the requirements of each country and lists of needs would then be forwarded to London, where the British would determine which goods could be supplied from Empire stocks. Those requirements not met in London would be forwarded to Washington, where U.S. authorities would consider those items which the British could not handle. All bulk cargoes of cereals and sugar would be sent directly to MESC for redistribution throughout the Middle East in accordance with the needs of the individual countries.[9]

Thus the Middle East Supply Center became a joint Anglo-American enterprise, one that buried the peacetime trade rivalries and subordinated each country's desire for trade to the military needs imposed by the war. In so doing, MESC was able to put together a program that would save vitally needed shipping space to provide military needs and at the same time sufficient space to fulfill civilian needs in the region. By 1943 about four-fifths of the civilian tonnage headed towards the Middle East had been eliminated. In spite of this marked decline the people of the region received sufficient food, for their agriculture, as well as their industries and economies, were geared up to support the war effort. The Center was responsible for this redirection of effort.[10]

On the recommendation of General Maxwell, the Department selected Frederick Winant to sit as the civilian representative on MESC. On arrival in Cairo, Winant was installed as chairman of the Executive Committee of the Middle East Supply Center.[11] As the ranking American in

MESC, Winant represented the office of the Lend-Lease Administration in the Middle East. He coordinated the efforts of MESC with that of the Administration in Washington. Winant held this position until mid-1943, when he returned to the United States. On his recommendation, an official with greater standing in national and international affairs was selected to replace him. James M. Landis, dean of the Harvard Law School, a member of President Roosevelt's "brain trust," and director of the Office of Civil Defense, was selected as Winant's replacement. Secretary Hull gave to Landis the rank of minister. With his rank, Landis began immediately to function as director of economic operations in the Middle East and as the principal American civilian representative to the MESC.[12] Landis arrived in Cairo in December 1943, following a stop in London to consult with American and British officials. On arrival in Cairo he began to work for a rapid subordination of American economic policy in the Middle East to the efforts of MESC. Another immediate benefit of his arrival was that he achieved an increased supply of American food for Iran, where a serious food shortage existed beginning in early 1943. By mid-1943 conditions in Iran had become alarming. Landis prepared a report on Iran for Harry Hopkins to take to the Tehran Conference and he also directed General Connolly in Iran to assign seventeen officers and ten enlisted men to assist the Iranians in solving problems related to the transport and supply of grain, sugar, fuel, and oil. The President subsequently approved Landis' policies with respect to Iran.[13]

But perhaps the greatest service performed by MESC was that of exercising control over shipping coming into Middle Eastern ports. As late as June 1941, following the closing of the Mediterranean, ships arrived at Red Sea and Persian Gulf ports loaded with badly needed military supplies as well as luxury goods that included silk stockings, cosmetics, automobiles, refrigerators, and other items unrelated to the war effort.[14] It was absolutely required that priority be given to the transport of military supplies to the British Army. This resulted in the curtailment of imports of nonessential items, because MESC adopted a strict licensing system. All requirements were reviewed not only by local supply committees but also by the MESC office at Cairo. Raw materials and equipment for industry came under the category of the Materials Division. Food Resources, Medicine Requirements, and the Transport Division divided the miscellaneous multiplicity of the remaining items. Each license was graded according to need, with "A" standing for essential; "B" for desirable but not urgent; "C" for nonessential; and "X" for undetermined.[15] With a well defined system of grading and licensing, MESC continued to allow trading companies to handle a large amount of the trade. But MESC purchased bulk goods such as grain, coal, tires, sugar, fats, oils, tea, coffee, canned milk, meat, and fish for its own account and then redistributed these items according to need. Because the roads and rail facilities in the Middle East were minimal and not up to handling the increased exchange of goods, MESC found it necessary to control freight and motor transport facilities.[16] In order to greatly reduce imports, thereby allocating more shipping space for military supplies, MESC also had to engage in a program for stimulating production of agricultural and industrial products within the region. The production of more grain to meet increased regional needs required scientific advice. The Center operated its own Agricultural Production section to exchange information required for stepped-up food production. For example, MESC found it necessary to combat the threat of locusts to regional crop production. Its Anti-Locust Unit reported to Cairo on breeding areas in various parts of the region. Poisoned bait was set out and many swarms were caught while still on the ground and destroyed. Aircraft also doused them with lethal sprays.[17]

By rational systems of grain collection, food distribution, and the opening up of new areas of production, MESC was able to increase regional food production. For example, new irrigation projects in Syria, Lebanon, and Iraq, and the cultivation of new acreage in Syria and Cyrenaica, new grain collection systems in Egypt, Iran, the Sudan, and the Levant, the shift from cotton crops to food crops in Egypt, the Levant, Iraq, Iran, and the Sudan, the introduction of the growing of potatoes and soya beans in Palestine and the Sudan all added immensely to regional food production, thereby freeing badly needed shipping space for military goods.[18]

The Supply Center also engaged in raising industrial production levels in the Middle East. Expansion took place in the more advanced countries such as Palestine, Egypt, Syria, Lebanon, Turkey, Iran, and Iraq. Palestine was a center of industrial activity. Shipyards in Palestine not only repaired Allied warships but also built two minesweepers. Shops, foundaries, and factories turned out a multiplicity of goods that included not only consumer products but also items for the military as well. Because there was a dearth of foreign manufactured goods, local suppliers took up the burden of supplying the needed spare parts and maintenance services to keep machinery and equipment in operation to turn out needed goods.[19]

Because there was a shortage of supplies, both agricultural and industrial, and an influx of money into the region, it was only natural that inflation should set in. Although none of the regional governments had the bureaucratic machinery to cope with runaway inflation, MESC was equipped to deal with the problem and used a system of controls—rationing and price control of essentials—to ensure that goods were not sold at exorbitant prices. The Center insisted that grain and other goods distributed to regional countries carried the condition that the government receiving the supplies must ensure that distribution was effected according to need.[20]

From the outset a large amount of the goods brought to the Middle East to meet regional demands came from the United States where such agencies as the Office of Economic Warfare worked in conjunction with the Lend-Lease Administration and the Foreign Economic Administration to meet these needs. Of course, MESC exercised ultimate control through the three Anglo-American supply committees — the Combined Production and Resources Board, the Combined Raw Materials Board, and the Combined Food Board.[21] These various committees determined what quantity of goods could be supplied from Allied stocks of materials for dispatch to the Middle East and the allocation of shipping to handle the exports.

Although MESC was a joint Anglo-American venture, it was inevitable that friction would arise between American exporters and the Middle East Supply Center which exercised control over American shipping. The United States had given to MESC control over its licensing, Lend-Lease, and shipping space allocations. Britain was unable to meet the civilian consumption needs of the people of the Middle East. Supply Center authorities suggested that the latter send their orders to the United States. In short order, American exports to the region rose to twice the prewar record of 1938 and exceeded the number of British exports. U.S. exporters were not happy that MESC exercised control over American exports to the region;[22] even in the Department of State there was a group who adopted a negative attitude toward MESC. This group viewed the Center as a British organization that aimed to perpetuate a state-controlled economy, one that was at odds with the American concept of free trade and with future American economic interests in the region.[23] In January 1944 Dean Acheson, Assistant Secretray of State for Economic Affairs, opposed the increase of American staff serving in MESC. He favored a gradual reversal of trade by rechanneling commerce through private avenues. Even Frederick Winant viewed the Middle East as a new area for American economic opportunity, one that should be open on the basis of equality and not restricted by discriminatory practices. Wallace Murray of NEA was opposed to the British effort to use MESC to continue the wartime controls and trade restrictions in the postwar era. James Landis voiced his opposition to the continuation of MESC in June 1944 when he asserted that MESC controls would work to the disadvantage of the United States in the postwar era.[24]

Thus, following the invasion of Normandy in June 1944, there began to appear strong differences between American and British economic planners. To the Americans the MESC schedules of restrictions and controls were anathema to the free enterprise system. The British hoped to use MESC in the postwar era to promote the cause of economic regionalism that would complement the emergence of the Arab League. With her position in the Middle East well established, Britain hoped to control these organizations and maintain a preferred position in the Middle East. For the British, economic coordination and planning had become a way of life at home and they believed that it must follow in the overseas area as well if Britain were to maintain her preferred position.[25]

With a consensus developing on economic policy for the Middle East that amounted to a desire to restore the Open Door policy, the Department of State sent an *aide-mémoire* to the British Embassy on September 28, 1944. It noted that the Middle East Supply Center had rendered valuable services to the war effort during the days when shipping space was extremely scarce. The joint Anglo-American operation had been successful, but conditions in the Middle East had changed. Shipping conditions had improved as the allocation of shipping space for civilian goods grew. The supply of civilian needs could now be met with increased imports. Given these changed circumstances, U.S. officials came to believe that "it is no longer necessary to maintain the extensive system of import controls developed by the Middle East Supply Center for that territory." While the Department proposed to continue the licensing system to control a select list of commodities that were still in short supply, it believed that with respect to other items the appropriate controls could be administered by the appropriate agencies in the United States. In closing, the note declared that James Landis would proceed to London and Cairo "to work out such details as may be necessary to put into operation the policies of the United States as described above."[26]

What is immediately apparent is that the State Department was aware that American exporters could begin to meet civilian needs in the Middle East at a time when British industry was still geared to war production. A removal of controls and restrictions would immediately open up new markets to American exporters.[27]

An early indication that the United States would end the system of controls that the Middle East Supply Center exercised on the import of goods into the Middle East came in the autumn of 1944. On September 4 Secretary of State Hull instructed American diplomats in Ankara, Baghdad, Beirut, Jerusalem, Tehran and Cairo that the Department was dispatching a special mission, headed by William S. Culbertson, to tour the Middle East with a view to developing long-range plans for increased commercial intercourse between the United States and the countries of that region. The mission would arrive in Cairo in early September, and later send members to visit Turkey, Iran, Iraq, Syria, and Palestine to make studies and recommend courses of action.[28]

John A. DeNovo tells us that the Culbertson Mission has generally been overlooked by historians of the American role in World War II.[29] But that mission was of great importance in establishing some guidelines that shaped American postwar economic planning for the Middle East.

Culbertson's report was taken seriously by those reponsible for the formulation of postwar policy. The author of this report and head of the mission was well qualified for his task. A lieutenant colonel serving at the Army Industrial College, his publication of four books on international trade had established him as an expert in that area. Secretary of State Hull requested and obtained for Culbertson the rank of ambassador. Culbertson's team of experts included Homer S. Fox, a noted State Department consultant on foreign trade, and Ray C. Miller, a trade expert provided by the Department of Commerce. The mission set out on its fact-finding investigation in August. Following a survey of French North Africa, Culbertson and his team proceeded to Cairo, where on September 17 Frederick Winant joined the mission. The mission surveyed the activities of MESC and in the next two months members of the Culbertson mission traveled to Tehran, Ankara, Damascus, Baghdad, Beirut, and Jerusalem, conferring with American and British officials along the way. The survey was completed by November 1944, and on the 15th Culbertson submitted his thirty-two-page report to Secretary Hull. He related that his mission had covered extensive ground, had been well received, and discussed matters with both public officials and private citizens.[30] The mission's report is not printed in *Foreign Relations*, but an excellent essay by John DeNovo gives a wealth of detail about it. The members were unanimous in the conclusion that all controls on trade must be removed. While they lauded the wartime efforts of MESC, they concluded that the controls exercised by this organization must cease, the better to serve American economic interests. They also recommended that the United States give greater encouragement to American citizens trying to expand their commercial contacts in the Middle East.[31]

Further indication of the American intent to terminate the Middle East Supply Center came in September 1945. Lieutenant Colonel Harold B. Hoskins, adviser on economic affairs and Counselor of Legation at Egypt, visited London and advised the British that the United States had originally set January 1, 1946, as the date for the termination of MESC. But the date was to be advanced to November 1, 1945. The British replied that they would like a formal notice of the date of termination and that it would be prepared to draft a statement of an announcement. On September 18, 1945, the Department addressed a memorandum to the British Embassy. It declared that the United States government agreed to the proposal for the issuance of a joint announcement effecting the end of the Middle East Supply Center on November 1, 1945. It addressed the problem of import controls on bulk commodities, asserting that controls should be removed and that "normal commercial channels" should be reopened at the earliest possible moment. It warned that if the British elected to continue centralized controls over the importation of these commodities, then the United States government would shape its export policy in such fashion as to obstruct the implementation of centralized procurement policies. While the U.S. government recognized the valuable service performed by the Center during the war, it also recognized the need to make a rapid transition toward the normalization of a private trade.[32]

The British had a different set of goals. Martin Wilmington relates that Britain hoped to promote Pan-Arab union in the Middle East and envisioned that the Middle East Supply Center would serve to promote economic unity in the region.[33] The British were thus somewhat reluctant to close down MESC. But at length, they proved willing, because British reconstruction following the war would largely depend upon American financial assistance. Phillip Baram concludes that with growing economic dependence on the United States, and with the Arab League already an established fact, the British agreed to close down MESC.[34] A joint statement was issued by the governments of the United States and Great Britain on September 26, 1945, announcing the dissolution of the Middle East Supply Center.[35]

Thus it was inevitable that the Middle East Supply Center would cease to function in the postwar era. The American tradition of private enterprise prevailed over the growing British dependence on state control, a dependence arising during the grim years of the war. The United States returned to the Open Door policy, while Britain continued to rely on state controls.

To be sure the Middle East Supply Center had been a success, for during the war years, internal production of food stuffs was increased to help meet the needs of peoples who had to bear reduced shipments of commodities due to the shortage of shipping space. The reduction of civilian imports was a tribute to the men who ran the affairs of MESC. The Center had no enforcement agency and could only recommend solutions and grade requirements according to need, but it did perform a most valuable task in assisting the Allies to achieve victory in the Middle East. Had MESC not provided the means to allocate materials and commodities for civilian needs, shipping space could not have been utilized to the optimum degree. Had civilian needs not been met, the peoples of the Middle East could have become disenchanted with the Allied cause, thrown in their lot with the Axis Powers and proven to be an impediment to the Allied war effort.

Although the Middle East Supply Center might have proven a valuable instrument in the postwar era in assisting with economic development in the Middle East, such was not to be. American plans for the postwar Middle East called for a return to a normalization of trade, reliance on the Open Door and utilization of private enterprise to meet regional needs. In planning for the postwar Middle East, state controls and economic barriers had no place in the State Department's policy papers.

Chapter 12

Preparations for a Postwar Policy in the Middle East

As the war progressed it became apparent that the United States did not have a comprehensive, region-wide policy to cover its activities in the Middle East. On September 27, 1943, Lieutenant Colonel Harold B. Hoskins, a Middle Eastern specialist with fluency in Arabic, recalls advising the President in this way: "As to the United States' political set-up in the Middle East I outlined the fact that we did not always have a coordinated political policy because our American ambassadors and ministers tended to think primarily in terms of American relations to the country to which each was accredited." Hoskins concluded "that at times there was a lack of a regional or area point of view in regard to various problems that extended over the whole Middle East area and beyond the confines of any one country."[1] That the United States was in the process of developing its policy on a country-by-country basis is evident from the record that shows that the State Department formulated policy guidelines as the situation arose. But an important question is whether or not the United States began to formulate a region-wide policy during the closing years of the war that transcended its interests in each country. The record indicates that the Department was in the process of forming a general postwar policy as early as 1943. For example, as early as January 23, 1943, John D. Jernegan of NEA wrote a paper on "American Policy in Iran." In a statement that set the tone for American policy vis-à-vis Iran, Jernegan also touched on the need for a postwar regional policy as well. He wrote: "So far, we have [maintained] our interest in winning the war. I wonder if we should not also begin, privately, to base our response upon our interest in winning the peace?" Jernegan raised the question if Iran did not constitute a "test case for the good faith of the United Nations and their ability to work out among themselves an adjustment of ambitions, rights and interests which will be fair not only to the Great Powers of our coalition but also to the small nations associated with us or brought into our sphere by circumstances."[2] Concern for the political and economic future of the small states in the Middle East seems to have been a primary consideration of the Department.

The movement of the small states of the Middle East toward an Arab union was given great impetus by British Foreign Secretary Anthony Eden, whose Mansion House speech on May 29, 1941, endorsed the strengthening of cultural, political, and economic ties among the Arab countries. Prime Minister Nuri Pasha of Iraq promptly issued a "blue book" entitled *Arab Independence and Union* in which he proposed the formation of an Arab League to be made up initially of a unified Syrian state — comprising Syria, Lebanon, Palestine, and Transjordan — and Iraq. Provision was made for other Arab states to adhere to the League. Anthony Eden made a second speech in February 1943 in the House of Commons, clearly endorsing the Arabs' effort to promote their own economic, cultural, and political unity. This endorsement caused Prime Minister Nuri Pasha of Iraq to engage in bilateral talks with the leading officials of Iraq, Transjordan, Saudi Arabia, Syria, Lebanon and Yemen, with a view to exchanging ideas on Arab union.[3]

While these exchanges were taking place, Cordell Hull made a nationwide radio address on American foreign policy. In this address he asserted that "all nations, large and small, which respect the rights of others, are entitled to freedom from outside interference in their internal affairs." He also commented on the future of dependent peoples who aspired to the right of self-determination of peoples. He declared: "It should be the duty of nations having political ties with such peoples of mandatories, of trustees, or of other agencies, as the case may be, to help the aspiring peoples to develop materially and educationally, to prepare themselves for the duties and responsibilities of self-government, and to attain liberty."[4]

During the exchanges between Nuri Pasha and other Arab leaders, Minister Alexander Kirk cabled the Department from Cairo, requesting instructions to guide him in presenting to the Arab leaders the American attitude on the concept of the Pan-Arab movement. He reported that he had had a conversation with Shaikh Youssef Yassin, acting Minister for Foreign Affairs of Saudi Arabia, who desired to know the American opinion of this movement.[5] At the time Cordell Hull was attending the Conference of Foreign Ministers in Moscow. On October 26 he cabled the Department instructions bearing on the reply to be made to Kirk. He wrote: "This government desires to see the independent countries of the Near East retain their freedom and strengthen their economic and social condition, and fully sympathizes with the aspirations of other Near Eastern countries for complete liberty." Concerning the formation of a greater Arab union, Hull observed: "If the peoples of the Near East should find it advantageous to unite of their own free will, it naturally follows from this government's basic attitude that such a development would be viewed with sympathy, always on the understanding that it should take place in accordance with the principles of the Atlantic Charter." Of the problems facing the Middle Eastern peoples, Hull noted: "It is realized that the countries concerned will shape their own decisions, but it seems to this government that the events and problems of the war years have shown that the Near Eastern countries need greater strength in the economic, social, and cultural domains, and that first steps toward unity might well have these ends in view."[6]

Hence, Edward R. Stettinius, acting Secretary of State, instructed Kirk to inform the Saudi official that the American attitude toward the nations of the Middle East

> is well known and has undergone no recent change. That attitude is, in brief, that we desire to see the independent Near Eastern countries retain their liberties and strengthen their economic and social condition. The aspirations of other Near Eastern countries for full independence have our complete sympathy. It naturally follows that if those peoples find it advantageous to unite of their own free will, we would view such a development with sympathy, always on the understanding that it takes place in accord with the principles set forth in the Atlantic Charter.[7]

This policy statement left no room for doubt about the American government's reaction to the hopes and aspirations of the peoples of the Middle East to practice self-determination.

The Saudi Arabian government again sought the views of the State Department at the time when a preliminary Arab conference was underway in July 1944. The Department's reply was couched in the same terms as the reply made in October 1943. Hull retired shortly thereafter, but he wrote later: "As I left office I entertained the strong hope that the Arab states of the Near East would soon begin to take the economic, social, and cultural steps we believed necessary as an approach toward political unity, that they would be able to compose the conflicting ambitions of their various leaders, and that, not too many years after the conclusion of the war, they would be able to bring stability, unity, and economic development to that historic corner of the world."[8]

Hull was speaking as a Wilsonian internationalist. His views were consonant with Point Twelve of President Wilson's Fourteen Points, which promised self-determination to the subject nationalities of the Ottoman Empire. This concept was later incorporated into Article XXII of the League of Nations Covenant, creating the system of mandatories.

In September and October 1944 the preliminary Arab Conference met at Alexandria. At length a formal meeting of the Arab states, consisting of delegates from Palestine, Egypt, Syria, Lebanon, Iraq, Trans-

jordan, Saudi Arabia, and Yemen, was convened. The Conference adopted a protocol for the purpose of forming a League of Arab States. The
Conference established numerous subcommittees on economic, cultural,
social and other matters. It passed resolutions recognizing the independence
of Lebanon and endorsing the rights of Arabs in Palestine. Subsequently, a
draft constitution for the Arab League was drawn up and signed by the
delegates of the seven member states on March 22, 1945. It provided for
the participation of a representative of the Palestine Arabs and for
cooperation with other Arab territories, such as the French North African
states then under French control and also the Persian Gulf sheikhdoms.
The pact of the League prohibited the use of force among the member
states, provided for consultation and mutual assistance in the event of
aggression against a member of state, and established a Council and a
Secretary General, with headquarters in Cairo.[9]

The creation of the Arab League was welcomed by both the British
and American governments. William Phillips, special assistant to the
Secretary of State, speaking at a banquet in New York City in honor of the
Regent of Iraq on June 2, 1945, said:

> The determination of the Arab people to reestablish their indepen-
> dence and to play a role in world affairs to which they feel them-
> selves entitled by reason of their brilliant past and their talents and
> industry, undoubtedly was one of the factors which motivated them
> during the first world war to fight for their freedom. Unquestionably
> the same determination contributed to their decision recently to form
> the League of Arab States. We welcome the development of Arab co-
> operation and are confident that the strengthening of the ties be-
> tween the various Arab countries will not only be to their common
> benefit but will also enable them to make important and constructive
> contributions to the great tasks awaiting the United Nations.[10]

In a memorandum to the Secretary of State dated August 29, 1945,
Loy W. Henderson, director of the Office of Near Eastern and African Affairs, echoed the sentiments of Phillips: "We have thus welcomed such
manifestations of Arab cooperation as the establishment of the League of
Arab States and the steps which have already been taken toward unity
between the Arabs in the economic, social, and cultural fields."[11]

To be sure, the political future of the peoples of the Middle East occupied much of the time of the planners at NEA, but the latter also devoted
themselves to the region's economic prospects. On May 2, 1945, the Coordinating Committee of the Department of State presented a paper entitled
"American Economic Policy in the Middle East." The paper contains the
very essence of the ideals that would become associated with the aims of
the so-called "free world." It called for the guarantee of the "right of people
to choose and maintain for themselves the types of political, social and
economic systems they desire." More to the point, it called for the

"creation of an equality of opportunity, as against a policy of exclusion, in commerce, transit, and trade...." As for the rights of Americans, it asserted that steps must be taken for the "general protection of American citizens [and the] protection and furtherance of legitimate American economic rights, existing or potential." In the political sphere, it declared that the United States should assist the independent countries of the Middle East to maintain their independence. With respect to Palestine, it maintained that that land "Is recognized as primarily a British responsibility, but we look forward to a just and reasonable solution at the proper time, after consultation with all interested parties."

With a view to creating more stable economies in the region's countries and improving the level of living for their peoples, the planners called for the increase of purchasing power by various means that included the extension of credit, the removal of trade restrictions, the improvement of American trade agreements with regional countries, and the offering of technical assistance in agriculture, trade, and industry. This plan envisioned improving agriculture, transportation, communications, and public health, and raising the level of living. The planners noted that the Western democratic free enterprise system as represented by the British was in competition with the closed, authoritarian system of the Soviet Union. The report indicated a suspicion of the Soviets, for it suggested they not only hoped to maintain security along their frontiers and prevent a coalition of capitalistic countries in the region against the Soviet Union, but that they also expected to extend the Soviet social and economic system throughout the Middle East. The best means of opposing a Soviet thrust into the region would be an increased standard of living which would remove the economic discontent that provides such a fertile seedbed for the spread of communist ideology. The report closed with a recommendation that the discriminatory regime of economic controls should be removed and replaced with a broad multilateral trade that would see the sale of American exports being paid for by the purchase of Middle Eastern goods. Too, the planners envisioned the influx of American capital to produce goods for local production and goods for export.[12]

That the United States anticipated a "forward" economic policy in the postwar Middle East is evident from a report by Harold B. Hoskins. Writing from Cairo on May 12, 1945, Hoskins urged that the Department plan for an economic conference that would encompass a broad range of problems such as the dollar exchange in the Middle East, the disposal of surplus property, the promotion of American trade in the region, the future of the Middle East Supply Center, future economic ties with the Pan-Arab Union, petroleum problems in the area, and the future of civil aviation.[13] Acting Secretary of State Joseph Grew replied to Hoskins' proposal on June 9, asserting that the Department did not favor the holding of such a conference. Grew asserted that the Culbertson Mission recommendations were still under consideration, and he pointed out that the Department had solicited recommendations and comments on the report of the Department's Coordinating Committee. Grew admitted that the Department favored broad discussions between the staffs of the various American missions engaged in implementing economic policy and the appropriate officials in Washington. Such discussions should address the promotion of sound long-range trading practices looking toward "maximum opportunites for private traders in this area" and consider "long-range trade possibilites" between the U.S. and the Middle East.[14]

That the United States contemplated a vigorous policy in the Middle East was further indicated by a memorandum by Under Secretary of State Dean Acheson, who wrote the Secretary of State on October 9. Acheson complained that congressional failure to authorize funds for use in the Middle East obstructed the Department's ability to meet the financial needs of King Ibn Saud of Saudi Arabia. He pointed out that the King required loans of about ten million dollars per year to meet fiscal obligations until such time as oil royalties would provide much needed revenue. Anticipating the Truman Doctrine which would make American economic resources available to Middle Eastern countries to counter Soviet intrusion into the region, Acheson endorsed the joint State, War, and Navy recommendation that the Congress create a fund of $100 million "for the purpose of furthering the political and strategic interests of the United States in the Middle East." In closing, Acheson recommended that the Secretary read closely the draft memorandum prepared by Gordon Merriam, chief of NEA, for President Harry S Truman.[15]

Shortly after his taking the reins of government, Truman received numerous memoranda from the Department concerning American policies in various regions. The NEA had provided the President with a wealth of data on the Middle East. Merriam's report, strongly endorsed by Dean Acheson, is comprehensive yet concise. The NEA chief referred to the Middle East as "a highly dangerous trouble spot." Of the ability of the United States to meet the challenge in this region, Merriam asserted that "we feel in the Department that this government is inadequately provided with the means for exerting its influence for peace and security in that area." Merriam was alluding to the Soviet threat to intrude its influence in the Middle East. Specifically, he pointed out that the Soviets had informed the Turkish government of its desire to revise the Montreux Convention governing the Straits and of its intention to terminate the Soviet-Turkish Treaty of Friendship and Neutrality. He declared that the Soviet Union had indicated an unwillingness to remove its troops from the northern part of Iran in keeping with her treaty obligation to do so. Merriam pointed out that while France had awarded independence to Syria and Lebanon, she was engaged in tactics designed to preserve a preferential French position in the countries of the Levant. He warned that the American oil concession in Saudi Arabia was in jeopardy unless the United States could supply the King's temporary needs for economic assistance. Merriam described the longstanding position of Britain and France in the Middle East as one that has left the masses of people in poverty, ignorance, and disease. Given the poor condition of the people and the decline of the British and French position in the region, Merriam warned that the Soviet Union is "showing marked interest in the area and is proceeding along its customary cautious but firm and calculating lines, to move into the picture. Hence, there is danger that the Near Eastern peoples, in the absence of any indication of a tangible nature that the United States is prepared to play an active role in raising their economic and cultural levels, will look to Soviet Russia for a cure of their economic and social ills and as the mainspring of power in the Near East."

The Middle East was centrally important to the United States, as evidenced by Merriam's reference to the mineral resources of the region and to its geographical position linking up East and West. It is imperative, Merriam, declared, that this region "should be in the hands of a people following the paths of democratic civilization rather than those of Eastern dictatorships." Presaging the time when Washington would extend aid to the region, Merriam asserted that "to serve our higher long-range ... purposes, our activities in the Near Eastern area must be based upon the political, educational and economic development of the native peoples and not merely upon the narror immediate interests of British or American economy." He pointed out that Whitehall had admitted that Britain could no longer keep order in the Middle East without the assistance of the United States. Of this caveat, Merriam proffered that "we are inclined to believe that a policy of inactivity or 'drift' on our part will result in a progressive deterioration of the influence of democratic civilization in the Near East." At the present time, Merriam stated, the United States was inadequately equipped to deal with the unfolding problems in the postwar Middle East. Merriam posited that long-range planning for the region would require an adequate means of implementing policy that would serve the nation's best interests. He avowed that the Department should suggest that Congress allocate $100 million per year for several years in order to restore stability to the crucial area of the Middle East.[16]

An examination of the recommendations of the Coordinating Committee of the State Department, of Harold Hoskins, of Dean Acheson, and of Gordon Merriam, allows one to draw certain conclusions. It is obvious that planners at the Department clearly envisioned the U.S. employment of government instrumentalities to create in the

postwar era a "free world," one in which democratic and capitalistic institutions would exist in a climate free of economic controls and
discriminating practices that would limit free trade in order that the United
States might expand its trade in the Middle East. But protection of
American economic interests was merely one facet of the larger plan, for
officials in the Department were only too aware that Britain and France
would experience a diminished position in the postwar Middle East, and
that unless the United States could fill this vacuum by extending economic
aid and technical assistance to the peoples of the region, the Soviet Union
would move in and establish hegemony. Soviet control of the Middle East
would be intolerable to the United States, for the region's mineral resources and transportation and communication routes were vital to the continued economic and strategic interests of the American people. It is
possible to conclude that planners at the Department of State were aware
that in the postwar era the United States would be required to fill the
vacuum of power caused by Britain's decline and to extend military
assistance, technical assistance, and even place its military forces
in the region to serve as a deterrent to the Soviet Union which even
in 1945 evinced a desire to expand its power in Turkey, Iran, and Greece.

To be sure, planners at the Department were anxious to expand the
American economic stake in the Middle East and knew of the opportunity
to obtain a share of markets long controlled by Britain and France. But
given the reality that the United States had suffered from a depressed
economy prior to the outbreak of World War II, it is possible that planners
looking to the days of peace to follow the six-year conflict hoped to give
the American economy an added stimulus by opening up markets in the
Middle East. All too often, writers on the left imply that the quest for new
economic opportunity and the profit motive are inherently evil. But is it
not part of the American heritage that new land, new opportunity, and the
hope of profit have run as major themes through American historical
development? Little did the American pioneers who ventured to the Middle East in the early years of the nineteenth century realize that in the years
following World War II the United States would find that the mineral
resources of the Middle East, that region's communication and transportation rules, and its geographical juxtasposition to the Soviet Union would
tie the destiny of the American people closely to the Middle East. That
State Department planners could envision the need for a more aggressive,
more "forward" American Middle Eastern policy in the aftermath of World
War II is a tribute to their awareness of the changes in that region during
the war years. No longer would the United States be able to stand in
splendid isolation and view this vital region from afar, languidly willing to
allow Great Britain to protect its peoples' destinies. To be sure, the United
States had no comprehensive, region-wide policy during the war, but

merely depended upon a policy determined by the needs of each country. Yet, within the last two years of the war, policy-planners at the Department of State slowly began to come to grips with this absence of a regional policy and to arrive at the realization that the United States would have to assume greater responsibility in the area following the war. The decline of Britain and France and the proximity of the Soviet Union to the region made it axiomatic that a more aggressive American policy for the Middle East would follow the end of hostilities.

Chapter Notes

CHAPTER 1

1. Thomas A. Bryson, *American Diplomatic Relations with the Middle East, 1784-1975: A Survey* (Metuchen, N.J., 1977), p. 2.

2. James A. Field, Jr., *America and the Mediterranean World, 1776-1882* (Princeton, N.J., 1969), and John A. DeNovo, *American Interests and Policies in the Middle East, 1900-1939* (Minneapolis, 1963), pp. 8-16.

3. *Niles Register*, July 21, 1821.

4. Lloyd Griscom, *Diplomatically Speaking: Memoirs of Constantinople and Persia* (New York, 1940), p. 134.

5. For the operaton of the missionary lobby on the Armenian issue, see Joseph L. Grabill, *Protestant Diplomacy and the Near East: Missionary Influence on American Policy, 1810-1927* (Minneapolis, 1971), and James B. Gidney, *A Mandate for Armenia* (Kent, Ohio, 1967).

6. Robert L. Daniel, *American Philanthropy in the Near East, 1820-1960* (Athens, Ohio, 1970), pp. 278-279, and Field, *America and the Mediterranean World*, pp. 166-68; 389-392.

7. See Bryson, *American Diplomatic Relations with the Middle East*; Field, *America and the Mediterranean World*; and DeNovo, *American Interests and Policies in the Middle East*.

8. See Thomas A. Bryson, *Tars, Turks, and Tankers: The Role of the U.S. Navy in the Middle East, 1800-1980* (Metuchen, N.J., 1980).

9. *Ibid.*

10. See Thomas A. Bryson, "Admiral Mark Lambert Bristol: An Open Door Diplomat in Turkey," *International Journal of Middle East Studies*, 5 (1974), 450-467.

11. John A. DeNovo, "A Railroad for Turkey: The Chester Project of 1908-1913," *Business History Review*, 33 (autumn 1959), 300-329.

12. Robert L. Daniel, "The Friendship of Woodrow Wilson and Cleveland Dodge," *Mid-America*, 43 (July 1961), 182-196, and Joseph L. Grabill, "Missionary Influence on American Relations with the Middle East, 1914-1923," *Muslim World*, 58 (1968), Part 1, 43-56, and Part 2, 141-54.

13. The best account of this subject is in Harry N. Howard, *The King-Crane Commission: An Inquiry in the Middle East* (Beirut, 1963).

14. The author is currently writing a biography of Admiral Bristol entitled *Admiral Mark L. Bristol: A Naval Diplomat*.

15. Bryson, *American Diplomatic Relations with the Middle East*, pp. 97-102.

16. DeNovo, *American Interests and Policies in the Middle East*, pp. 210-228.

17. *Ibid.*, pp. 297-302, and Bryson, *American Diplomatic Relations with the Middle East*, pp. 88-89.

18. DeNovo, *American Interests and Policies in the Middle East*, p. 346, and Bryson, *American Diplomatic Relations with the Middle East*, pp. 90-92.

19. Phillip J. Baram, *The Department of State in the Middle East, 1919-1945* (Philadelphia, 1978), p. 52.

20. DeNovo, *American Interests and Policies in the Middle East*, p. 393.

CHAPTER 2

1. United States Department of State, *Foreign Relations of the United States: The Conferences at Washington, 1941-1942, and Casablanca, 1943* (Washington, 1968), pp. 21-26 (hereinafter cited as FRUSCon Washington & Casablanca); see also Winston S. Churchill, *The Grand Alliance* (Boston, 1950), pp. 644-651.

2. FRUSCon Washington & Casablanca, p. 64, and Churchill, *The Grand Alliance*, pp. 663-64.

3. Churchill, *The Grand Alliance*, pp. 664-665.

4. FRUSCon Washington & Casablanca, pp. 71-72, and Forrest C. Pogue, *George C. Marshall: Ordeal and Hope* (New York, 1967), pp. 267-268.

5. FRUSCon Washington & Casablanca, pp. 162-164.

6. *Ibid.*, pp. 185-186.

7. Churchill, *The Grand Alliance*, pp. 704-705, and James MacGregor Burns, *Roosevelt: The Soldier of Freedom*, 1940-1945 (New York, 1970), p. 180.

8. Herbert Feis, *Churchill, Roosevelt, Stalin: The War They Waged and the Peace They Sought* (Princeton, 1967), pp. 37-40, and Gaddis Smith, *American Diplomacy during the Second World War, 1941-1945* (New York, 1966), pp. 22-24; for a good explanation of the reasons behind the Europe First policy, see Dwight D. Eisenhower, *Crusade in Europe* (New York, 1948), pp. 27-28.

9. Pogue, *Ordeal and Hope*, p. 306, and Smith, *American Diplomacy During the Second World War*, p. 25.

10. William Hardy McNeill, *America, Britain, and Russia: Their Cooperation and Conflict, 1941-1946* (New York, 1970 ed), p. 192, Pogue, *Ordeal and Hope*, p. 306, Burns, *Roosevelt*, p. 230, and Eisenhower, *Crusade in Europe*, p. 47.

11. Pogue, *Ordeal and Hope*, pp. 314-316, and Arthur Bryant, *The Turn of the Tide: A History of the War Years Based on the Diaries of Field-Marshal Lord Alanbrooke* (New York, 1957), p. 285.

12. Pogue, *Ordeal and Hope*, pp. 307-318, McNeill, *America, Britain, and Russia*, pp. 174-175, Feis, *Churchill, Roosevelt, and Stalin*, pp. 41-42, Burns, *Roosevelt*, p. 231, Winston S. Churchill, *The Hinge of Fate* (Boston, 1950), pp. 314-320, and Sherwood, *Roosevelt and Hopkins*, pp. 521-535; see also Bryant, *The Turn of the Tide*, p. 286.

13. Pogue, *Ordeal and Hope*, p. 319, McNeill, *America, Britain, and Russia*, pp. 174, 1975 and Burns, *Roosevelt*, p. 231.

14. Churchill, *The Hinge of Fate*, pp. 332-338.

15. *Ibid.*, pp. 346, 353, 355-356, Pogue, *Ordeal and Hope*, pp. 326-328, and McNeill, *American, Britain, and Russia*, pp. 178-179.

16. FRUSCon Washington & Casablanca, pp. 422-435, Pogue, *Ordeal and Hope*, pp. 329-333, and Bryant, *The Turn of the Tide*, pp. 326-327.

17. Churchill, *The Hinge of Fate*, pp. 382-383, and Bryant, *The Turn of the Tide*, p. 329.

18. Pogue, *Ordeal and Hope*, p. 334.

19. *Ibid.*, pp. 337-341, and Churchill, *The Hinge of Fate*, p. 434.

20. Churchill, *The Hinge of Fate*, p. 433, and Pogue, *Ordeal and Hope*, pp. 337-341.

21. Sherwood, *Roosevelt and Hopkins*, pp. 603-605.

22. *Ibid.*, pp. 609-610, Churchill, *The Hinge of Fate*, pp. 445-446, Pogue, *Ordeal and Hope*, pp. 344-345, and Bryant, *The Turn of the Tide*, pp. 342-343.

23. Pogue, *Ordeal and Hope*, pp. 345-347, Churchill, *The Hinge of Fate*, p. 447, Sherwood, *Roosevelt and Hopkins*, pp. 609-612, Feis, *Churchill, Roosevelt, and Stalin*, pp. 42-44, and McNeill, *America, Britain, and Russia*, p. 196.

24. McNeill, *America, Britain, and Russia*, p. 197, Churchill, *The Hinge of Fate*, pp. 449-450, and Eisenhower, *Crusade in Europe*, p. 71.

25. Pogue, *Ordeal and Hope*, pp. 348-349, and Burns, *Roosevelt*, pp. 287-290.

26. Robert Murphy, *Diplomat Among Warriors* (New York, 1964), p. 101.

27. Arthur Layton Funk, *Torch: The Allied Landings and the Algiers Putsch, 1942* (Lawrence, Kansas, 1974), p. 30.

28. With respect to the American Vichy policy see Paul Farmer, *Vichy: Political Dilemma* (New York, 1955), W.L. Langer, *Our Vichy Gamble* (New York, 1947), Louis Gottschalk, "Our Vichy Fumble," *Journal of Modern History*, 26 (1948), 47-56, Ellen Hammer, "Hindsight on Vichy," *Political Science Quarterly*, 61 (1948), 175-188, and Admiral W.D. Leahy, *I Was There* (New York, 1950).

29. Murphy, *Diplomat*, p. 81, Luella J. Hall, *The United States and Morocco, 1776-1956* (Metuchen, N.J., 1971), p. 893, and Langer, *Our Vichy Gamble*, pp. 107-108.

30. Funk, *Torch*, p. 9.

31. Murphy, *Diplomat*, pp. 71-81, and Langer, *Our Vichy Gamble*, p. 135.

32. Leon Borden Blair, "Amateurs in Diplomacy: The American Vice Consuls in North Africa, 1941-1943," *Historian*, 25 (August 1973), 607-620, Murphy, *Diplomat*, pp. 89-91, and Langer, *Our Vichy Gamble*, p. 140.

33. Blair, "Amateurs in Diplomacy," 610-611, Hall, *United States and Morocco*, p. 899, Kenneth W. Pendar, *Adventures in Diplomacy: Our French Dilemma* (New York, 1966 ed.), pp. 4, 16, 43, and 76, and Langer, *Our Vichy Gamble*, pp. 228-229.

34. Murphy, *Diplomat*, pp. 101-104.

35. *Ibid.*, pp. 106-107.

36. Pendar, *Adventures in Diplomacy*, p. 430. The reader will also wish to consult J. Rives Childs, *Foreign Service Farewell: My Years in the Near East* (Charlottesville, Va., 1969), pp. 114-16, for an account of the American chargé at Tangier.

37. Pendar, *Adventures in Diplomacy*, p. 76.

38. Murphy, *Diplomat*, pp. 109-112, and Hall, *United States and Morocco*, p. 903.

39. Funk, *Torch*, pp. 35-36.

40. Murphy, *Diplomat*, pp. 113-119.

41. *Ibid.*, pp. 118-120, Mark W. Clark, *Calculated Risk* (New York, 1950), pp. 68-877, and Hall, *United States and Morocco*, pp. 914-915.

42. Murphy, *Diplomat*, p. 121.

43. *Ibid.*, p. 122.

44. *Ibid.*, p. 124.

45. Clark, *Calculated Risk*, pp. 95-102.

46. Murphy, *Diplomat*, pp. 125-132.

47. *Ibid.*, pp. 132-133.

48. For the best account of the TORCH landings, see Samuel E. Morison, *Operations in North African Waters, October 1942-June 1943* (Boston, 1947); see also the fourth chapter of Bryson, *Tars, Turks, and Tankers.*

49. Murphy, *Diplomat*, pp. 135-138.

50. *Ibid.*, pp. 138-141, Clark, *Calculated Risk*, pp. 111-112, and Hall, *United States and Morocco*, pp. 921-923.

51. Murphy, *Diplomat*, pp. 142-143, and Clark, *Calculated Risk*, pp. 122-125, 130.

52. Eisenhower, *Crusade in Europe*, pp. 108, 109-110.

53. Murphy, *Diplomat*, p. 145, and United States Department of State, *Foreign Relations of the United States*, 1943, II, 23-24.

54. Murphy, *Diplomat*, pp. 145-146.

55. *Ibid.*, pp. 151-152.

56. *Ibid.*, pp. 162, 167; also see Forrest C. Pogue, *George C. Marshall: Organizer of Victory* New York, 1973), p. 10.

57. Murphy, *Diplomat*, p. 163, and Burns, *Roosevelt*, p. 315.

58. FRUSCon Washington & Casablanca, pp. 521-522.

59. Murphy, *Diplomat*, p. 165.

60. Churchill, *Hinge of Fate*, p. 676. On Marshall's views, see Pogue, *Organizer of Victory*, p. 15; also see McNeill, *America, Britain, and Russia*, pp. 264-265.

61. FRUSCon Washington & Casablanca, pp. 509, 512.

62. For example, see Marshall's statement on January 14 to the assembled Combined Chiefs: *Ibid.*, p. 545.

63. *Ibid.*, pp. 538-540, 570.

64. Burns, *Roosevelt*, pp. 317-318, and Pogue, *Organizer of Victory*, pp. 21-28; see also McNeill, *America, Britain, and Russia*, p. 263, on the differences of opinion held by the American chiefs.

65. FRUSCon Washington & Casablanca, pp. 760-761.

66. Pogue, *Organizer of Victory*, p. 30, and FRUSCon Washington & Casablanca, p. 628.

67. FRUSCon Washington & Casablanca, pp. 707-719, Sherwood, *Roosevelt and Hopkins*, pp. 690-691, and Churchill, *Hinge of Fate*, p. 692.

68. Burns, *Roosevelt*, p. 319.

69. McNeill, *America, Britain, and Russia*, p. 267, Feis, *Churchill, Roosevelt, and Stalin*, pp. 107-108, Pogue, *Organizer of Victory*, p. 31 and Sherwood, *Roosevelt and Hopkins*, p. 675.

70. McNeill, *America, Britain, and Russia*, pp. 269-272.

71. Burns, *Roosevelt*, p. 321, and Sherwood, *Roosevelt and Hopkins*, p. 680.

72. Murphy, *Diplomat*, pp. 169-181.

73. Sherwood, *Roosevelt and Hopkins*, p. 694.

74. Cordell Hull, *The Memoirs of Cordell Hull* (2 vols, New York, 1948), II, 1512.

CHAPTER 3

1. Hull, *Memoirs*, II, 1499, 1511, 1512.

2. Bryson, *American Diplomatic Relations with the Middle East*, pp. 107-108, and Joseph William Walt, "Saudi Arabia and the Americans, 1928-1951," Ph.D. dissertation, Northwestern University, 1960.

3. Hull, *Memoirs*, II, 1512, and United States Department of State, *Foreign Relations of the United States* (hereinafter cited as FRUS), 1942, IV, 559-585.

4. Walt, "Saudi Arabia and the Americans," pp. 184-197.

5. FRUS, 1942, IV, 559-561.

6. *Ibid.*, 830-832.

7. Walt, "Saudi Arabia and the Americans," pp. 295-296.

8. FRUS, 1942, IV, 561-566.

9. *Ibid.*, 566-567, and Walt, "Saudi Arabia and the Americans," pp. 284-285.

10. FRUS, 1942, IV, 566, and Walt, "Saudi Arabia and the Americans," p. 287.

11. Walt, "Saudi Arabia and the Americans," p. 288.

12. FRUS, 1942, IV, 576-585.

13. Walt, "Saudi Arabia and the Americans," pp. 151-177, Baram, *The Department of State in the Middle East*, pp. 210-211, Benjamin Shwadran, *The Middle East, Oil, and the Great Powers* (New York, 1955), pp. 303-306, George W. Stocking, *Middle East Oil* (Nashville, 1970), pp. 89-96, and Robert W. Stookey, *America and the Arab States* (New York, 1975), p. 69.

14. Shwadran, *The Middle East, Oil, and the Great Powers*, pp. 309-09.

15. FRUS, 1943, IV, 854-855.

16. *Ibid.*, 855.

17. Irvine H. Anderson, "Lend-Lease for Saudi Arabia: A Comment on Alternative Conceptualizations," *Diplomatic History*, 3 (fall 1979), 413-423; see Roosevelt to Stettinius, 18 Feb. 1943, FRUS, 1943, IV, 859.

18. FRSU, 1943, IV, 861-867.

19. Walt, "Saudi Arabia and the Americans," pp. 221, 226-227.

20. *Ibid.*, pp. 289-292.

21. FRUS, 1943, IV, 906-911.

22. Walt, "Saudi Arabia and the Americans," pp. 291-297.

23. FRUS, 1943, IV, 886-903, and Walt, "Saudi Arabia and the Americans," pp. 222-228.

24. Shwadran, *The Middle East, Oil, and the Great Powers*, pp. 310-311, and Stocking, *Middle East Oil*, p. 98.

25. Herbert Feis, *Petroleum and American Foreign Policy* (Stanford, Calif., 1944), pp. 14-18.

26. FRUS, 1943, IV, 925-930, and Shwadran, *The Middle East, Oil and the Great Powers*, p. 312.

27. FRUS, 1943, IV, 930-931, and Shwadran, *The Middle East, Oil, and the Great Powers*, p. 314.

28. Gerald D. Nash, *United States Oil Policy, 1890-1964* (Pittsburgh, 1968), pp. 171-172, and Shwadran, *The Middle East, Oil, and the Great Powers*, p. 314.

29. Nash, *United States Oil Policy*, p. 1973, Shwadran, *The Middle East, Oil, and the Great Powers*, pp. 314-315, Stocking, *Middle East Oil*, pp. 98-99, and Shoshana Klebanoff, *Middle East Oil and U.S. Foreign Policy* (New York, 1974), p. 23.

30. Baram, *The Department of State in the Middle East*, pp. 214-215, Shwadran, *The Middle East, Oil, and the Great Powers*, pp. 319-320, Stocking, *Middle East Oil*, p. 100, and Nash, *United States Oil Policy*, p. 174.

31. Shwadran, *The Middle East, Oil, and the Great Powers*, pp. 320-21, and FRUS, 1944, V, pp. 24-25.

32. Bryson, *American Diplomatic Relations with the Middle East*, p. 125,

Hull, *Memoirs*, II, 1534, FRUS, 1944, V, 563-564, Evan M. Wilson, "The Palestine Papers, 1943-1947," *Journal of Palestine Studies*, 2 (summer 1973), 41; and Richard P. Stevens, *American Zionism and United States Foreign Policy* (New York, 1962), p. 80.

33. Shwadran, *The Middle East, Oil and the Great Powers*, pp. 322-331, Nash, *United States Oil Policy*, p. 174, Stocking, *Middle East Oil*, p. 101, and Klebanoff, *Middle East Oil and U.S. Foreign Policy*, pp. 25-29.

34. Baram, *The Department of State in the Middle East*, p. 217.

35. Shwadran, *The Middle East, Oil, and the Great Powers, p. 331, and* Stocking, *Middle East Oil*, pp. 101-102.

36. Shwadran, *The Middle East, Oil, and the Great Powers*, pp. 332-334, and Stocking, *Middle East Oil*, pp. 101-102.

37. Shwadran, *The Middle East, Oil, and the Great Powers*, pp. 335-336, and Stocking, *Middle East Oil*, pp. 102-103.

38. Stocking, *Middle East Oil*, pp. 105-107.

39. Shwadran, *The Middle East, Oil, and the Great Powers*, p. 337.

40. FRUS, 1943, IV, 943-944, and Hull, *Memoirs*, II, 1513-1514.

41. FRUS, 1943, IV, 679, and Hull, *Memoirs*, II, 1514.

42. FRUS, 1943, IV, 691, 703, 710, and Hull, *Memoirs*, II, 1514-1516.

43. FRUS, 1943, IV, 947, 948, Baram, *The Department of State in the Middle East*, p. 229, and Hull, *Memoirs*, II, 1521.

44. Nash, *United States Oil Policy*, p. 176, and Klebanoff, *Middle East Oil and U.S. Foreign Policy*, p. 43.

45. Raymond F. Mikesell, and Hollis B. Chenery, *Arabian Oil: America's Stake in the Middle East* (Chapel, N.C. 1949), pp. 96-100, Hull, *Memoirs*, II, 1525, Nash, *United States Oil Policy*, p. 177, and Klebanoff, *Middle East Oil and U.S. Foreign Policy*, p. 44.

46. Nash, *United States Oil Policy*, p. 178, and Mikesell and Chenery, *America's Stake in the Middle East*, p. 96.

47. See Bryson, *American Diplomatic Relations with the Middle East*, pp. 125-127, and William A. Eddy, *F.D.R. Meets Ibn Saud* (New York, 1954), pp. 34-36.

Chapter 4

1. DeNovo, *American Interests and Policies in the Middle East*, pp. 54-55 and 282-283.

2. Hull, *Memoirs*, II, 1599; a good work on this period is Richard Anthony Pfau, "The United States and Iran, 1941-1947: Origins of Partnership," Ph.D. dissertation, University of Virginia, 1975.

3. Michael Kahl Sheehan, *Iran: The Impact of United States Interests and Policies, 1941-1954* (New York, 1968), p. 6.

4. T.H. Vail Motter, *The Persian Corridor and Aid to Russia* (Washington, DC, 1952), p. 6.

5. *Ibid.*, pp. 7, 88-91, 213, 241-242, 264, 282, 308, 316, 328, 331-377, 381.

6. FRUS, 1942, IV, 311-312.

7. *Ibid.*, 314.

8. *Ibid.*, 315.

9. Motter, *The Persian Corridor and Aid to Russia*, pp. 331-378.

10. *Ibid.*, pp. 99-123, 183, 188.

11. *Ibid.*, pp. 316-329.

12. *Ibid.*, p. 139.

13. *Ibid.*, pp. 125-138.

14. FRUS, 1943, IV, 377-379.

15. FRUS, 1942, IV, 120-121.

16. *Ibid.*, 121-122.

17. *Ibid.*, 126-127. Motter asserts that the shortage was in large measure due to intense hoarding by Iranians and by seizure of grain by the Soviets in their zone of occupation: Motter, *The Persian Corridor and Aid to Russia*, p. 452.

18. United States Department of State, *Foreign Relations of the United States* (hereinafter cited as FRUS), 1942, IV, 158-164. During the ensuing year the U.S. and Britain imported 30,000 tons of wheat and 24,000 tons of barley to aid the Iranians: Motter, *The Persian Corridor and Aid to Russia*, pp. 452-453.

19. FRUS, 1942, IV, 140-141.

20. *Ibid.*, 289.

21. *Ibid.*, 208-209, and Motter, *The Persian Corridor and Aid to Russia*, pp. 455-456.

22. *Ibid.*, pp. 458-459.

23. Rouhollah K. Ramazani, *Iran's Foreign Policy, 1941-1973* (Charlottesville, VA., 1975), pp. 86-87.

24. FRUS, 1942, IV, 276-277.

25. Ramazani, *Iran's Foreign Policy*, pp. 89-90.

26. *Ibid.*, p. 72.

27. FRUS, 1942, IV, 223, 247; see Pfau, "United States and Iran," p. 48.

28. FRUS, 1942, IV, 215-232.

29. *Ibid.*, 232-233, Motter, *The Persian Corridor and Aid to Russia*, p. 163, and Ramazani, *Iran's Foreign Policy*, p. 2.

30. FRUS, 1942, IV, 248, 260.

31. Ramazani, *Iran's Foreign Policy*, p. 73.

32. *Ibid.*, pp. 73, 74, Sheehan, *Iran*, p. 18 and George Lenczowski, *Russia and the West in Iran, 1918-1948* (Ithaca, N.Y., 1949), p. 272.

33. Bryson, *American Diplomatic Relations with the Middle East*, p. 138.

34. FRUS, 1942, IV, 235, 241; see also Pfau, "United States and Iran," pp. 81-84, for General Greely's performance of his job.

35. FRUS, 1942, IV, 252, and Ramazani, *Iran's Foreign Policy*, pp. 74-75.

36. Ramazani, *Iran's Foreign Policy*, p. 75.

37. Sheehan, *Iran*, p. 18.

38. Ramazani, *Iran's Foreign Policy*, pp. 75-76.

39. J.C. Hurewitz, *Middle East Dilemmas: The Background of United States Policy* (New York, 1953), p. 29.

40. FRUS, 1942, IV, 238; for more on Millspaugh's mission, see Arthur C. Millspaugh, *Americans in Persia* (Washington, D.C., 1946), and Hassan Mojedhi, "Arthur C. Millspaugh's Two Missions to Iran and Their Impact on American-Iranian Relations," Ph.D. dissertation, Ball State Univesity, 1975.

41. FRUS, 1942, IV, 244.

42. *Ibid.*, 253, 262, and Ramazani, *Iran's Foreign Policy*, pp. 77, 78.

43. Millspaugh, *Americans in Persia*, pp. 47, 61.

44. *Ibid.*, pp. 129-132.

45. *Ibid.*, p. 137.

46. *Ibid.*, pp. 137-184.

47. Ramazani, *Iran's Foreign Policy*, pp. 78-85, and FRUS, 1943, IV, 538-539.

48. Millspaugh, *Americans in Persia*, p. 224.

49. FRUS, 1943, IV, 532-548, and Lenczowski, *Russia and the West in Iran*, p. 270.

50. FRUS, 1942, IV, 264-265, and Motter, *The Persian Corridor and Aid to Russia*, p. 437.

51. FRUS, 1942, IV, 267, 268.

52. Motter, *The Persian Corridor and Aid to Russia*, p. 442.

53. FRUS, 1942, IV, 274-275.

54. Motter, *The Persian Corridor and Aid to Russia*," p. 442, and Sheehan, *Iran*, p. 31.

55. FRUS, 1943, IV, 334-335; also see Pfau, "United States and Iran," pp. 107-140 on the formulation of U.S. policy in wartime Iran.

56. FRUS, 1943, IV, 377-378.

57. *Ibid.*, 413, 414.

58. Lenczowski, *Russia and the West in Iran*, p. 280.

59. Lewis V. Thomas and Richard N. Frye, *The United States and Turkey and Iran* (Cambridge, Mass., 1951), p. 231.

60. Motter, *The Persian Corridor and Aid to Russia*, p. 445.

61. FRUS, 1943, IV, 363-370.

62. *Ibid.*, 419-426.

63. Hull, *Memoirs*, II, 1507, and Don Lohbeck, *Patrick J. Hurley* (Chicago, 1956), p. 225.

64. Lohbeck, *Patrick J. Hurley*, p. 226.

65. FRUS, 1944, V, 343-344, and Hull, *Memoirs*, II, 1506-1507, T.H. Motter asserts that Hurley's influence was important in shaping President Roosevelt's thinking on Iran: Motter, *The Persian Corridor and Aid to Russia*, pp. 442-443. But Russell Buhite contradicts this view, commenting that Hurley was a mere gadfly, with little influence on the President concerning the Middle East: Buhite, *Patrick Hurley and American Foreign Policy* (Ithaca, N.Y., 1973), pp. 314-315.

66. Hull, *Memoirs*, II, 1508.

67. *Ibid.*, p. 1508, Ramazani, *Iran's Foreign Policy*, p. 97, and FRUS, 1943, IV, 625-626.

68. Ramazani, *Iran's Foreign Policy*, p. 97.

69. Eduard M. Mark, "Allied Relations in Iran, 1941-1947: The Origins of a Cold War Crisis," *Wisconsin Magazine of History*, 59 (autumn 1975), 55.

70. *Ibid.*, 56.

71. FRUS, 1944, V, 452.

72. *Ibid.*, 452-253; also see Richard A. Pfau, "Avoiding the Cold War: The United States and the Iranian Oil Crisis, 1944," *Essays in History*, 18 (1974), 106.

73. Pfau, "Avoiding the Cold War," 106, and FRUS, 1944, V, 453-454.

74. FRUS, 1933, V, 455.

75. *Ibid.*, 456-457.

76. *Ibid.*, 457-461, Pfau, "Avoiding the Cold War," 107-109, and Ramazani, *Iran's Foreign Policy*, pp. 99-100.

77. FRUS, 1944, V, 462-463.

78. Pfau, "Avoiding the Cold War," 111.

79. Ramazani, *Iran's Foreign Policy*, pp. 107-108.

80. Mark, "Allied Relations in Iran," 59-62.

81. George E. Kirk, *The Middle East in the War, 1939-1946* (London, 1952), pp. 24, 367-369, 474, and Joyce Kolko and Gabriel Kolko, *The Limits of Power: The World and United States Foreign Policy, 1945-1954* (New York, 1972), p. 236.

82. Gabriel Kolko, *The Politics of War: The World and United States Foreign Policy, 1943-1945* (New York, 1968), pp. 297, 310, 495.

83. Hull, *Memoirs*, II, 1501, 1504-1509.

84. Millspaugh, *Americans in Persia*, pp. 8, 47, 233, 208-209; 230-231.
85. Lenczowski, *Russia and the West in Iran*, pp. 279, 283.

CHAPTER 5

1. Hull, *Memoirs*, II, 1528, Bryson, *American Diplomatic Relations with the Middle East*, pp. 90-91, Richard P. Stevens, *American Zionism and United States Foreign Policy* (New York, 1962), pp. 62-64, Frank E. Manuel, *The Realities of American-Palestine Relations* (Washington, D.C., 1949), p. 290, DeNovo, *American Interests and Policies in the Middle East*, p. 339, and FRUS, 1924, II, 203-222.
2. Manuel, *The Realities of American-Palestine Relations*, p. 310-311, and Samuel Halperin, *The Political World of American Zionism* (Detroit, 1961), pp. 12, 17.
3. Phillip J. Baram, *The Department of State in the Middle East, 1914-1945* (Philadelphia, 1978), pp. 251-254, DeNovo, *American Interests and Policies in the Middle East*, pp. 342-344, and Manuel, *The Realities of American-Palestine Relations*, pp. 305-307.
4. Hull, *Memoirs*, II, 1928.
5. Bryson, *American Diplomatic Relations with the Middle East*, p. 124.
6. Stevens, *American Zionism and United States Foreign Policy*, p. 3; Manuel, *The Realities of American-Palestine Relations*, p. 310, and Halperin, *The Political World of American Zionism*, p. 126.
7. Stevens, *American Zionism and United States Foreign Policy*, pp. 6-13, and Halperin, *The Political World of American Zionism*, pp. 129-133.
8. Stevens, *American Zionism and United States Foreign Policy*, pp. 17-32.
9. *Ibid.*, pp. 33-34.
10. Evan M. Wilson, "The Palestine Papers, 1943-1947," *Journal of Palestine Studies*, 2 (summer 1973), 37.
11. United States Department of State, *Foreign Relations of the United States* (hereinafter cited as FRUS), 1943, IV, 747-751, 781-785.
12. *Ibid.*, 776-780.
13. *Ibid.*, 805-806, and Hull, *Memoirs*, II, 1531-1532.
14. Hull, *Memoirs*, II, 1953, and FRUS, 1943, IV, 751-753, 755.
15. FRUS, 1943, IV, 773-775.
16. *Ibid.*, 786-787.
17. Wilson, "The Palestine Papers," 38, and Hull, *Memoirs*, p. 1532.
18. FRUS, 1943, IV, 790-792.
19. FRUS, 1945, III, 699, Hull, *Memoirs*, II, 1533, and Wilson, "The Palestine Papers," 39.
20. Baram, *The Department of State in the Middle East*, p. 282, Wilson, "The Palestine Papers," 39-40, Hull, *Memoirs*, II, 1534, Stevens, *American Zionism and United States Foreign Policy*, p. 79; and FRUS, 1943, IV, 823-824.
21. FRUS, 1944, V, 600-603.
22. FRUS, 1943, IV, 795, Hull, *Memoirs*, II, 1532-1533, and Stevens, *American Zionism and United States Foreign Policy*, pp. 74-75.
23. FRUS, 1943, IV, 807-810.
24. *Ibid.*, 811-814.
25. *Ibid.*, 816-821.
26. *Ibid.*, 822.
27. Hull, *Memoirs*, II, 1934.

28. Stevens, *American Zionism and United States Foreign Policy*, pp. 37-39, Manuel, *The Realities of American-Palestine Relations*, p. 311, Herbert Feis, *Birth of Israel: The Tousled Diplomatic Bed* (New York, 1969), p. 15, and FRUS, 1944, V, 560-561.

29. FRUS, 1944, V, 564.

30. *Ibid.*, 565, 568.

31. *Ibid.*, 570.

32. *Ibid.*, 563.

33. *Ibid.*, 563-564.

34. *Ibid.*, 577, 582, 583.

35. *Ibid.*, 567.

36. *Ibid.*, 574-576.

37. *Ibid.*, 581-582, and Hull, *Memoirs*, II, 1535-1536.

38. FRUS, 1944, V, 591.

39. *Ibid.*, 586-587.

40. Baram, *The Department of State in the Middle East*, p. 293

41. FRUS, 1944, V, 591, 596, 597.

42. Manuel, *The Realities of American-Palestine Relations*, p. 312, Hull, *Memoirs*, p. 1536, and Stevens, *American Zionism and United States Foreign Policy*, pp. 53-54.

43. FRUS, 1944, V, 590-591, Wilson, "The Palestine Papers," 42 and Hull, *Memoirs*, II, 1536.

44. Stevens, *American Zionism and United States Foreign Policy*, pp. 54-55.

45. *Ibid.*, p. 57.

46. FRUS, 1944, V, 606-609.

47. Hull, *Memoirs*, II, 1937.

48. FRUS, 1944, V, 615, and Stevens, *American Zionism and United States Foreign Policy*, pp. 83-84.

49. FRUS, 1944, V, 616, 619, 621, 622.

50. *Ibid.*, 622-626.

51. *Ibid.*, 631-633.

52. *Ibid.*, 637, Stevens, *American Zionism and United States Foreign Policy*, p. 59, and Manuel, *The Realities of American-Palestine Relations*, p. 313.

53. FRUS, 1944, V, 638.

54. *Ibid.*, 640-642.

55. *Ibid.*, 643-644.

56. *Ibid.*, 645-646.

57. Baram, *The Department of State in the Middle East*, p. 315.

58. *Ibid.*, p. 295, Manuel, *The Realities of American-Palestine Relations*, p. 313, and FRUS, 1944, V, 652.

59. FRUS, 1944, V, 648-649.

60. *Ibid.*, 655-657.

61. Wilson, "The Palestine Papers," 43.

62. FRUS, 1945, VIII, 681-682.

63. William A. Eddy, *FDR Meets Ibn Saud* (New York, 1954), pp. 29-30.

64. *Ibid*, pp. 33-37, and FRUS, 1945, VIII, 2-3.

65. Stevens, *American Zionism and United States Foreign Policy*, p. 90.

66. FRUS, 1945, VIII, 690-691.

67. Stevens, *American Zionism and United States Foreign Policy*, p. 91.

68. FRUS, 1945, VIII, 693.

69. *Ibid.*, 693-694.

70. *Ibid.*, 695.

71. *Ibid.*, 697.

72. *Ibid.*, 692-707.

73. Wilson, "The Palestine Papers," 44.

74. FRUS, 1945, VIII, 707-709, and Baram, *The Department of State in the Middle East*, p. 296.

75. FRUS, 1945, VIII, 705-706.

76. Stevens, *American Zionism and United States Foreign Policy*, p. 125.

77. FRUS, 1945, VIII, 704-705, and John Snetsinger, *Truman, the Jewish Vote and the Creation of Israel* (Stanford, Calif., 1974), p. 16.

78. Wilson, "The Palestine Papers," 45-46, and Harry S Truman, *Memoirs: Years of Trial and Hope* (New York, 1955), II, 132-135.

79. FRUS, 1945, VIII, 705-707, 709, Stevens, *American Zionism and United States Foreign Policy*, p. 130, and Walter Millis and E.S. Duffield, eds., *The Forrestal Diaries* (New York, 1951), pp. 188-189.

80. Wilson, "The Palestine Papers," 46 and FRUS, 1945, VIII, 717.

81. FRUS, 1945, VIII, 716-717.

82. *Ibid.*, 719, and Truman, *Memoirs*, II, 136.

83. FRUS, 1945, VIII, 737-739.

84. William B. Quandt, "United States Policy in the Middle East: Constraints and Choices," in Paul Y. Hammond and Sidney S. Alexander, eds., *Political Dynamics in the Middle East* (New York, 1972), p. 497.

85. Stevens, *American Zionism and United States Foreign Policy*, p. 137, Millis and Duffield, eds., *The Forrestal Diaries*, p. 323, and George F. Kennan, *Memoirs, 1925-1950* (Boston, 1967) I, 380.

86. Hull, *Memoirs*, II, 1530-1534; 1536-1537.

87. Sumner Welles, *Where Are We Heading?* (New York, 1946), pp. 264-265.

88. Howard M. Sachar, *Europe Leaves the Middle East, 1936-1954* (New York, 1972), pp. 453-454.

89. Smith, *American Diplomacy During the Second World War*, pp. 113-114, Burns, *Roosevelt*, p. 397, and John C. Campbell, "American Efforts for Peace," in Malcolm H. Kerr, ed., *The Elusive Peace in the Middle East* (Albany, N.Y., 1975), p. 252.

90. Truman, *Memoirs*, II, 132, and Merle Miller, *Plain Speaking: An Oral Biography of Harry S. Truman* (New York, 1974), p. 214.

CHAPTER 6

1. DeNovo, *American Interests and Policies in the Middle East*, pp. 322-337.

2. United States Department of State, *Foreign Relations of the United States* (hereinafter cited as FRUS), 1942, IV, 647-48, Hull, *Memoirs*, II, 1540-1541, Kirk, *The Middle East in the War*, p. 121, Baram, *The Department of State in the Middle East*, p. 130, and Sachar, *Europe Leaves the Middle East*, 282-283.

3. Baram, *The Department of State in the Middle East*, p. 130.

4. FRUS, 1942, IV, 586-587.

5. *Ibid.*, 588-589.

6. *Ibid.*, 591, and Hull, *Memoirs*, II, 19542.

7. FRUS, 1942, IV, 594-595.

8. *Ibid.*, 606.

9. *Ibid.*, 606.

10. *Ibid.*, 606-607.

11. *Ibid.*, 613.

11. *Ibid.*, 613.
12. *Ibid.*, 619, and Hull, *Memoirs*, II, 1542.
13. FRUS, 1942, IV, 623, 626.
14. *Ibid.*, 619-620, and Hull, *Memoirs*, II, 1542.
15. Hull, *Memoirs*, II, 1542-1543.
16. FRUS, 1942, IV, 636-637.
17. *Ibid.*, 617, 644.
18. Baram, *The Department of State in the Middle East*, pp. 132-133.
19. Hull, *Memoirs*, II, 1543, and FRUS, 1942, IV, 641-664.
20. FRUS, 1942, IV, 669, Hull, *Memoirs*, II, 1543, and Sachar, *Europe Leaves the Middle East*, p. 295.
21. FRUS, 1943, IV, 956.
22. *Ibid.*, 960-961.
23. *Ibid.*, 963-964.
24. *Ibid.*, 971.
25. *Ibid.*, 974, 975, 976.
26. *Ibid.*, 978, 980, 982.
27. *Ibid.*, 987.
28. *Ibid.*, 987-988.
29. *Ibid.*, 993.
30. *Ibid.*, 994-995.
31. Hull, *Memoirs*, II, 1544.
32. FRUS, 1943, IV, 1001-1007.
33. *Ibid.*, 1011, and Hull, *Memoirs*, II, 1544.
34. FRUS, 1943, IV, 1013-1019, and Sachar, *Europe Leaves the Middle East*, pp. 305-307.
35. FRUS, 1943, IV, 1022, and Hull, *Memoirs*, II, 1944.
36. FRUS, 1943, IV, 1023, and Hull, *Memoirs*, I, 1545.
37. FRUS, 1943, IV, 1037.
38. Kirk, *The Middle East in the War*, pp. 282-283.
39. FRUS, 1943, IV, 1040-1041.
40. *Ibid.*, 1045.
41. *Ibid.*, 1045-1046.
42. *Ibid.*, 1049, and Hull, *Memoirs*, II, 1545.
43. FRUS, 1943, IV, 1055.
44. FRUS, 1944, V, 774-775.
45. *Ibid.*, 775.
46. *Ibid.*, 779, 786.
47. *Ibid.*, 791-795.
48. Sachar, *Europe Leaves the Middle East*, p. 313.
49. FRUS, 1944, V, 795-796.
50. *Ibid.*, 799-800.
51. *Ibid.*, 801-802.
52. *Ibid.*, 810.
53. *Ibid.*, 812-813.
54. FRUS, 1945, VIII, 1034-1935.
55. *Ibid.*, 1042-1043.
56. *Ibid.*, 1044-1045.
57. *Ibid.*, 1046, 1047.
58. *Ibid.*, 1049-11051. The force consisted of some 18,000 Druze and Circassian troops under French control.
59. *Ibid.*, 1051.
60. *Ibid.*, 1052.

61. *Ibid.*, 1056-1058.
63. *Ibid.*, 1060-1061.
64. Sachar, *Europe Leaves the Middle East*, pp. 314-315.
65. FRUS, 1945, VIII, 1075-1078.
66. *Ibid.*, 1080, and Sachar, *Europe Leaves the Middle East*, p. 318.
67. FRUS, 1945, VIII, 1085.
68. Sachar, *Europe Leaves the Middle East*, p. 318.
69. Winston S. Churchill, *Triumph and Tragedy* (Boston, 1953), p. 563.
70. FRUS, 1945, VIII, 1085-1086.
71. *Ibid.*, 1092.
72. *Ibid.*, 1095.
73. *Ibid.*, 1098.
74. *Ibid.*, 1103-1104.
75. *Ibid.*, 1109.
76. *Ibid.*, 1113.
77. *Ibid.*, 1116, 1117.
78. *Ibid.*, 1118-1121.
79. *Ibid*, 1121.
80. *Ibid.*, 1121-1122.
81. *Ibid.*, 1124, and Sachar, *Europe Leaves the Middle East*, p. 320.
82. FRUS, 1945, VIII, 1125, and Kirk, *The Middle East in the War*, p. 297.
83. FRUS, 1945, VIII, 1130, 1131-1132.
84. *Ibid.*, 1134, 1135, 1136.
85. *Ibid.*, 1140-1141, Sachar, *Europe Leaves the Middle East*, p. 324, and Joseph C. Grew, *Turbulent Era: The Diplomatic Record of Forty Years, 1904-1945* (London, 1953), pp. 1516-1519.
86. FRUS, 1945, VIII, 1141-1142.
87. *Ibid.*, 1151-1152.
88. *Ibid.*, 1152-1154.
89. *Ibid.*, 1154-1155, Sachar, *Europe Leaves the Middle East*, p. 327, and Kirk, *The Middle East in the War*, p. 303.
90. FRUS, 1945, VIII, 1176, 1183, and Sachar, *Europe Leaves the Middle East*, p. 327.

CHAPTER 7

1. Hull, *Memoirs*, II, 1201, and Kirk, *The Middle East in the War*, pp. 405-442.
2. United States Department of State, *Foreign Relations of the United States* (hereinafter cited as FRUS), 1943, II, 23-24, 47, and Hull, *Memoirs*, II, 1208-1209.
3. FRUS, 1943, II, 44-46, 48-51, and Hull, *Memoirs*, II, 1208-1209.
4. FRUS, 1943, II, 77-81.
5. *Ibid.*, 67-70.
6. *Ibid.*, 74-76.
7. *Ibid.*, 79-80, and Hull, *Memoirs*, II, 1215-1216.
8. FRUS, 1943, II, 108-109.
9. *Ibid.*, 111-112.
10. *Ibid.*, 113-114, and Hull, *Memoirs*, II, 1216-1217.
11. Hull, *Memoirs*, II, 1218-1219, and FRUS, 1943, II, 115-116.
12. FRUS, 1943, II, 122-123, and Hull, *Memoirs*, II, 1219-1230.

13. Hull, *Memoirs*, II, 1220, and FRUS, 1943, II, 134-135.
14. Hull, *Memoirs, II, 1220-1221, and FRUS, 1943, II, 141-142.*
15. Hull, *Memoirs*, II, 1221-1222.
16. *Ibid.*, 1225.
17. *Ibid.*, 1225, FRUS, 1943, II, 175-177, and Winston S. Churchill, *Closing the Ring* (Boston, 1951), pp. 180-182.
18. FRUS, 1943, II, 182, and Churchill, *Closing the Ring*, p. 182.
19. Hull, *Memoirs*, 1225-1226, and FRUS, 1943, II, 183-184.
20. FRUS, 1943, II, 184-185, Hull, *Memoirs*, II, 1241-42, and Robert Lee Hamburger, "Franco-American Relations, 1940-1962: The Role of United States Anticolonialism and Anticommunism in the Formulation of United States Policy on the Algerian Question," Ph.D. dissertation, University of Notre Dame, 1970, p. 30.
21. Hull, *Memoirs*, II, 1242, 1243.
22. *Ibid.*, 1245.
23. FRUS, 1944, III, 683, and Hamburger, "Franco-American Relations," p. 31.
24. FRUS, 1944, III, 735-736.
25. *Ibid.*, 745. Caffery was confirmed as ambassador to France on November 25, 1944.
26. Hamburger, "Franco-American Relations," p. 32.
27. FRUS, 1943, II, 112.
28. Murphy, *Diplomat Among Warriors*, p. 168.
29. FRUS, 1944, III, 773.
30. FRUS, 1945, IV, 667-669.
31. Gallagher, *The United States and North Africa*, pp. 95-97.
32. FRUS, 1945, VIII, 30-31.
33. *Ibid.*, 31-32.
34. *Ibid.*, 32.
35. *Ibid.*, 32.
36. Hamburger, "Franco-American Relations," pp. 36-37.
37. Hall, *The United States and Morocco*, pp. 943, 1002, Burns, *Roosevelt*, p. 322, and Kirk, *The Middle East in the War*, p. 412. But Leon Borden Blair in his *Western Window on the Arab World* (Austin, Texas, 1970), pp. 96-97 and 301, questions the claim that Roosevelt encouraged the Moroccan leader to expect U.S. assistance in ending the French protectorate at the conclusion of the war.
38. Hall, *The United States and Morocco*, pp. 989-999, and Gallagher, *The United States and North Africa*, p. 99.
39. Hall, *The United States and Morocco*, pp. 1002-1003.
40. *Ibid.*, p. 956, and Blair, *Western Window on the Arab World*, p. 100.
41. Hall, *The United States and Morocco*, p. 1003, and Blair, *Western Window on the Arab World*, p. 101.
42. Hall, *The United States and Morocco*, p. 1005.
43. *Ibid.*, pp. 1005-1006, and Clark, *Calculated Risk*, p. 159.
44. Blair, *Western Window on the Arab World*, pp. 97-98.
45. *Ibid.*, p. 101.
46. FRUS, 1944, V, 527-528.
47. *Ibid.*, 533-534.
48. FRUS, 1943, IV, 745-746.
49. Hall, *The United States and Morocco*, pp. 1006-1007.
50. *Ibid.*, p. 1007.
51. FRUS, 1943, IV, 743-744.
52. FRUS, 1944, V, 533-534.

53. Hall, *The United States and Morocco*, p. 1008.
54. *Ibid.*, p. 1009.
55. *Ibid.*, p. 1011.
56. FRUS, 1944, V, 539-553.
57. FRUS, 1945, VIII, 601-655, and *Department of State Bulletin*, October 21, 1945, 613-618.
58. Gallagher, *The United States and North Africa*, pp. 71-85-89.
59. Alal al-Fasi, *The Independence Movements in North Africa*, (New York, 1970), pp. 73-74, 75-77.
60. FRUS, 1947, V, 673-674.
61. FRUS, 1946, VII, 62-63.
62. L. Carl Brown, "The United States and the Maghrib," *Middle East Journal*, 30 (summer 1976), 288-289.

CHAPTER 8

1. DeNovo, *American Interests and Policies in the Middle East*, pp. 320-321, 347-350.
2. Sachar, *Europe Leaves the Middle East*, pp. 168-169, Kirk, *The Middle East in the War*, p. 65, and United State Department of State, *Foreign Relations of the United States* (hereinafter cited as FRUS), 1941, III, 486-487.
3. FRUS, 1941, III, 487-488.
4. *Ibid.*, 489.
5. *Ibid.*, 491-492.
6. *Ibid.*, 492-293.
7. *Ibid.*, 496.
8. *Ibid.*, 498.
9. *Ibid.*, 497-499.
10. *Ibid.*, 499-500.
11. *Ibid.*, 501-502.
12. Sachar, *Europe Leaves the Middle East*, p. 170.
13. Kirk, *The Middle East in the War*, pp. 75-76.
14. Sachar, *Europe Leaves the Middle East*, p. 1975.
15. FRUS, 1941, III, 503.
16. *Ibid.*, 503-504.
17. *Ibid.*, 506-507.
18. *Ibid.*, 507-508.
19. *Ibid.*, 508-509, Kirk, *The Middle East in the War*, pp. 74-75, and Sachar, *Europe Leaves the Middle East*, p. 193.
20. FRUS, 1941, III, 511.
21. *Ibid.*, 513.
22. *Ibid.*, 513-514.
23. Smith, *American Diplomacy during the Second World War*, p. 105.
24. Henry Nettleton Fisher, *The Middle East* (New York, 1969), p. 487.
25. Baram, *The Department of State in the Middle East*, p. 175.
26. FRUS, 1942, IV, 343.
27. *Ibid.*, 344.
28. *Ibid.*, 345-346.
29. *Ibid.*, 643-644.
30. FRUS, 1943, IV, 636-638.
31. Baram, *The Department of State in the Middle East*, p. 175.
32. FRUS, 1942, IV, 347.

33. *Ibid.*, 347-348.
34. *Ibid.*, 348-353.
35. FRUS, 1943, IV, 639-640.
36. *Ibid.*, 642.
37. *Ibid.*, 645-647.
38. *Ibid.*, 647-648.
39. *Ibid.*, 649-650.
40. *Ibid.*, 650-651.
41. *Ibid.*, 653-654.
42. *Ibid.*, 654-655.
43. Baram, *The Department of State in the Middle East*, pp. 176-177.
44. FRUS, 1944, V, 500-501.
45. *Ibid.*, 501-502.
46. *Ibid.*, 502-503.
47. FRUS, 1945, VIII, 586.
48. *Ibid.*, 49-51.
49. *Ibid*, 587.

CHAPTER 9

1. DeNovo, *American Interests and Policies in the Middle East*, p. 366.
2. *Ibid.*, p. 368.
3. Baram, *The Department of State in the Middle East*, p. 184; also see Phillip Baram's article, "Undermining the British: Department of State Policies in Egypt and the Suez Canal Before and During World War II," *Historian,* 46 (August 1978), 631-649.
4. Kirk, *The Middle East in the War*, p. 199.
5. United States Department of State, *Foreign Relations of the United States* (hereinafter cited as FRUS), 1941, III, 267-268.
6. *Ibid.*, 272.
7. *Ibid.*, 273-274.
8. *Ibid.*, 277-278.
9. Deborah Wing Ray, "The Takoradi Route: Roosevelt's Prewar Venture beyond the Western Hemisphere," *Journal of American History,* 62 (September 1975), 341.
10. *Ibid.*, 343-355.
11. *Ibid.*, 287.
12. FRUS, 1941, III, 287.
13. *Ibid.*, 292-293.
14. *Ibid.*, 294.
15. *Ibid.*, 296, and Ray, "The Takoradi Route," 355.
16. Baram, *The Department of State in the Middle East*, pp. 187-88.
17. Thomas A. Bryson, *An American Consular Officer in the Middle East in the Jacksonian Era: A Biography of William Brown Hodgson, 1801-1871* (Atlanta, 1979), Chapter 5.
18. FRUS, 1941, III, 299-302.
19. *Ibid.*, 301.
20. *Ibid.*, 304.
21. *Ibid.*, 305.
22. *Ibid.*, 306, 309.
23. *Ibid.*, 307-308.
24. *Ibid.*, 310-311.

25. *Ibid.*, 312-313.
26. *Ibid.*, 314.
27. *Ibid.*, 314-315.
28. *Ibid.*, 316.
29. Baram, *The Department of State in the Middle East*, p. 188.
30. FRUS, 1941, III, 336.
31. *Ibid.*, 338, 339.
32. Baram, *The Department of State in the Middle East*, p. 190.
33. FRUS, 1943, IV, 66-67.
34. *Ibid.*, 68-69.
35. *Ibid.*, 35.
36. *Ibid.*, 72.
37. *Ibid.*, 64.
38. *Ibid.*, 65.
39. *Ibid.*, 65.
40. FRUS, 1944, V, 62-67.
41. Baram, *The Department of State in the Middle East*, p. 191; see also Hull's letter to Minister Hassan, regarding disposal of U.S. installations in Egypt: FRUS, 1945, VIII, 89-90.
42. FRUS, 1944, V, 67-69.
43. *Ibid.*, 69-70.
44. FRUS, 1945, VIII, 89-90.
45. *Ibid.*, 95-96.
46. FRUS, 1942, IV, 63-64, and Kirk, *The Middle East in the War*, pp. 207-208.
47. FRUS, 1942, IV, 65-66, and Kirk, *The Middle East in the War*, p. 209.
48. Kirk, *The Middle East in the War*, p. 209.
49. FRUS, 1942, IV, 66-67, and Kirk, *The Middle East in the War*, p. 210.
50. FRUS, 1942, IV, 67.
51. *Ibid.*, 67, and Kirk, *The Middle East in the War*, p. 210.
52. FRUS, 1942, IV, 68-69, and Baram, *The Department of State in the Middle East*, p. 188.
53. Baram, *The Department of State in the Middle East*, p. 189.
54. General R.L. Maxwell was chief of the United States Military Mission in North Africa, with headquarters in Cairo, and was responsible for assisting British troops in the use of American Lend-Lease supplies sent to Egypt.
55. FRUS, 1942, IV, 69-70.
56. *Ibid.*, 71.
57. FRUS, 1941, III, 317-318.
58. *Ibid.*, 319-320.
59. FRUS, 1942, IV, 97-99.
60. For an excellent summary of the matter of jurisdiction over American military and civilian personnel in Egypt, see the memorandum in FRUS, 1945, VIII, 91-95.
61. FRUS, 1942, IV, 89.
62. *Ibid.*, 89-90.
63. *Ibid.*, 90-91.
64. *Ibid.*, 93.
65. FRUS, 1943, IV, 73-76.
66. *Ibid.*, 76-78.
67. *Ibid.*, 80-81.
68. FRUS, 1942, IV, 72-87, Kirk, *The Middle East in the War*, pp. 213-224, and Ray, "The Takoradi Route," 355.

CHAPTER 10

1. Bryson, *American Diplomatic Relations with the Middle East*, p. 77.
2. DeNovo, *American Interests and Policies in the Middle East*, pp. 236-237. The author is currently writing a biography of Admiral Bristol.
3. United States Department of State, *Foreign Relations of the United States* (hereinafter cited as FRUS). 1941, III, 815.
4. *Ibid.*, 818.
5. *Ibid.*, 819-820.
6. *Ibid.*, 825.
7. *Ibid.*, 828-829.
8. *Ibid.*, 833.
9. *Ibid.*, 835-836, 837-838.
10. *Ibid.*, 841-849.
11. *Ibid.*, 853, 855, 857-858.
12. *Ibid.*, 864,867-68, 873-74.
13. *Ibid.*, 875-876.
14. *Ibid.*, 882,884, 898, 899, 900.
15. *Ibid.*, 902, 903, 905, 906-921.
16. *Ibid.*, 921-922, 923-925, and Hull, *Memoirs*, II, 1366.
17. FRUS, 1941, III, 922-923, 929.
18. FRUS, 1942, IV, 677-678.
19. *Ibid.*, 679-680.
20. *Ibid.*, 680.
21. *Ibid.*, 681-682.
22. *Ibid.*, 683-684.
23. *Ibid.*, 685-693.
24. *Ibid.*, 700-708.
25. FRUS, 1943, IV, 1094-1095, for an excellent summary of the development of American policy *vis-à-vis* Turkey on Lend-Lease, see *ibid.*, 1099-1100.
26. *Ibid.*, 1111.
27. FRUS, 1944, V, 906, 912-913.
28. FRUS, 1945, VIII, 1299-1309.
29. Edward Weisband, *Turkish Foreign Policy, 1943-1945* (Princeton, N.J., 1973), pp. 95-103.
30. FRUS, 1941, III, 936-937.
31. *Ibid.*, 940-941.
32. *Ibid.*, 941-943.
33. *Ibid.*, 945.
34. Weisband, *Turkish Foreign Policy*, pp. 104-105, and FRUS, 1941, III, 958-962, 964-965.
35. FRUS, 1941, III, 966, 971.
36. FRUS, 1942, IV, 728-729.
37. *Ibid.*, 730-732, 734.
38. *Ibid.*, 740-741.
39. *Ibid.*, 719, 722-724.
40. *Ibid.*, 742-743.
41. *Ibid.*, 747, 748-749, 781-788.
42. FRUS, 1943, IV, 1154.
43. *Ibid.*, 1166.
44. FRUS, 1944, V, 821, and Weisband, *Turkish Foreign Policy*, pp. 257-258.

45. FRUS, 1944, V, 825-826.

46. *Ibid.*, 826, 831, 851 and Weisband, *Turkish Foreign Policy*, p. 260.

47. Weisband, *Turkish Foreign Policy*, pp. 107-109.

48. FRUS, 1943, IV, 1118-1119.

49. See United States Department of State, *Foreign Relations of the United States: The Conferences at Washington, 1941-1942, and Casablanca, 1943*, pp. 487-849 (hereinafter cited as FRUSCon Washington & Casablanca), Harry N. Howard, *Turkey, the Straits and U.S. Policy* (Baltimore, 1974), p. 172, Sherwood, *Roosevelt and Hopkins* p. 683, Winston S. Churchill, *The Hinge of Fate* (Boston, 1950), pp. 669-703, Weisband, *Turkish Foreign Policy*, pp. 119-124, Feis, *Churchill Roosevelt, Stalin*, pp. 105-107, McNeill, *America, Britain and Russia*, pp. 265-273, and Pogue, *Organizer of Victory*, pp. 188-35.

50. FRUSCon Washington & Casablanca, pp. 491-492 and McNeill, *America, Britain, and Russia*, p. 265.

51. FRUSCon Washington & Casablanca, pp. 539-40, 571, 584.

52. Pogue, *Organizer of Victory*, p. 21.

53. FRUSCon Washington & Casablanca, p. 634.

54. *Ibid.*, 643, and Sherwood, *Roosevelt and Hopkins*, p. 683.

55. *Ibid.*, pp. 772, 774, Churchill, *Hinge of Fate*, p. 692, Howard, *Turkey*, p. 172, McNeill, *America, Britain, and Russia*, p. 272, and Weisband, *Turkish Foreign Policy*, pp. 123-124.

56. Churchill, *Hinge of Fate*, pp. 706-712, FRUS, 1943, IV, 1960-1062, Weisband, *Turkish Foreign Policy*, pp. 133-138, and McNeill, *America, Britain, and Russia*, p. 272.

57. Weisband, *Turkish Foreign Policy*, p. 145.

58. FRUSCon Washington & Casablanca, pp. 25, 36, 224-225.

59. Weisband, *Turkish Foreign Policy*, pp. 152-153.

60. *Ibid.*, pp. 153-161.

61. United States Department of State, *Foreign Relations of the United States: The Conferences at Washington and Quebec, 1943* (1970), p. 463.

62. *Ibid.*, pp. 704-705.

63. *Ibid.*, p. 1131, Howard, *Turkey*, p. 177, Weisband, *Turkish Foreign Policy*, p. 163, and Hull, *Memoirs*, II, 1368.

64. Pogue, *Organizer of Victory*, p. 251.

65. Hull, *Memoirs*, II, 1369, Howard, *Turkey*, p. 179, and Weisband, *Turkish Foreign Policy*, p. 175.

66. United States Department of State, *Foreign Relations of the United States: The Conferences at Cairo and Tehran, 1943*, (1961), pp. 117, 121 (hereinafter cited as FRUSCon Cairo & Tehran).

67. Weisband, *Turkish Foreign Policy*, p. 179, Hull, *Memoirs*, II, 1369, and FRUSCon Cairo & Tehran, 1943, pp. 164-167, 174-175.

68. FRUSCon Cairo & Tehran, 1943, pp. 476-482, Howard, *Turkey*, p. 183, and Weisband, *Turkish Foreign Policy*, pp. 195-196.

69. Churchill, *Closing the Ring*, pp. 367-368.

70. FRUSCon Cairo & Tehran, 1943, pp. 565-568, 585-593, Churchill, *Closing the Ring*, pp. 389-393, and Howard, *Turkey*, p. 186.

71. FRUSCon Cairo & Tehran, 1943, pp. 651-652, and Howard, *Turkey*, p. 187.

72. FRUSCon Cairo & Tehran, 1943, pp. 662-667.

73. Weisband, *Turkish Foreign Policy*, pp. 202-203.

74. Churchill, *Closing the Ring*, pp. 415-416.

75. Sherwood, *Roosevelt and Hopkins*, p. 800.

76. Weisband, *Turkish Foreign Policy*, p. 209.

77. *Ibid.*, pp. 201-202, 206.
78. *Ibid.*, pp. 213-214, Howard, *Turkey*, p.192, and Hull, *Memoirs*, II, 1370.
79. Weisband, *Turkish Foreign Policy*, p. 222.
80. *Ibid.*, pp. 220-225, Hull, *Memoirs*, II, 1370-1371, and Howard, *Turkey*, pp. 195-196.
81. Weisband, *Turkish Foreign Policy*, pp. 228-229, and Howard, *Turkey*, p. 199.
82. FRUS, 1943, IV, 1079-1081.
83. Weisband, *Turkish Foreign Policy*, pp. 232-236.
84. *Ibid.*, pp. 237-256.
85. *Ibid.*, pp. 261-265.
86. *Ibid.*, pp. 266-268.
87. *Ibid.*, p. 268, FRUS, 1944, V, 860-863, Howard, *Turkey*, pp. 201-207, and Hull, *Memoirs*, II, 1374-1376.
88. Weisband, *Turkish Foreign Policy*, p. 269.
89. *Ibid.*, p. 270, and Hull, *Memoirs*, II, 1374.
90. Weisband, *Turkish Foreign Policy*, p. 270, and Hull, *Memoirs*, II, 1374.
91. Howard, *Turkey*, pp. 164, 208-209.
92. Weisband, *Turkish Foreign Policy*, p. 305, and George S. Harris, *Troubled Alliance: Turkish-American Problems in Historical Perspective, 1945-1971* (Washington, D.C., 1972), p. 15.
93. Harris, *Troubled Alliance*, pp. 15-17.
94. *Ibid.*, p. 19.

CHAPTER 11

1. Martin W. Wilmington, *The Middle East Supply Centre* (Albany, N.Y., 1971), p. 4; see Wilmington's article "The Middle East Supply Center: A Reappraisal," *Middle East Journal*, 6 (1952), 344; also see Baram, *The Department of State in the Middle East*, p. 159, and Kirk, *The Middle East in the War*, p. 173.
2. Wilmington, *The Middle East Supply Centre*, pp. 4-50.
3. United States Department of State, *Foreign Relations of the United States* (hereinafter cited as FRUS), 1942, IV, 1.
4. *Ibid.*, 2.
5. *Ibid.*, 2-3.
6. *Ibid.*, 3-4.
7. *Ibid.*, 4-12.
8. *Ibid.*, 12
9. *Ibid.*, 14-15.
10. Wilmington, *The Middle East Supply Centre*, pp. 21, 61.
11. FRUS, 1942, IV, 16-17, Baram, *The Department of State in the Middle East*, p. 16, Motter, *The Persian Corridor and Aid to Russia*, pp. 450-451, and Wilmington, *The Middle East Supply Centre*, p. 64.
12. FRUS, 1943, IV, 9, Wilmington, *The Middle East Supply Centre*, p. 65, and Motter, *The Persian Corridor and Aid to Russia*, p. 45.
13. Motter, *The Persian Corridor and Aid to Russia*, pp. 452-457.
14. Kirk, *The Middle East in the War*, p. 179.
15. Wilmington, *The Middle East Supply Centre*, p. 86.
16. *Ibid.*, p. 90.
17. Kirk, *The Middle East in the War*, p. 184, and Wilmington, *The Middle East Supply Centre*, pp. 123-124.

18. Wilmington, *The Middle East Supply Centre*, pp. 120-121.
19. *Ibid.*, 109-110, and Kirk, *The Middle East in the War*, pp. 185-186.
20. Kirk, *The Middle East in the War*, p. 187.
21. *Ibid.*, p. 175.
22. Wilmington, *The Middle East Supply Centre*, pp. 73, 75, 76.
23. Baram, *The Department of State in the Middle East*, p. 161.
24. *Ibid.*, pp. 162-164.
25. *Ibid.*, pp. 163-164, Wilmington, *The Middle East Supply Centre*, pp. 152-156, and Kirk, *The Middle East in the War*, pp. 188-189, 191-192.
26. FRUS, 1944, V, 41-52.
27. Wilmington, *The Middle East Supply Centre*, pp. 161-162.
28. FRUS, 1944, V, 38.
29. John A. DeNovo, "The Culbertson Economic Mission and Anglo-American Tensions in the Middle East, 1944-1945," *Journal of American History*, 63 (March 1977), 913.
30. FRUS, 1944, V, 39-40.
31. DeNovo, "The Culbertson Economic Mission," pp. 922-936.
32. FRUS, 1945, VIII, 85-86.
33. Wilmington, *The Middle East Supply Centre*, pp. 152-158.
34. Baram, *The Department of State in the Middle East*, p. 166.
35. FRUS, 1945, VIII, 87.

Chapter 12

1. United States Department of State, *Foreign Relations of the United States* (hereinafter cited as FRUS), 1943, IV, 813-814.
2. *Ibid.*, 331-336.
3. FRUS, 1945, VIII, 27.
4. United States *Department of State Bulletin*, September 18, 1943, 173-179.
5. FRUS, 1943, IV, 852-853.
6. Hull, *Memoirs*, II, 1547.
7. FRUS, 1943, IV, 853-854.
8. FRUS, 1945, VIII, 28, and Hull, *Memoirs*, II, 1547.
9. FRUS, 1945, VIII, 28; for the Alexandria Protocol and the Pact of the Arab League, see J.C. Hurewitz, *The Middle East and North Africa in World Politics: A Documentary Record* (New Haven, Conn., 1979), II, 732-738.
10. FRUS, 1945, VIII, 29.
11. *Ibid.*, 29.
12. *Ibid.*, 34-39.
13. *Ibid.*, 39-42.
14. *Ibid.*, 42-43.
15. *Ibid.*, 43-44.
16. *Ibid.*, 45-48.

Bibliography

DOCUMENTS

J.C. Hurewitz, ed. *The Middle East and North Africa in World Politics: A Documentary Record.* 2 vols. New Haven, Conn.: Yale University Press, 1979.

United States. Department of State. *Foreign Relations of the United States, 1941,* III, (1959).

————. ————. *Foreign Relations of the United States, 1942,* IV (1963).

————. ————. *Foreign Relations of the United States, 1943,* IV (1964).

————. ————. *Foreign Relations of the United States, 1944,* V (1965).

————. ————. *Foreign Relations of the United States, 1945,* VIII (1969).

————. ————. *Foreign Relations of the United States: The Conferences at Washington, 1941-1942, and Casablanca, 1943* (1968).

————. ————. *Foreign Relations of the United States: The Conferences at Washington and Quebec, 1943* (1970).

————. ————. *Foreign Relations of the United States: The Conferences at Cairo and Tehran, 1943* (1961).

————. ————. *Foreign Relations of the United States: The Conference at Quebec, 1944* (1972).

MEMOIRS

Childs, J. Rives. *Foreign Service Farewell: My Years in the Near East.* Charlottesville: University Press of Virginia, 1969.

Clark, Mark W. *Calculated Risk.* New York: Harper, 1950.

Eisenhower, Dwight D. *Crusade in Europe.* Garden City, N.Y.: Doubleday, 1948.

Grew, Joseph C. *Turbulent Era: A Diplomatic Record of Forty Years, 1904-1945.* 2 vols. London: Hammond, Hammond, 1953.

Griscom, Lloyd. *Diplomatically Speaking: Memoirs of Constantinople and Persia.* New York: Literary Guild of America, 1940.

Hull, Cordell. *The Memoirs of Cordell Hull.* 2 vols. New York: Macmillan, 1948.

Kennan, George F. *Memoirs, 1925-1950.* 2 vols. New York: Little, Brown, 1967.

Murphy, Robert. *Diplomat Among Warriors.* Garden City, N.Y.: Doubleday, 1964.

Pendar, Kenneth W. *Adventures in Diplomacy: Our French Dilemma.* New York: Da Capo, reprint 1966.

Truman, Harry S. *Memoirs: Years of Trial and Hope.* 2 vols. Garden City, N.Y.: Doubleday, 1955.

BIOGRAPHY

Bryant, Arthur. *The Turn of the Tide: A History of the War Years Based on the*

Diaries of Field-Marshall Lord Alanbrooke, Chief of the Imperial General Staff. Garden City, N.Y.: Doubleday, 1957.

Buhite, Russell. *Patrick J. Hurley and American Foreign Policy*. Ithaca, N.Y.: Cornell University Press, 1973.

Burns, James MacGregor. *Roosevelt: The Soldier of Freedom, 1940-1945*. New York: Harcourt Brace Jovanovich, 1970.

Lohbeck, Don. *Patrick J. Hurley*. Chicago: Henry Regnery, 1956.

Pogue, Forrest C. *George C. Marshall*. 4 vols. New York: Viking, 1973.

Sherwood, Robert E. *Roosevelt and Hopkins*. New York: Harper, 1948.

SECONDARY SOURCES

al-Fasi, Alal. *The Independence Movement in North Africa*. New York: Octagon Books, 1970.

Antonius, George. *The Arab Awakening: The Story of the Arab National Movement*. New York: Putnam, 1946.

Baram, Phillip J. *The Department of State in the Middle East 1919-1945*. Philadelphia: University of Pennsylvania Press, 1978.

Blair, Leon Borden. *Western Window on the Arab World*. Austin: University of Texas Press, 1970.

Bryson, Thomas A. *American Diplomatic Relations with the Middle East, 1784-1975: A Survey*. Metuchen, N.J.: Scarecrow Press, 1977.

_____. *Tars, Turks, and Tankers: The Role of the United States Navy in the Middle East, 1800-1980*. Metuchen, N.J.: Scarecrow Press, 1980.

Campbell, John C. *Defense of the Middle East: Problems of American Policy*. New York: Harper, 1960.

Churchill, Winston S. *Closing the Ring*. Boston: Houghton Mifflin, 1951.

_____. *The Grand Alliance*. Boston: Houghton Mifflin, 1950.

_____. *The Hinge of Fate*. Boston: Houghton Mifflin, 1950.

Daniel, Robert L. *American Philanthropy in the Near East, 1820-1960*. Athens: Ohio University Press, 1970.

DeNovo, John A. *American Interests and Policies in the Middle East, 1900-1939*. Minneapolis: University of Minnesota Press, 1963.

Farmer, Paul. *Vichy: Political Dilemma*. New York: Columbia University Press, 1955.

Feis, Herbert. *The Birth of Israel: The Tousled Diplomatic Bed*. New York: Norton, 1969.

_____. *Petroleum and American Foreign Policy*. Stanford, Calif.: Stanford University Press. 1944.

_____. *Roosevelt, Churchill, Stalin: The War They Waged and the Peace They Sought*. Princeton, N.J.: Princeton University Press, 1967.

Field, James A., Jr. *America and the Mediterranean World, 1776-1882*. Princeton, N.J.: Princeton University Press, 1969.

Fisher, Sydney Nettleton. *The Middle East: A History*. New York: Knopf, 1960.

Gallagher, Charles F. *United States and North Africa: Morocco, Algeria, Tunisia*. Cambridge, Mass.: Harvard University Press, 1963.

Gardner, Lloyd C. *Economic Aspects of New Deal Diplomacy*. Madison: University of Wisconsin Press, 1964.

Grabill, Joseph L. *Protestant Diplomacy and the Near East: Missionary Influence on American Policy, 1810-1927*. Minneapolis: University of Minnesota Press, 1971.

Hall, Luella J. *The United States and Morocco, 1776-1956*. Metuchen, N.J.: Scarecrow Press, 1971.

Halperin, Samuel. *The Political World of American Zionism*. Detroit: Wayne State University Press, 1961.

Harris, George S. *Troubled Alliance: Turkish-American Problems in Historical Perspective, 1945-1971*. Stanford, Calif.: Hoover Institution on War and Peace, 1972.

Hoskins, Halford L. *The Middle East: Problem Area in World Politics*. New York: Macmillan, 1957.

Howard, Harry N. *Turkey, the Straits, and U.S. Policy*. Baltimore: Johns Hopkins University Press, 1974.

Hurewitz, J.C. *Middle East Dilemmas: The Background of United States Policy*. New York: Harper, 1953.

Khouri, Fred J. *The Arab-Israeli Dilemma*. Syracuse, N.Y.: Syracuse University Press, 1968.

Kirk, George E. *The Middle East in the War*. London: Oxford University Press, 1952.

Klebanoff, Shoshana. *Middle East Oil and U.S. Foreign Policy with Special Reference to the U.S. Energy Crisis*. New York: Praeger, 1974.

Kolko, Gabriel. *The Politics of War: The World and United States Foreign Policy, 1943-1945*. New York: Random House, 1968.

Kolko, Joyce, and Gabriel Kolko. *The Limits of Power: The World and United States Foreign Policy, 1945-1954*. New York: Harper & Row, 1972.

Kuniholm, Bruce R. *The Origins of the Cold War in the Near East: Great Power Conflict and Diplomacy in Iran, Turkey, and Greece*. Princeton, N.J.: Princeton University Press, 1980.

Langer, William. *Our Vichy Gamble*. New York: Knopf, 1947.

Lenczowski, George. *The Middle East in World Affairs*. Ithaca, N.Y.: Cornell University Press, 1956.

————. *Russia and the West in Iran, 1918-1948*. Ithaca, N.Y.: Cornell University Press, 1949.

Lilienthal, Alfred M. *The Other Side of the Coin: An American Persepctive of the Arab-Israeli Conflict*. New York: Devin-Adair, 1965.

McNeill, William Hardy. *America, Britain, and Russia: Their Cooperation and Conflict, 1941-1946*. New York: Johnson Reprint Corp., reprint 1970.

Manuel, Frank E. *The Realities of American-Palestine Relations*. Washington, D.C.: Public Affairs Press, 1949.

Meo, Leila. *Lebanon, Improbable Nation: A Study in Political Development*. Bloomington: Indiana University Press, 1965.

Mikesell, Raymond F., and Hollis B. Chenery. *Arabian Oil: America's Stake in the Middle East*. Chapel Hill: University of North Carolina Press, 1949.

Miller, Merle. *Plain Speaking: An Oral Biography of Harry S. Truman*. New York: Putnam, 1974.

Millis, Walter, and E.S. Duffield, eds. *The Forrestal Diaries*. New York: Viking, 1951.

Millspaugh, Arthur C. *Americans in Persia*. Washington, D.C.: Brookings Institution, 1946.

Morison, Samuel E. *History of the United States Naval Operations in World War II: Operations in North African Waters*. Boston: Little, Brown, 1947-62.

Mosley, Leonard. *Power Play: Oil in the Middle East*. New York: Random House, 1973.

Motter, T.H. Vail. *The Persian Corridor and Aid to Russia*. Washington, D.C.: U.S. Gov. Printing Office, 1952.

Nash, Gerald D. *United States Oil Policy, 1890-1964*. Pittsburgh: University of Pittsburgh Press, 1968.

Ramazani, Rouhollah K. *Iran's Foreign Policy, 1941-1973: A Study of Foreign Policy in Modernizing Nations.* Charlottesville: University Press of Virginia, 1975.

Reitzel, William. *The Mediterranean: Its Role in American Foreign Policy.* New York: Harcourt, Brace, 1948.

Sachar, Howard M. *Europe Leaves the Middle East, 1936-1954.* New York: Knopf, 1972.

Sheehan, M.K. *Iran: Impact of United States Interests and Policies, 1941-1954.* Brooklyn, N.Y.: Theo Gaus's Sons, 1968.

Shwadran, Benjamin. *The Middle East, Oil and the Great Powers.* New York: Praeger, 1955.

Smith, Gaddis. *American Diplomacy During the Second World War.* New York: Wiley, 1966.

Snetsinger, John. *Truman, The Jewish Vote and the Creation of Israel.* Stanford, Calif.: Hoover Institution Press, 1974.

Speiser, Ephraim. *The United States and the Near East.* Cambridge, Mass.: Harvard University Press, 1952.

Stevens, Richard P. *American Zionism and United States Foreign Policy.* New York: Pageant Press, 1962.

Stocking, George W. *Middle East Oil: A Study in Political and Economic Controversy.* Nashville, Tenn.: Vanderbilt University Press, 1970.

Stookey, Robert W. *America and the Arab States: An Uneasy Encounter.* New York: Wiley, 1975.

Thomas, Lewis V., and Richard N. Frye. *The United States and Turkey and Iran.* Cambridge, Mass.: Harvard University Press, 1951.

Twitchell, K.S. *Saudi Arabia: With an Account of the Development of Its Natural Resources.* Princeton, N.J.: Princeton University Press, 1958.

Weisband, Edward. *Turkish Foreign Policy, 1943-1945.* Princeton, N.J.: Princeton University Press, 1973.

Welles, Sumner. *Where Are We Heading?* New York: Harper, 1946.

Wilmington, Martin W. *The Middle East Supply Centre.* Albany: State University Press of New York, 1971.

ARTICLES

Anderson, Irvine H. "Lend-Lease for Saudi Arabia: A Comment on Alternative Conceptualizations," *Diplomatic History*, 3 (fall 1979), 413-423.

Baram, Phillip. "Undermining the British: Department of State Policies in Egypt and the Suez Canal before and During World War II," *Historian*, 40 (August 1978), 631-649.

Blair, Leon Borden. "Amateurs in Diplomacy: The American Vice Consuls in North Africa, 1941-1943," *Historian*, 35 (August 1973), 607-620.

Brown, L. Carl. "The United States and the Maghrib," *Middle East Journal*, 30 (summer 1976), 273-290.

Bryson, Thomas A. "Admiral Mark Lambert Bristol: An Open Door Diplomat in Turkey," *International Journal of Middle East Studies* 5 (1974), 450-467.

Daniel, Robert L. "The Friendship of Woodrow Wilson and Cleveland Dodge," *Mid-America*, 43 (July 1961), 182-196.

DeNovo, John A. "The Culbertson Economic Mission and Anglo-American Tensions in the Middle East, 1944-1945," *Journal of American History*, 63 (March 1977), 913-936.

Grabill, Joseph L. "Missionary Influence on American Relations with the Near East,

1914-1923," *Muslim World,* 58 (April 1968), 141-154.

Mark, Eduard M. "Allied Relations in Iran, 1941-1947: The Origins of a Cold War Crisis," *Wisconsin Magazine of History.* 59 (autumn 1975), 51-63.

Pfau, Richard. "Avoiding the Cold War: The United States and the Iranian Oil Crisis, 1944," *Essays in History,* 18 (1974), 104-114.

_____. "The Legal Status of American Forces in Iran," *Middle East Journal,* 28 (spring 1974), 141-153.

Quandt, William B. "United States Policy in the Middle East: Constraints and Choices," in Paul Y. Hammond and Sidney S. Alexander, eds., *Political Dynamics in the Middle East.* New York: American Elsevier, 1972.

Ray, Deborah Wing. "The Takoradi Route: Roosevelt's Prewar Venture beyond the Western Hemisphere," *Journal of American History,* 62 (September 1975), 340-358.

Wilmington, Martin W. "The Middle East Supply Centre," *Middle East Journal,* 6 (1952), 144-166.

Wilson, Evan M. "The Palestine Papers, 1943-1947," *Journal of Palestine Studies,* 2 (summer 1973), 33-54.

Unpublished Dissertations

Hamburger, Robert Lee. "Franco-American Relations, 1940-1962: The Role of United States Policy on the Algerian Question," Ph.D dissertation, University of Notre Dame, 1970.

Pfau, Richard Anthony. "The United States and Iran, 1941-1947: Origins of Partnership," Ph.D. dissertation, University of Virginia, 1975.

Walt, Joseph William, "Saudi Arabia and the Americans, 1923-1951," Ph.D. dissertation, Northwestern University, 1960.

Index